Robert Ryman

OCTOBER Books

Broodthaers, edited by Benjamin H. D. Buchloh

AIDS: Cultural Analysis/Cultural Activism, edited by Douglas Crimp

Aberrations: An Essay on the Legend of Forms, by Jurgis Baltrušaitis

Against Architecture: The Writings of Georges Bataille, by Denis Hollier

Painting as Model, by Yve-Alain Bois

The Destruction of Tilted Arc: Documents, edited by Clara Weyergraf-Serra and Martha Buskirk

The Woman in Question, edited by Parveen Adams and Elizabeth Cowie

Techniques of the Observer: On Vision and Modernity in the Nineteenth Century, by Jonathan Crary

The Subjectivity Effect in Western Literary Tradition: Essays toward the Release of Shakespeare's Will, by Joel Fineman

Looking Awry: An Introduction to Jacques Lacan through Popular Culture, by Slavoj Žižek

Cinema, Censorship, and the State: The Writings of Nagisa Oshima, by Nagisa Oshima

The Optical Unconscious, by Rosalind E. Krauss

Gesture and Speech, by André Leroi-Gourhan

Compulsive Beauty, by Hal Foster

Continuous Project Altered Daily: The Writings of Robert Morris, by Robert Morris

Read My Desire: Lacan against the Historicists, by Joan Copjec

Fast Cars, Clean Bodies: Decolonization and the Reordering of French Culture, by Kristin Ross

Kant after Duchamp, by Thierry de Duve

The Duchamp Effect, edited by Martha Buskirk and Mignon Nixon

The Return of the Real: The Avant-Garde at the End of the Century, by Hal Foster

October: The Second Decade, 1986–1996, edited by Rosalind Krauss, Annette Michelson, Yve-Alain Bois, Benjamin H. D. Buchloh, Hal Foster, Denis Hollier, and Silvia Kolbowski

Infinite Regress: Marcel Duchamp 1910–1941, by David Joselit

Caravaggio's Secrets, by Leo Bersani and Ulysse Dutoit

Scenes in a Library: Reading the Photograph in the Book, 1843–1875, by Carol Armstrong

Bachelors, by Rosalind Krauss

Neo-Avantgarde and Culture Industry: Essays on European and American Art from 1955 to 1975, by Benjamin H. D. Buchloh

Suspensions of Perception: Attention, Spectacle, and Modern Culture, by Jonathan Crary

Leave Any Information at the Signal: Writings, Interviews, Bits, Pages, by Ed Ruscha

Guy Debord and the Situationist International: Texts and Documents, edited by Tom McDonough

Random Order: Robert Rauschenberg and the Neo-Avant-Garde, by Branden W. Joseph

Decoys and Disruptions: Selected Writings, 1975–2001, by Martha Rosler

Prosthetic Gods, by Hal Foster

Fantastic Reality: Louise Bourgeois and a Story of Modern Art, by Mignon Nixon

Women Artists at the Millennium, edited by Carol Armstrong and Catherine de Zegher

"The Beautiful Language of My Century": Reinventing the Language of Contestation in Postwar France, 1945–1968, by Tom McDonough

The Artwork Caught by the Tail: Francis Picabia and Dada in Paris, by George Baker

Robert Ryman: Used Paint, by Suzanne P. Hudson

Robert Ryman

Used Paint

Suzanne P. Hudson

An OCTOBER Book

The MIT Press
Cambridge, Massachusetts
London, England

MIT Press books may be purchased at special quantity discounts for business or sales promotional use. For information, please e-mail <special_sales@mitpress.mit.edu>, or write to Special Sales Department, The MIT Press, 55 Hayward Street, Cambridge, MA 02142.

Support for this publication has been provided by The Publications Committee, Department of Art and Archaeology, Princeton University.

This book was set in Bembo Std by Graphic Composition, Inc., Bogart, Georgia. Printed and bound in Spain.

Library of Congress Cataloging-in-Publication Data

Hudson, Suzanne Perling, 1977–
Robert Ryman : used paint / Suzanne P. Hudson.
p. cm.
"An October book."
Includes bibliographical references and index.
ISBN 978-0-262-01280-5 (hardcover : alk. paper)
1. Ryman, Robert, 1930– —Criticism and interpretation. I. Title.
ND237.R83H83 2009
759.13—dc22

2008029435

10 9 8 7 6 5 4 3 2

Illustration credits are found on pages 293 to 302.

In the Fall of 1968 I did my first show at Konrad Fischer's gallery in Dusseldorf. The exhibition consisted of six paintings on paper panels, nine panels to a painting. The panels were crated and shipped to Dusseldorf. In the process of getting them though customs (in order to avoid the duty that is to be paid on "Art" arriving in the country), Konrad had listed them as "paper" and not as paintings. But the customs official said "But? It is expensive paper (handmade) so you will have to pay so much!" "Yes, it is expensive paper," Konrad said, "but it has been used." The customs official agreed that it had indeed been used. So the paintings arrived designated as "Used Paper." Since that time I have wondered about the possibility of paintings being defined as "Used Paint." Then there could be "Used Bronze," "Used Canvas," "Used Steel," "Used Lead . . ."

—Robert Ryman, "Robert Ryman," Art Now: New York *3, no. 3, (September 1971).*

Contents

Acknowledgments

Robert Ryman: Used Paint closely examines how people learn, and I wish to thank those who have taught me more than they probably realize. This undertaking was conceived while studying with Hal Foster at Princeton University, and I am indebted to him for his incisive criticality, sly humor, and longstanding faith in my work. His objections are the ones that I still anticipate and hope to forestall, long after completion of the dissertation from which this book emerged. At Princeton, I also had the great fortune to work with Carol Armstrong, whose keen intelligence has improved virtually every one of these pages, and Brigid Doherty, Branden Joseph, and John Wilmerding. All provided models—of scholarship, pedagogy, and generosity—worthy of emulation. Additionally, I appreciate the richly satisfying classes given by Michael Jennings and Tom Levin and the community offered by Kaira Cabañas, Kate Nesin, and Julia Robinson.

I am grateful to Princeton's Department of Art and Archaeology—especially to Diane Schulte and Susan Lehre—for tremendous support during the time I was there (and then some). Indeed, I owe a sincere debt to the Publications Committee, Department of Art and Archaeology, Princeton University for a very generous subvention. Portions of this book have been published in *Art Journal* and *October;* my thanks extend to these journals. To the editors of *October,* too, I am gratified by the espousal of this project in book form. Recognition also goes to the engaged audiences who first responded to some of these materials in presentations at the Bard College Center for Curatorial Studies, College Art Association, Frick Museum, George Washington University, New School for Social Research, Princeton University, Smithsonian American Art Museum, Syracuse University, University of Illinois at Urbana-Champaign, and Whitney Museum of American Art. A special note of acknowledgment is reserved for Kathryn Potts, Frank Smigiel, Margie Weinstein, and all of my former Whitney colleagues.

This book was completed at the University of Illinois, Urbana-Champaign, in residence at The Phillips Collection Center for the Study of Modern Art. Jonathan Fineberg's enthusiasm has been wonderfully implacable. Rachael DeLue, Jennifer Greenhill, Jordana Mendelson, Ruth Perlin, and Terri Weissman enriched my first years at Illinois and The Phillips, as have Alexander Dumbadze, Anne Ellegood, and Joshua Shannon, my D.C. gang. In practical terms, I could not have obtained the many permissions—or done a million other things—without the grace and pluck of Laura Bandy, Jessica Cash, Margaret Ewing, and Andrea Ferber, who all helped at various stages. At the MIT Press, Roger Conover has produced the book I have hoped to publish, and I could not be more pleased with his skill, insight, and patience. Earnest thanks go to Marc Lowenthal and Anar Badalov. I am also thankful for Deborah Cantor-Adams and Rosemary Winfield, whose deft editorial interventions saved me from myself.

To this book's subject, Robert Ryman, I offer my thanks for his willingness to talk at length about his work and for the work itself. My heartfelt gratitude extends to Amy Baker Sandback and David Gray for numerous, immensely helpful conversations and for archival matters over many years. And I appreciate Phyllis Tuchman's and Ellsworth Kelly's insights. I further benefited from the assistance of many libraries, galleries, museums, and collections, the munificence of which are reflected in the book's photographs and citations, as well as from the aid of Timothy McCarthy at Art Resource Inc., Alan Baglia at Artists Rights Society, and everyone at PaceWildenstein. And thanks to Richard Meyer for a truly helpful exchange at just the right time and to Elise Adibi for lively dialogue throughout. For their astute reading and manifold contributions—particularly their honesty and friendship—I thank Johanna Burton, Anne Byrd, William McManus, and Lisa Turvey.

Lastly, I treasure my family, for whom I am the most grateful of all. To my parents, Karen and David Perling, and to my brother Michael, I offer this book as a small compensation for the times I've been too busy to properly acknowledge all that you do. Carolyn and Van Hudson have been sources of warmth. It is dedicated to—and would have been impossible without—Drew Hudson, who shares so profoundly in my successes and failures alike. Since our undergraduate days at Berkeley, he has been my first reader, whether he wanted to serve as such or not, and my work has improved immeasurably because of his involvement. It is with all my devotion that I can give to him the last word.

A Note on the Illustrations

Robert Ryman's work is exceedingly difficult to reproduce. There are too many white squares on white pages and, whether photographed in black and white or in color, these paintings almost make allegations of invisibility stick. (As a friend once suggested, the reader has many "blank" pages for notes in a book like this.) Some catalogues have tried to make up for the flattening of surface details by shooting works from the side and under raking light. Others have used wide installation shots or microdetails, and still more have abandoned reproductions altogether.

Christel Sauer has recently complained—with good reason—that "it is almost impossible to reproduce Ryman's paintings in a suitable manner (even though this has been tried, time and again). The white paint he uses and the subtle nuances of his color application do not easily allow a technical reproduction."[1] Because of this, critics have written ample amounts of description, an infelicitous route for entirely other reasons since it is so very difficult to find the right words to describe the paintings. When this strategy fails, Ryman is often brought in for an interview.

The principal issue is that Ryman's painting disallows photographic duplication. Ryman's experience of learning about art from art is an increasingly uncommon experience if one accepts André Malraux's dematerialized *musée imaginaire*. Much art history happens through a representational understanding born of the museum without walls—the reduction of vast "heterogeneity," in Douglas Crimp's terms, into "a single perfect similitude."[2] In contrast, Ryman stunts transcription by virtue of the irreproducibility of his works. Additionally, Ryman accords primacy to the viewing of works in person. In their resistance to duplication, his works perform a reflexive manner of critique—one that has an internal relation to Ryman's practice. Still—and maybe for this very reason—it seems important to provide as complete a visual record as possible (free from an exhibition checklist), and many works are published here for the first time. Through this book, I wish to make Ryman's works more available to more reviewers. With an acknowledgment of the relative poverty of the images that follow, then, I can only echo Ryman and encourage firsthand apprehension: "You have to see the real thing," Ryman contends. "Books leave you with the wrong impression. Seeing a real painting is the only way to do it."[3]

Robert Ryman

Introduction

Time magazine, November 22, 1968. Nestled between a feature on Catholicism's "silent schism" in the wake of Pope Paul VI's ban on contraception and a seasonal wish for the *Apollo 8* crew's "Christmas at the Moon" was an unsigned piece on the contemporary art scene. Readers were informed that many young artists were flooding New York galleries with a new kind of work that as yet lacked even a label: "Some call it 'antiform,' for its outlines—or rather, its conspicuous efforts to avoid them. Others call it 'process art,' for it proudly shows off the marks of the process by which it was made. Another term is 'conceptual art,' for in every case, the concept behind the piece is infinitely more impressive than the workmanship."[1] Although the new works by Robert Ryman, Richard Tuttle, James Lee Byars, Walter de Maria, Robert Morris, Bruce Nauman, Keith Sonnier, and others defied classification, *Time* nonetheless averred that the terms of their welcome were patent: Conflating reception with supposed ambition, their art was "deliberately made hard to understand: subtle, cerebral, elusive, private, intense."[2]

Time upheld Ryman as a primary example of this critical predicament, discussing him first. A "shy, quiet" transplant from the South, Ryman lived in "Manhattan lofts and tenements and painted 'naked' pictures. That is to say, he covers rectangles of metal, canvas or paper with white paint and then, instead of framing them or stretching them, he mounts them as close to the wall as

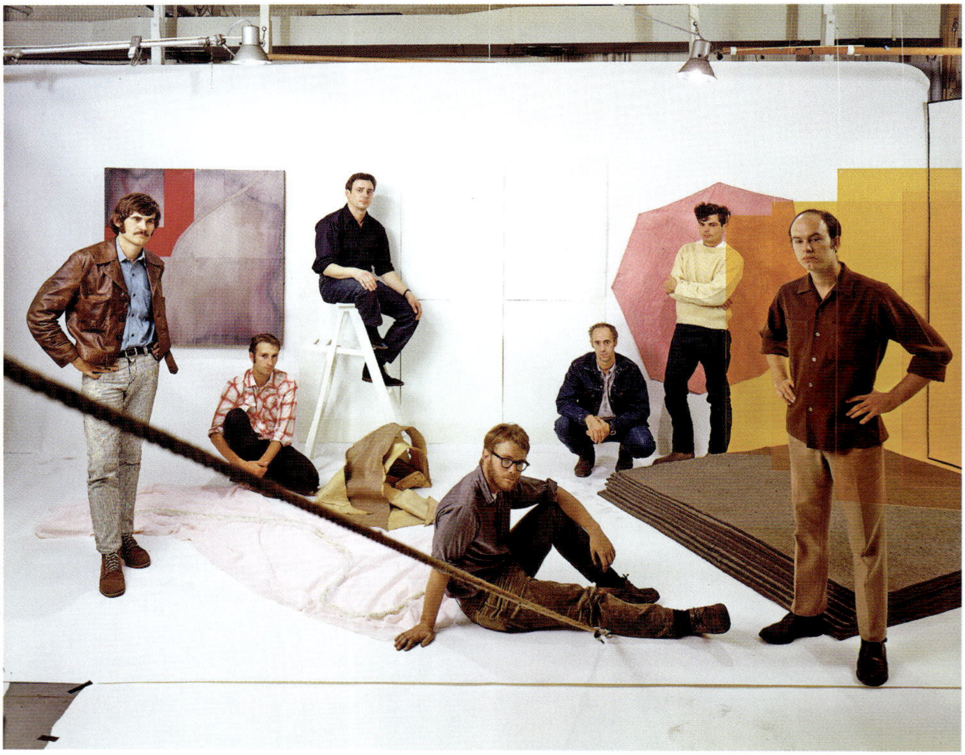

Group portrait in *Time* magazine (1968). Image contains (left to right) Keith Sonnier, Bruce Nauman, Robert Ryman, Bill Bollinger, Robert Morris, Richard Tuttle, David Lee. *Murillo*, ca. 1968, appears behind Ryman.

he can get them, sometimes stapling them directly to the plaster. The effect is unnerving. The wall seems to have developed a gaping hole."[3] Thus, the psychic consequence of Ryman's "naked" pictures: "Ryman's pictures are so unsettling, in fact, that some who see them for the first time laugh outright."[4] Resonating with the proverbial conceit of the emperor's new clothes, *Time*'s concentration on bareness emphasized the farcical blatancy rather than the ethical transparency or obdurate materiality of Ryman's "nakedness." By virtue of their "maddeningly artless look,"[5] Ryman's paintings fulfilled an additional function by introducing *Time*'s constituency to what, in 1968, comprised an aesthetic form.

Time asserted that Ryman's painting—and the art of his peers—was art because it made "the viewer look, and feel, and think. The artist may speak from underground, but he retains, in an elliptical way, his traditional role."[6] In jettisoning both ontological certainties and qualitative pronouncements (in favor of intentionality, however winsomely bohemian), art that looked artless could be art, even as it posed a challenge to normative viewing and the philosophical subtext with which it was supported. But one lingering question was whether art like Ryman's was solely about ideas. Or did the registration of the process by which the work was made become its content? By drawing together artists associated with process and conceptual art and by reading Ryman through this enfolding, *Time* unwittingly dramatized the tensions at the core of Ryman's subsequent reception. Much writing on Ryman oscillates between his materialism and conceptualism, all the while assuming that they are mutually incompatible positions. I argue that Ryman's material experimentation manifests its own signs—not merely as "process" but as embodied thinking.

Labor—Ryman's facility or the suspected lack thereof and his seemingly unimpressive workmanship—is specifically at stake in the *Time* piece. Although Ryman was hardly alone in receiving this critique, the extent to which his practice manages to elicit it decades later is remarkable. His paintings are white squares, after all—the kind of "DIY [do it yourself] wall tiles"[7] that are routinely satirized as supercilious and vacuous in the media by the likes of Morley Safer. The plot of Yasmina Reza's play *Art* turns on a man's purchase of a large, expensive white canvas that is defaced when an infuriated friend draws a "little skier with a woolly hat"[8] on its presumptively snowy base. Reza turns the non-objective field of the painting into the literal ground for representation so that the perceived offense to the character's sensibility mimics the audience's own outrage. A physical act of vandalism counters the affective trauma that the work enacts by loosening the definitions of modern art and (and maybe even more ominously) identifying the cultural elites that validate it and buy it. In a statement that could have come straight from the lips of the glib, nay-saying character in *Art,* Vivien Raynor once indicted Ryman's work by saying, "This is art for souls wealthy enough to own temperature-controlled penthouses with live-in gnomes to keep it pristine."[9]

Here and elsewhere, the question is just what constitutes a painting and not only in relation to positions that might be characterized as boorish by anyone with one foot in the academy or the art market. Even so, we would do well to remember Leo Steinberg's famous registration of anxiety before the work of Jasper Johns. Of the artist's "puzzling" encaustics, the apparent banality of which had frustrated many, Steinberg writes:

> My own first reaction was normal. I disliked the show and would gladly have thought it a bore. Yet it depressed me and I wasn't sure why. Then I began to recognize in myself all the classical symptoms of a philistine's reaction to modern art. I was angry at the artist, as if he had invited me to a meal only to serve something uneatable, like tow and paraffin. I was irritated at some of my friends for pretending to like it—but with an uneasy suspicion that perhaps they did like it, so that I was really mad at myself for being so dull, and at the whole situation for showing me up.[10]

At issue is an anxiety about deception and duplicity. The feeling is that something has been sacrificed and devalued, whether tradition, method, or technical proficiency; there is also the concomitant intimation of a troubling of values, where deprivation goes unredeemed.

Robert Ryman, *Untitled* (c. 1960). Oil on stretched cotton canvas.

These responses to the avant-garde are familiar, which does not preclude their sincerity, defang their vitriol, or mask the incredulity with which they have been restated about Ryman. As one reviewer of Ryman's massive traveling 1993 retrospective exhibition guffawed in a local paper after seeing it in London: "Frustrated artists tempted to cut off their ears or revert to painting by numbers should take heart—and a tin of white emulsion. Got that? Right, now buy a large sheet of hardboard, arm yourself with a big paintbrush and carefully cover the hardboard with the white paint. Then when it's dry, put a nice frame around it and tote it to the Tate." And then the taunting *coup de grâce:* "You certainly shouldn't have too much trouble persuading the 'experts' to hang it on the gallery's hallowed walls because they've already accepted about half a dozen similar ones by Robert Ryman."[11]

But my point is that uncertainty in judgment (as Steinberg went on to celebrate) can abet as many possibilities as it excludes—in viewing or making. The oft-heard criticism "But *I* could do this!" is worth taking seriously and not only because of its cultural biases for art as auratic, graced with the uniquely magical touch of its creator, and for artists who are beholden to specified, verifiable performances of expertise. Such a can-do exclamation resonates differently for Ryman because it was the suggestion from which his work began.

Born in 1930 in Nashville, Tennessee, Ryman enrolled in the Tennessee Polytechnic Institute in Cookville, Tennessee, in 1948, and transferred to the George Peabody College for Teachers the following year to study music. In 1950, he enlisted in the United States Army Reserve Corps, where he played tenor saxophone in the Army Reserve Corps Band and briefly toured the southern states during the Korean War. From his perch in Alabama, his troupe offered "anything that the army wanted music for, we played within a certain radius—marching, parades, service clubs, officers clubs, dances,"[12] and Ryman occasionally moonlighted in local clubs. When released from active duty in 1952, he took his $250 payout, bought a bus ticket, and moved to New York City to play jazz. To this end, he studied with Lenny Tristano, a blind pianist whom the popular press dubbed the "Schoenberg of jazz" for the economy of his decidedly atonal music.[13] By late June 1953, almost exactly a year after he arrived in the city, Ryman took a temporary job as a vacation relief guard at the Museum of Modern Art on the suggestion of Betsy Jones, a friend whom he met through a singing group called the Heathertones.

This was the first of many "flunky"[14] jobs that Ryman held to pay for rent and lessons; in fact, it sustained him for the next seven years. Admittedly the MoMA job was better than average because it allowed him to keep his mornings free for music and painting. The staff also let Ryman practice his instrument in MoMA's empty auditorium, which was helpful given his small apartment and its paper-thin walls. Ryman later described this appointment as "the beginning of an education, a very good education," adding that it "was the best thing that I could have done."[15]

Ryman confronted the story of modern painting as assembled and narrated by Alfred Barr, an art historian and the first director of the Museum of Modern Art. He sketched on pilfered office supplies in the museum galleries during his shifts, responding to the works' provocations rather than reproducing them wholesale. His daily contact with the European works of Paul Cézanne, Henri Matisse, and Pablo Picasso was critical to him, and contemporary American paintings (works by Jackson Pollock, Willem de Kooning, and Mark Rothko) entered the collection in rapid succession, often in Dorothy Miller's watershed shows. In addition to drawing in the galleries, Ryman began to paint in earnest at home. By 1954, Ryman had "put away"[16] his saxophone.

Ryman is self-taught, a musician gone painter in the modernist museum. Unlike previous generations of artists who were trained to incorporate a canon by copying the old masters and imitating their techniques, Ryman's introduction to practice within the white walls of the Modern had little to do with explicit emulation of tradition. Neither was it directed by a mentor. Instead, it was inadvertently shaped by a widespread institutional ethos of experiential learning, whereby museum educators such as Victor D'Amico, the director of the education department for over three decades and the head of the People's Art Center where Ryman studied briefly, promoted values of thinking and making "outside the lines." Disdainful of coloring books because they encouraged "neatness" and imitative "discipline" at the expense of expression, D'Amico likened copying to "counterfeiting or stealing."[17]

D'Amico's opinions, published by the museum's Department of Education and Creative Teaching, influenced a wide range of institutional practices. During the years of Ryman's employment, the museum's culture was openly acquisitive, a stance brought about by a practical allegiance to its 1929 State of New York educational charter, which declared that the mission of the institution was to create and educate a community—of viewers, artists, and patrons—for modern art. Barr curated installations with didactic wall texts, while D'Amico's education programs translated John Dewey's ideas of creative education into a curriculum for art instruction. He highlighted the charter's pedagogical directives in the galleries, on the printed pages of museum publications like those cited above, and through related programs. Frequently imaged as a "laboratory" in which the community was encouraged to participate, the museum succeeded, for a time (that is long past), in giving consequence to this rhetoric.

The Museum of Modern Art encouraged Ryman's education and fostered his personal ties with other members of its small community. Not insignificantly—given her staunch, well-deserved criticism of Museum of Modern Art policy in the early 1970s, first and foremost under the auspices of the Art Workers' Coalition (AWC)—Lucy Lippard characterized the museum of this era as "intimate." She worked as a library assistant from 1958 to 1960, when she was, in her words, "apolitical and fresh out of college"[18] and felt more or less positive about her time there: "Everybody knew each other. There wasn't a lot of hierarchical bullshit, on the surface, anyway," she recalls. "Everybody came into the Library, of course. I was the page and I indexed magazines and I filled vertical files on individual artists, and I looked at every single thing that went under my nose and I got an incredible education."[19]

Ryman and Lippard met at a reopening party after the MoMA fire in 1958 and were married in 1961.[20] Ryman also met Mark Rothko around 1957 (probably in the cafeteria), Dan Flavin in 1959 (he had begun working as a guard), and Sol LeWitt in 1960 (he had taken a job as a desk assistant and eventually taught drawing for D'Amico in 1964). LeWitt and Ryman became closer in the following years as neighbors on Manhattan's Lower East Side, along with Robert and Sylvia Mangold and Eva Hesse and Tom Doyle.

Since Ryman's time at the Museum of Modern Art (followed by a brief stint as a page in the New York Public Library's arts division, his last job before dedicating himself to painting full-time), his origin story has been retold frequently, sometimes following the "immaculate conception theory,"[21] as Lippard quipped, and usually in a way that emphasizes precocity. (Lippard felt that Ryman "was just a natural. He could have done anything.")[22] In 2005, his friend Jan Dibbets exclaimed that when he first met Ryman, he was "amazed that someone who had once been a passionate musician had, completely of his own accord, with no intermediary steps, discovered this art of painting. And that right from the beginning, with his very first attempts, he had produced paintings that were all unmistakably 'Rymans.'"[23]

Ryman's origins matter, even as his practice seems to forgo Oedipal confrontation and direct dialogism. Instead, it is marked by a careful working over of painting's conventions in their most radically reduced (to white paint and a support structure) and paradoxically inverted and expanded possibilities. This increasingly methodical testing of material possibilities came slowly. The more he worked, the more he knew what could be done and how his work related to that of his peers. But from the first, he painted to see what would happen when, say, a brush made contact with a support. As Ryman recounts of his first foray in 1953 (see *Untitled,* 1953, page 64 in this book):

> There was a little art-supply store on the corner [at 60th Street and Lexington Avenue, near Ryman's apartment across from Bloomingdale's department store on Manhattan's Upper East Side]. I went there and bought a couple of canvasboards and some oil paint—they didn't have acrylic paint at the time—and some brushes, and I thought I would try and see what would happen. I wanted to see what the paint would do, how the brushes would work. That was the first step. I just played around. I had nothing really in mind to

> paint. I was just finding out how the paint worked, colors, thick and thin, the brushes, surfaces.[24]

Through such a reduction to matter and to the opportunities that are implicit in wielding implements and redistributing substances, Ryman's paintings exhibit a way of making apart from representing, and he produces paintings as objects as much as images or as images without illusions.

Ryman's paintings have never used paint for depiction. He did not pass through a landscape phase, try for the human figure, or abstract from objects. Even his first paintings, such as those made in the aftermath of the art-supply store visit (discussed in chapter 2), establish a disinterest in representation; so Dibbets's avowal of the early, unmistakable "Rymans." Nor does color—or the lack thereof—function mimetically, symbolically, metaphorically, or even emotively. Despite his near exclusive use of white paints since the late 1950s, Ryman is adamant that his paintings are not monochromes. His use of white, as Phyllis Tuchman summarizes, allows for the heightened visibility of other elements and "can be hot or cold, light or dark. It can exist as oil, acrylic, casein, enamel, or pastel, among many other mediums, and can be applied in all sorts of ways and with a variety of implements."[25] Besides, there is always the color of the support—the gray of steel, the buttery brown of aged paper, or the chalky white of bleached cotton—that must be considered in concert with the paint.

Ryman also claims that his paintings, as images without illusions, are not abstract, which makes the ground (and its color, texture, and receptivity to paint, among other things) significant. In the tradition of Kasimir Malevich and Piet Mondrian, Ryman calls his paintings "realist"—a lexical and philosophical designation that I keep hold of, taking Ryman at his word to better understand the position he constructs—as they open onto and often explicitly annex the light, space, and walls of the galleries in which they are sited as part of their compositions.[26] This means, for instance, that a shadow cast by a deeply projecting stretcher is as much a part of the work as the painted field on the support that produces it. In this, they are not ideational, securely optical, or readymade paintings. Facture and the quality of paint qua paint loom large and constitute the subtle variations between and among serial works. To quote Ryman on differences within what seems a repetitive act: "Monet did a lot of waterlilies, and he also did some haystacks, a number of haystacks, that were very similar, but very unique, and I think it's the same with me."[27]

Slight distinctions from work to work, or even within the field of a single painting where the painted activity continues unabated onto its edges, solicit a phenomenological engagement that occurs in both space and dilating swells of time. An impatient, cursory glance yields little, while presumptuous critical ascriptions all too often mislead. As Robert Storr wrote in 1986: "Robert Ryman's paintings pose a special challenge to critical writing. An art of incremental shifts in emphasis within a strictly limited repertoire of abstract elements, Ryman's work confounds ideological exegesis and disdains the melodrama of stylistic rupture upon which so much criticism thrives."[28] A decade later, Storr had not changed his mind about Ryman's import (or the difficulties involved in conveying it in prose).[29] In his comprehensive Museum of Modern Art catalogue accompanying Ryman's 1993 retrospective, Storr announced—some forty pages into his essay—that "writing about Ryman is notoriously difficult. While words may point out formal and painterly subtleties, they can never fully render them. Transcription is not translation."[30]

Since the time of Ryman's early shows, this problematic has gone a long way to explain the dearth of material on the artist. For a generation of critics who were torn between the existential poetics exemplified by Harold Rosenberg's "The American Action Painters" (published in *Art News* in 1952) and the pseudo-scientific formalism of Clement Greenberg's medium specificity (active from the early 1940s, consolidated with the publication of *Art and Culture* in 1961, and later promulgated by Michael Fried), Ryman's work occupied a no-man's land outside of these two mainstream conceptions of American abstraction. Nonetheless, terms to handle the works were hardly in short supply in the 1960s and 1970s (discussed in chapter 4). The problem became whether those designations offered any insights into Ryman's production.

Although Ryman admits to being tremendously influenced by Willem de Kooning and Mark Rothko in the 1950s, when he was beginning to paint

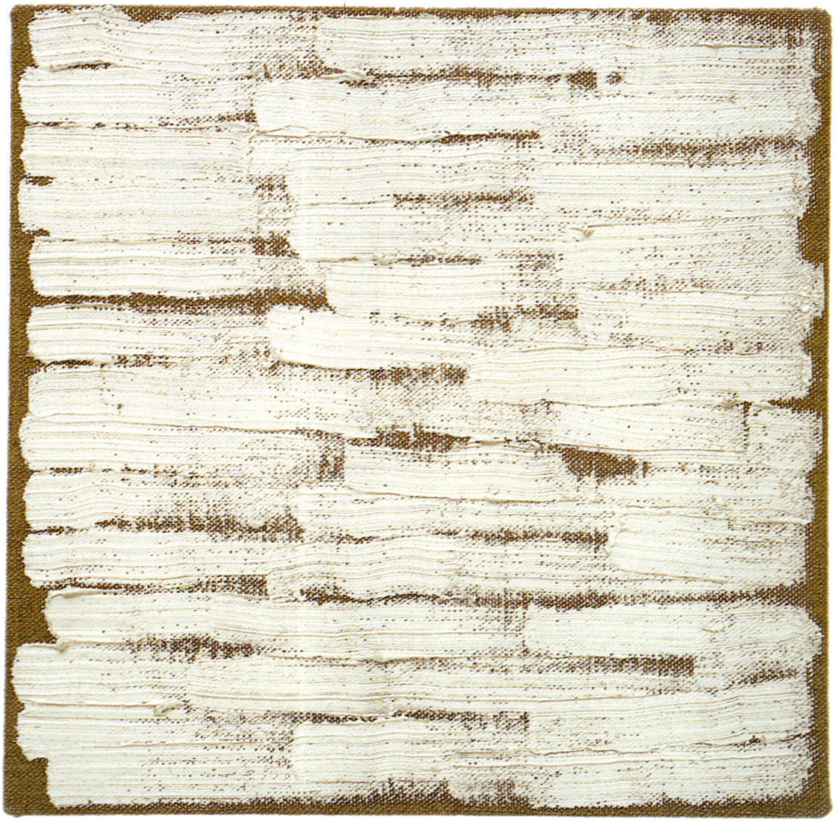

Robert Ryman, *Untitled* (c. 1965). Oil on stretched sized linen canvas.

seriously, he was never affiliated with the New York School. The historical circumstances that delayed the making known of Ryman's works also complicate group affiliations, whether with the New York School or otherwise. Ryman contributed a painting to a MoMA staff exhibition in the museum's penthouse in 1958, and his work appeared in group exhibitions, including a Christmas show at the artist-run 10th Street Brata Gallery in 1958 and 1959, the American Abstract Artists Twenty-eighth Annual Exhibition at New York University's Loeb Student Center in 1964, and the Dan Flavin-curated Eleven Artists show at the Kaymar Gallery in 1964 (where Ryman was shown in the company of Flavin, Jo Baer, Walter Darby Bannard, Donald Judd, Sol LeWitt, Larry Poons, and Frank Stella). But he was not showing with any regularity or being written about with any concentration until almost a decade after his first outings. By the late 1960s, too, painting's outlier status was yet another distraction.

Ryman's inclusion in Lawrence Alloway's conceptually oriented Systemic Painting exhibit at the Guggenheim Museum in 1966 was a boon in spite of the catalogue's few references to his participation; he was one of only two artists without an exhibition history or a bibliography.[31] He installed his first one-man exhibition in April 1967 at the Paul Bianchini Gallery at the suggestion of gallery assistant Dorothy Herzka. Nothing was sold, even though the paintings were inexpensive. As Ryman recollected: "But I brought an old acquaintance of mine who happened to be in town to look at my paintings. He didn't think much of them, but he saw a little Rembrandt drawing that Paul had in his office, and eventually bought it. Paul was so pleased about that (because he was going broke too—he folded a couple of months after my show) that he gave me $100. So something came from the show, and at that time $100 meant a lot."[32]

In May, he was included in the company of Ad Reinhardt, Dan Graham, Robert Mangold, and others in the Fifteen People Present Their Favorite Book show at Joseph Kosuth's Lannis Gallery, New York, where Robert Morris contributed his favorite book, the 1967 *New York Telephone Company Yellow Pages;* Carl Andre contributed Friedrich Waismann's *Introduction to Mathematical Thinking;* and Ryman gamely supplied Henry Miller's *Tropic of Cancer.*[33]

The year 1969 proved a crossroads, with solo shows at the Fischbach Gallery in New York and at the European triumvirate of Galerie Konrad Fischer (Düsseldorf), Galerie Heiner Friedrich (Munich), and Galerie Yvon Lambert (Paris).[34] He was also included in the watershed When Attitudes Become Form: Works, Concepts, Processes, Situations, Information exhibit, which was curated by Harold Szeeman at the Kunstmuseum Bern; Op losse schroeven: situaties en cryptostructuren curated by Wim Beeren at the Stedelijk Museum, Amsterdam (it traveled as Verborgene Strukturen to Museum Folkwang, Essen); and in the Anti-Illusion: Procedures/Materials exhibit, which was curated by Marcia Tucker and James Monte at the Whitney Museum of American Art, New York. Following his contribution to Susan Tumarkin Goodman's 1970 Jewish Museum show, Using Walls, Ryman was granted a Guggenheim retrospective in 1972, with "over 30 paintings and 10 prints and drawings."[35] By exhibiting paintings from only 1965 to 1972 and excluding anything earlier (and likely facture-laden), this first large-scale presentation of recent work neatly sanitized Ryman's production and annulled a decade's worth of painting.[36] While a coinciding John Weber Gallery show, Robert Ryman: Early Painting, sought to redress this void, it was overwhelmed by the larger retrospective uptown.

Ryman's visibility in both sites coincided with the popularization of minimalism (articulated chiefly in and as sculpture) and conceptualism in the 1960s and early 1970s. It was largely under these later rubrics (and not those of 1950s abstract expressionism) that Ryman's aesthetic was subsumed. Even as early as 1972, however, the uncomfortable fit between Ryman and these admittedly internally inconsistent, heterogeneous fields (on this count, *Time* got it right) was becoming more apparent.

In the Guggenheim catalogue published for Ryman's retrospective, Diane Waldman names him as a minimalist but then recants, writing that "although Ryman is aligned with the Minimalist movement, he has more recently been claimed for both Process and Conceptual art. These shifting classifications, if somewhat arbitrary, do nonetheless point out the fact that he eludes categorization."[37] In a review for the same Guggenheim show, Peter Schjeldahl championed minimalist painting as "the finest and most enduring legacy of

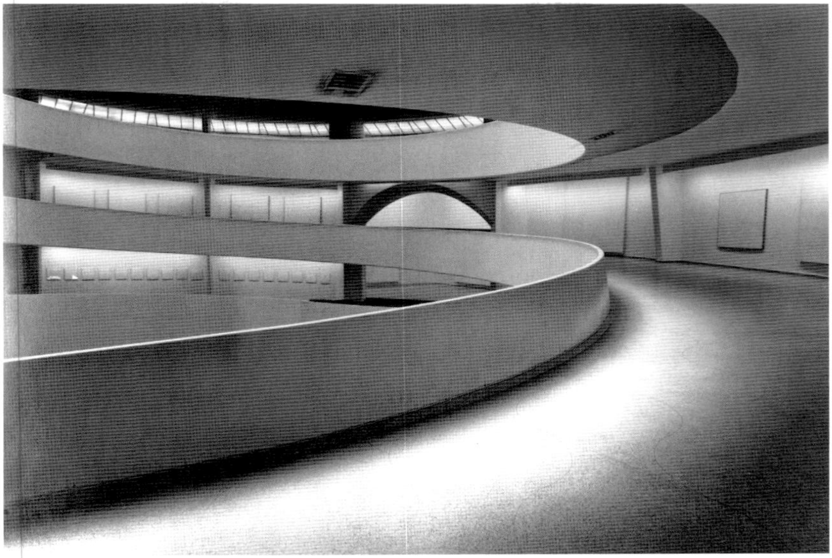

Installation view of Robert Ryman (1972), The Solomon R. Guggenheim Museum, New York.

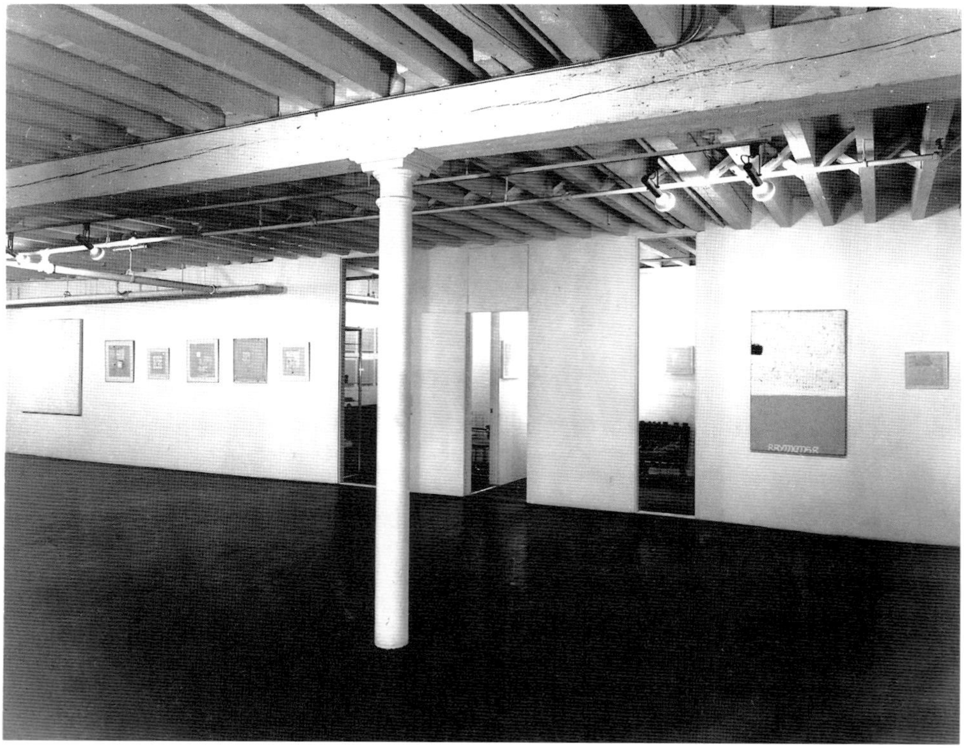

Installation view of Robert Ryman: Early Paintings (1972), John Weber Gallery, New York.

the [minimalist] movement," counting Ryman within this paradigm and yet revoking its claim with belletristic flourish: "But Ryman does not even 'elude' these categories [minimalism or postminimalism] so much as cut across them with a simple will to make personal, direct and beautiful paintings, a will whose pressure and resourcefulness emanate from all his work like a steady white light."[38]

Against this assignation or repudiation of Ryman as a minimalist—and how, much less in what ways, this taxonomy makes a difference—the point remains that Ryman kept making paintings that operate outside of any classificatory structure. In this, I agree with Storr when he writes that

> Ryman's endeavor [is not] bound to the idea or moment of Minimalism, which his paintings of the late 1950s and early 1960s anticipated and his present work survives. Beginning where Malevich left off while avoiding the routine serial production which has claimed many of his contemporaries, Ryman has continued to create paintings that matter-of-factly refute end-game esthetics, slipping the noose of Greenbergian and post-Greenbergian formalist teleologies just as surely as they, in their turn, obviate recourse to the metaphysical apologetics of earlier abstract schools.[39]

A 1969 press release for his Fischbach show asserts that "while Ryman has been associated with the dubiously labeled Minimal and Anti-form Movements, his work has developed in a self-imposed isolation and determinedly personal progression. Its intense nonchalance has proved disconcerting and uncategorizable."[40] In a comparable vein, Patrick Frey once dubbed Ryman an "absolute loner in American painting,"[41] while Naomi Spector insisted that he "cannot be categorized into any movement."[42]

Because of his practice's longevity and his longstanding exemption from categorical limitations (then or now, however generational he may be), questions of historical recapitulation matter. Indeed, irrespective of his nonaffiliations, I would not claim for Ryman the reified position of a historicist of one. That Ryman's practice is not divorced from aesthetic or social history I assume as axiomatic. But any claims for connection to that history must be grounded in the particularity of paint and the effects that it fosters, painting by painting. These effects might exceed the apprehension of a white paint surface sutured to a wall, but that is where they must be given form. Only then can larger questions about the meaning of putting white pigment on a linen canvas be addressed.

Painting in Ryman's hands has continued as a series of propositions that are born out of an engagement with the materiality of paint, the properties of support structures, and notions of how such objects relate to their beholders in an exhibition space. Meaning is revealed in practical concerns and the consequences of specific material choices so that the basic possibilities of the medium are worked again and again and again. For Yve-Alain Bois, Ryman stands guard at the tomb of modern painting, constructing and deconstructing painting as tradition, exposing the limits of critical discourse in his wake: "He is perhaps the *last modernist painter,* in the sense that his work is the last to be able graciously to maintain its direction by means of modernist discourse, to be able to fortify it if necessary, but above all radically to undermine it and exhaust it through excess."[43]

Although Ryman's practice deconstructs tenets of modernist painting and reveals the performance of manual dexterity that has long guaranteed it, it does not stand for the finality (however mythic) of modernism. Instead of a dialectical process, I see a chiasmatic structure of interwoven and overlapping parts. I likewise propose a differential model in which Ryman's paintings are particular, not interchangeable, and have meaningful variations.

Still, many writers, Bois chief among them, have theorized painting's endgame and Ryman's place within it. The crucial quote (with Bois citing Hubert Damisch) follows:

> The fiction of the end of art (or of painting) is understood as a "confusion between the end of the game itself (as if a game could really have an end) and that of such and such a match (or series of matches)." One can conclude then that, if the match "modernist painting" is finished, it does not necessarily mean that the game

> "painting" is finished: many years to come are ahead for this art. But the situation is even more complicated: for the match "modernist painting" was the match of the end of painting; it was both a response to the feeling of the end and a working through of the end. And this match was historically determined—by the fact of industrialization (photography, the commodity, etc.). To claim that the "end of painting" is finished is to claim that this historical situation is no longer ours, and who would be naïve enough to make this claim when it appears that reproducibility and fetishization have permeated all aspects of life: have become our "natural" world?[44]

In such defining essays as "Painting: The Task of Mourning," from which the preceding excerpt is taken, and "Ryman's Tact," where Bois argues that Ryman reveals the institutions of painting, Bois positions Ryman as blindingly repeating modernism's undermined terms, resulting in a revelation of the essential arbitrariness of painting that modernism sought to deny.[45]

Maurice Berger has since restated Bois's position, reading Ryman as akin to the likes of Peter Halley and Sherrie Levine as a kind of postmodern cipher: "Robert Ryman's stringent paintings serve as a paradigm of minimalism's cultural deconstruction. Like the fabrications of minimalist sculpture, Ryman's canvases, while elegant, nevertheless question modernist notions of 'creativity,' 'originality,' and the expression of the artist's 'temperament.'"[46] While Ryman deflates hyperbolic notions of expression, his works are marked by the play of facture, a point that is hard to confirm or refute in relation to Berger's text and particularly in relation to his assertion that Ryman's paintings are devoid of his hand (which to Berger appears to "glide mechanistically over the canvas"), as he does not reproduce or refer with any specificity to a single Ryman painting.[47] Meanwhile, for Douglas Crimp, Ryman's project is similarly "a systematic, single-minded, persistent attempt to rid painting once and for all of its idealist trappings."[48] This implies that painting is synonymous with and inextricable from models of modernist transcendence and hyperbolic subjective engagement with the materials of painting, wherein those materials are transubstantiated and meant to signify apart from their articulation of surface.

Though I do not see Ryman's work as rehearsing painting's end, neither do I suppose that it implies or guarantees its longevity, the equally deterministic (if buoyantly antediluvian) position to which Storr subscribes. In his opposition to a perceived authoritarian entrenchment, Storr enacts an equally ideological stance. His reactionary, if generous, Ryman "is an empiricist of beauty" who is "demonstrating [painting's] infinite fecundity."[49] In this, Storr acts in binary lock-step with the "several sects" of critics who have diagnosed "painting's auto-extinction." For Storr, Bois and others "seek to give positive meaning to the present by forecasting negative scenarios for the future."[50]

However compelling the oratory on either side, this in-fighting is not analytical discourse, especially when it remains at the level of personal denigration and seems unmotivated by the work at hand.[51] Much writing on Ryman's practice therefore feels obliquely occasioned by it rather than causally related to it. Any meaningful elaboration of his work must be rooted in specific practices apart from the work's significance (often abstracted beyond recognition) for those whose minds were made up long before seeing Ryman's paintings.

Against antiaesthetic historicism and anticonceptual hedonism, this book asserts Ryman's pragmatism. I do not make a case for painting's extinction or for its continuation. Instead, my claim is that Ryman's assumption of the possibility of painting's viability keeps it an open inquiry, the resolution of which is perpetually deferred. Querying what a painting is every time that he makes one, Ryman in his experiential practice aligns with John Dewey's conception of "learning by doing," where ideas and things, concepts and materials, are indivisible. As Dewey writes: "Here is the organic relation of theory and practice. . . . [One learns] not simply [by] doing things, but [by] getting also the *idea* of what he does; getting from the start some intellectual conception that enters into his practice and enriches it; while every idea finds, directly or indirectly, some application in experience and has some effect upon life."[52]

What Ryman learns in one painting—whether success or failure—becomes a way to understand and deal effectively with what follows. Dewey affirms: "The method of intelligence manifested in the experimental method demands keeping track of ideas, activities, and observed consequences. Keeping track is a matter of reflective review and summarizing, in which there is both discrimination and record of the significant features of a developing experience. To reflect is to look back over what has been done so as to extract the net meanings which are the capital stock for intelligent dealing with further experiences."[53]

Knowledge is the concrete consequence of a test, not something hypostatized or cordoned off from experience. In Dewey's formulation of the experimental method, importance is attached "to ideas as ideas."[54] But the "ideas or hypotheses are tested by the consequences which they produce when they are acted upon."[55] As such, Ryman's painting crucially derives from a series of encounters—formal, material, institutional, and social—through which actions unfold out of and respond to a discrete set of circumstances, options, and concerns that are different for every painting. Results that are achieved in the practice of painting are primary. For Ryman, the painted sign, the support on which it is put down, the edge that rims it and connects it to the wall, and the wall that finally completes the circuit form the empirical relay that justifies the painting's existence and (potentially) generates it as a painting.

Ryman's testing of materials and their effects to produce "painting" is elaborated throughout what follows in a division of chapters into Ryman's diachronic, sometimes overlapping investigations of primer, paint, support structures, edges, and the walls on which his works hang. Contingent on the work that Ryman was doing at decisive moments and the particular problems with which he was engaged, the chapters move back and forth temporally, rendering the chapter divisions porous. Attention shifts from Ryman's paintings to matters of context and discourse, with material rubrics annexed for the chapters' titles and mined as their conceptual motivations and institutional frames. But most of Ryman's paintings can be read through the framework of any chapter or all chapters, and the constituents can collapse into one another. They become inextricable in Ryman's practice and do exactly that in chapter 5.

My organization acknowledges the precariousness with which to think Ryman's practice together with pragmatism, or better, Ryman as painting pragmatism. His artworks cannot be illustrative of this theory since pragmatism

Robert Ryman, *Test* (1986). Lascaux acrylic (synthetic polymer paint) and graphite on gatorboard panel.

undercuts and renders logically impossible an applicationist model that would allow objects to be descriptive of it. Pragmatism, William James maintained, is a method as opposed to a meaning—a way of doing philosophy as opposed to a philosophy as such.[56] But this method serves to undo many staples of philosophy—verbal solutions, self-evident reasons, fixed principles, and closed systems.[57] Charles Peirce underscores the pragmatist antipathy to metaphysics in a manner that makes James seem positively mild in his disaffection (James would simply ask what the differences in believing in opposing notions actually are and conclude that if "the alternatives mean practically the same thing . . . all dispute is idle").[58] Peirce writes that metaphysics "is a subject much more curious than useful, the knowledge of which, like that of a sunken reef, serves chiefly to enable us to keep clear of it."[59]

The issue becomes how to reconcile pragmatic doing with discursive meaning. Can the former be held apart from any and all interpretive programs, as Ryman himself seems to claim? And even if tenable, is such a neat bifurcation desirable? Here is Jean Frémon: "As a matter of fact, it appears these paintings [of Ryman's] are made for themselves. . . . They are not signs, they do not aspire to that." To be sure, "everything is a sign as soon as it is shown, discussed, reproduced, bought-sold, where, how, by whom, in what company." The distinction for Frémon is that although much art aspires to the condition of the sign, "Ryman's paintings do as little as possible"[60] to assist transcription. My concession is that significance needs to stay motivated, resist both capricious rationales and exogenous connections, and be as mobile as making. In short, pragmatic making entails pragmatic meaning, functioning conclusively but not infallibly as a rubric for approaching Ryman. Or such is my hope.

But pragmatism here is also historically specific. It is apposite in relation to Ryman's work since it markedly influenced the Museum of Modern Art's early "laboratory" years. At the most basic level, my positioning of Ryman as a pragmatist means that Ryman's painting remains for him a perpetual experiment and that each painting is the upshot of his trials. What a painting *is* is commensurate with what a painting *does,* so that ideas are hypotheses to be tested and revised against the consequences, in painting, that they have produced.

In this spirit of testing, each chapter that follows may well be read as an attempt to work through an aspect of Ryman's practice, meaning that this project is less about constructing a normative monograph about Ryman than offering a series of interlocking essays on Ryman. And yet the chapters are still roughly chronological. Chapter 1 is a prehistory that leads to the 1950s, chapter 2 begins in the 1950s, chapter 3 details the 1960s, chapter 4 attends to the late 1960s and 1970s, and chapter 5 travels to the 1980s and 1990s. As noted above, most paintings are equally resonant in multiple interpretive sites; some years are retraced as well. For example, I seek in chapter 1 to understand the 1950s through the institutional context in which Ryman learned to paint and then in chapter 2 to present a close examination of the paintings from those years.

Accordingly, chapter 1 ("Primer") offers a history of Alfred Barr's museum and Victor D'Amico's education department during the years of Ryman's employment at the Museum of Modern Art. It looks at questions of pedagogy as they played out in the educational contexts of both museum-sponsored art courses and the galleries where Ryman worked. This discussion (in which Ryman's position is epigrammatic) lays the foundation for the rest of the book as a kind of briefing—the base color that underlies the values that it regulates—on the conditions in which his work began. Taking seriously how and where people learn (D'Amico through Dewey at Columbia, Barr at Princeton and Harvard, and Ryman through the Museum of Modern Art shaped by D'Amico and Barr), this chapter argues for pragmatism as an intellectual and philosophical tradition that is mediated by the institution and assimilated by the artist for reasons that are as concrete in their motivation as they were broad in their application.

Following chapter 1's institutional narrative—which questions what the differing modes of instruction and active reception of ideas *do* in the institution, painting, or painting in the institution—chapter 2 ("Paint") seeks to understand Ryman's earliest paintings in relation to his museum learning experiences. This is a hard association to ignore for innumerable reasons, especially a surviving cache of drawings that Ryman created while working in the galleries. What do these drawings show? How exactly did Ryman work? How are ideas translated into and through material form, and how does an institutional intercession of pragmatism model an artist who is learning to paint through its terms? How did Ryman learn to paint, and what does this education suggest about the works produced thereafter?

Chapter 3 ("Support") considers Ryman's definition of painting as born of conventions and their effects rather than period notions of medium or claims for its ontology as voiced most strenuously by Clement Greenberg. Support is the guiding principle for Ryman, and this chapter reads Ryman's use of support structures literally through, among other things, his works on unstretched canvas. In addition, it privileges the support as a philosophical intention. The coincident painting of Ellsworth Kelly—whose model of antisubjective, acompositional abstraction was based on missing referents that are regrounded in the history of painting—provides a foil for Ryman's work as it was developing. Ryman's paintings engage not the history of painting—whether of style, medium, or critical position—but its *practice.* Like all such comparisons in the book, contrasts were selected not on the basis of proximity (even if in cases like Eva Hesse there was a personal connection to Ryman) but according to the logic of heuristic function—how their work helps better articulate the specificity and the associations of Ryman's efforts. In one sense, they are utterly random; in another, they are the furthest things from it.

This midpoint of the book reflects a turning point in his career between prepublic (chapters 1, 2, and 3) and public (chapters 4 and 5) Ryman. Although Ryman was developing ideas about what, for him, constituted a painting, he was doing so largely without critical appraisal until the late 1960s. This midpoint also bridges the institutional and the discursive. The final chapters take as their object the reception of Ryman's paintings (and his response to criticism) and posit a pragmatic relation both between Ryman and his painting and between his paintings and their viewers.

Once exhibited, Ryman's works were apprehended in many contradictory and discordant ways, and chapter 4 ("Edge") offers a reception history of Ryman's paintings as they became known in the late 1960s. It addresses the seminal Sixteen Americans show at the Museum of Modern Art to ask generationally resonant questions about what counted as a painting for Ryman's publics—and about which method of critical engagement with that painting was the most appropriate. This elaboration of the discursive field within which Ryman's works became visible is marked by what I call *the edge*—the uncomfortable feeling that viewers experience when they confront works that exceed a field's given framework. Here, I focus on Sixteen Americans' exhibitor Frank Stella. Where Stella's paintings baited but sought to refuse circumscription, Ryman's paintings are arhetorical, which embarrassed overdetermined criticism—and these two strategies have radically different outcomes.

Ryman's work from this period likewise pressures the delimiting function of the edge, opening his works beyond the picture plane and into the world. His paintings increasingly imply connections to their environments and to each other (that is, the project as a whole), a point that also appears in the criticism under discussion. In chapter 5 ("Wall"), I explore this "beyond" by juxtaposing Ryman's method of installation (and its bearing on his work's categorization as painting) with that of the work of Eva Hesse. Hesse worked outside painting in the gap between painting and sculpture, a move that Ryman chose not to make. Further, Ryman understands his paintings as beholden to realism, where spatial and institutional viewing parameters become key.

Finally, Ryman's works open onto a distinct model of painting that has philosophical ramifications for painting more generally. Pragmatism allows for a differential model of modern representation and of subjectivity in representation. Ryman's pragmatism issues from a position of antiskeptical fallibilism that believes in the possibility of painting's prospects but is besieged by doubt. Ryman's works are neither prognostic indicators nor proleptic foreclosures, but ways of keeping painting an open question without delimiting what results might follow.

1

Primer

Not long into his tenure as a guard at the Museum of Modern Art in 1953, Robert Ryman was enticed by a staff discount to take an adult course in experimental painting at the People's Art Center in MoMA's Department of Education. This brief engagement provided his only formal art education—excluding a mechanical drawing class at the American Art School that he dropped almost as soon as he started.[1] The precise date of the MoMA painting course is unknown (records from these years for the People's Art Center are incomplete), and Ryman put so little stock in the episode's value that he claims to have forgotten most of its specifics, other than that he likely drew from a model, worked with collage, and gained some insights into materials and techniques.[2] The fact nonetheless remains that Ryman did learn to paint in the institution, if not solely—or even primarily—in the context of the People's Art Center.

While most of his peers enrolled at the Art Students League or in school programs, thanks in large part to the GI Bill and the advancing preeminence of postwar master of fine arts (MFA) degrees, Ryman shunned formalized education in favor of a different sort of indoctrination. For him, art was less a profession to be assumed or a set of preordained skills to be studied, reproduced, and mastered than a site of creative experimentation where materials could be tested. Ryman, as he has always maintained, wanted to see "how the paint worked."[3]

Ryman tested constitutive materials, queried technical strategies, and observed the ways that paint moves across a supporting surface. By careful looking and by doing the thing to be learned, he assimilated technical competence over time. Ryman's approach to painting was not contingent on an academic calendar but tendered through shifting arrangements of pictures. Thus it belies a connection to an ethos of modernist self-discovery through materials and their consolidation as forms, where, as Howard Singerman articulates (echoing Johannes Itten and the John Dewey-inflected Bauhaus programs more generally): "Each formal discovery was a self-discovery; this is why modernism can be, or rather has been, simultaneously formalist and expressionist: formal innovation is a discovering and instantiation of the self."[4]

Particular to Ryman's alignment of his practice with materials (rather than discursive constructions or nominative associations) is the congruency between this mode of formal and subjective discovery and its practical confirmation within the Museum of Modern Art of the 1950s. Artists elsewhere might have been indoctrinated (as Singerman argues, artists were not teaching artists a "particular métier" or material tradition but "about it, along its frame"),[5] but Ryman was educated by objects and through the ways in which they were configured. Thomas Crow writes that Ryman's concerns "depended on the newly authoritative history of twentieth-century painting which [the Museum of Modern Art] had done [the] most to create" and that this like "any history promulgated by a museum will entail the necessary fiction that works of art generate other works of art with little mediation of historical context, which cannot be displayed on its walls."[6] Crow continues: "Ryman made his art out of the same assumption; he could form a valid project through the *consumption* of certain ideas about what mattered in recent practice, while forgoing anything like a traditional apprenticeship in the *production* of paintings."[7]

Working in the galleries from 1953 to 1960 proved to be adventitious to—and determinant of—Ryman's education in ways that he could not have foreseen. But even before his hire, Ryman, recently having moved to New York, started visiting galleries and museums "like a tourist."[8] At the Museum of Modern Art, he "looked at the collection. I was completely open to everything because I didn't know anything. I was totally naïve, and so I just looked and looked."[9] Soon he was scheduling periodic looking-blocks in front of a rotating cast of artworks during his work hours: "I would concentrate on different paintings each week or so, you know. Sometimes I would be into the Cézannes. Other times I would concentrate on the Matisses or the Picassos or other things."[10] As is discussed in chapter 2, he was also sketching while on duty and painting on his own time, maintaining an openness to other works.

An argument can be made that Ryman's evolution from tourist to student (which occurred in tandem with his conversion from musician to painter) had much to do with the museum's culture in the 1950s. The accessibility and usefulness of its objects helped viewers learn to see creatively, think independently, gain knowledge of the manual crafts necessary to complete a work of art for oneself, and integrate the production and consumption of art into everyday life. A score of contemporaneous museum publications—including the textbook *Creative Teaching in Art* (first published in 1942, reprinted seven times by 1951, and revised in 1953) and the Art for Beginners series of books inaugurated in the late 1940s—are exemplary in this regard and crucial for our understanding of museum pedagogy.[11] With titles like *How to Make Objects of Wood* and *How to Draw and Paint,* these arts and crafts primers grew out of the museum's educational programs as developed by its education director, Victor D'Amico.[12]

The series introduction, as reproduced in *How to Make Modern Jewelry,* states that the "books are intended as self-instruction manuals for persons working on their own, and as aids to the trained teacher in directing large groups."[13] Projects begin with something appropriate for the novice and proceed in order of difficulty. They require a minimum of tools (even the jewelry-making guide, the most utensil-heavy of the bunch, stresses that most of its requirements are "simple and not expensive with the exception of a blowtorch or kiln in Projects XIII and XIV").[14] As experience allows, students work on increasingly complex projects without needing supplementary materials.

Likewise telling is *Art for the Family,* which demystifies art, medium by medium, "for anyone who can hold a brush or work a pair of scissors or fasten things together, or wants to."[15] In a section entitled "Everybody Can Paint," the authors of *Art for the Family* (D'Amico and two of his colleagues) explain that in addition to learning to use paint, through painting you could "learn new and wonderful things about yourself and the world around you."[16] To this end, the book details what materials and tools to buy (for example, bristle brushes, a cellulose sponge, a plastic or metal water bowl or coffee can, and a smock), where to buy them at local suppliers, and what to do with them: "Use brushes of different sizes. Make lines. Make dots. Drop paint from your brush onto the paper. Paint with your sponge. Make lines in the paint with your brush handle. Try painting on a wet paper. Try a colored paper. Cut your paper in a different shape and see how this changes your painting. Make more paintings, trying different experiments."[17] More "experiments" with their related "discoveries" follow, teaching students "from three to thirty, or nine to ninety" about perspective and other fundamentals: "Experiment: Look down a street with houses on each side, or look down a railroad track. Discovery: Do the sides of the street or the railroad tracks appear to come together in the distance? Do the houses seem to follow the line of the street? Do the houses farther away seem to be higher up than the nearer ones?"[18]

Once work has been produced, the authors propose staging a family art gallery where each person can learn from others' works without actually copying them ("*Don't copy anyone . . . anything* . . . Don't even copy nature").[19] That way, the authors suggest, you will nurture your own vision, and if you "keep a record of what you do,"[20] you can chart growth over time. (Without rendering this too pat an analogy, it is worth mentioning that many decades and paintings later, Ryman still had a wall in his studio devoted to just such a record.) Focal here is an underlying premise: "*There is no one way to paint. There are a lot of ways.* There is *your* way."[21]

Although the didacticism of this permissive, subject-oriented mission is confined to the page in these books, comparable messages were simultaneously communicated in the galleries. Notions of self-learning were flourishing there to such an extent that they threatened the primacy of the Education Department's programs (discussed below). On one level, my argument is uncomplicated: Ryman's acquisition of the skills of looking and painting were made

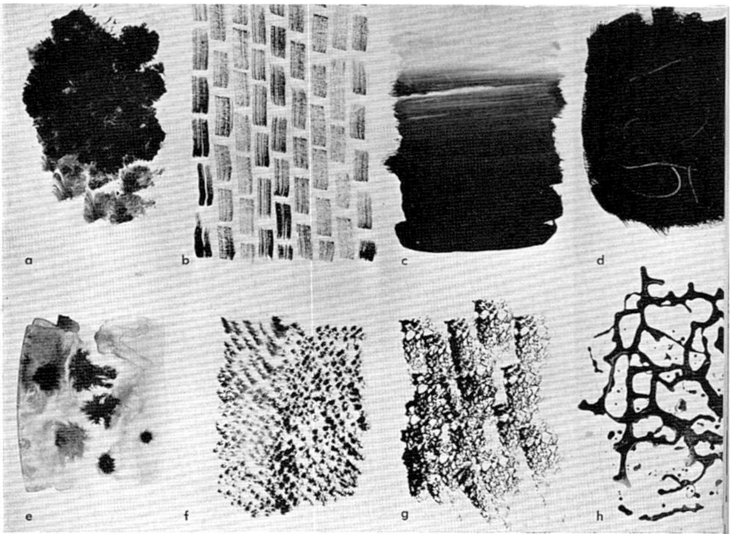

Discover what you can do with paint

Here are some ways of exploring with paint. Try out your colors. Wet your brush and press it on the sponge to take out the extra water. Dip it in a color and put the paint on the paper. The paint in the coasters will stay clean if you remember to wash your brush and press it on the sponge whenever you change to a new color. Try each color. Mix them together and invent new colors. Brush one color on top of another that has already dried on your paper. Use more water with a color and see what happens. Use brushes of different sizes. Make lines. Make dots. Drop paint from your brush onto the paper. Paint with your sponge. Make lines in the paint with your brush handle. Try painting on a wet paper. Try a colored paper. Cut your paper in a different shape and see how this changes your painting. Make more paintings, trying different experiments.

Adult experiment
a. dabbing one color over another
b. dry brush strokes
c. blending from light to dark
d. scratching through paint with brush handle
e. dropping color on wet background
f. stippling
g. sponge painting
h. pouring paint and letting it run

19

Victor D'Amico, Frances Wilson, and Moreen Maser, *Art for the Family* (1954).

possible by the museum. As a pragmatist institution during the period under consideration, MoMA nudged its installations and related programs, publications, and courses toward such educational purposes under the aegis of Victor D'Amico and Alfred Barr, whose own educational background predisposed him to reorient where and how learning could take place. In short, the gallery became the classroom, and Barr thought about both sites through the model of the laboratory. After studying at the Fogg Museum and teaching at Wellesley College, where laboratory work was favored in the arts as well as sciences, Barr transmitted the notion of problem solving to the topics that structured his lectures and then to the organization of the museum.

For Barr, modern artwork could have provisional historical significance—future anteriority. Therefore, it could be managed like its classical counterparts in a conditional bet on what might, in the end, count. The work would not be reified—made mute or static—when it passed into Barr's archival respository, however. Instead, it remained a working "laboratory" that was subject to testing, transformation, reordering, and retrospective refinement over time. When this antifoundational conception is applied to the mechanisms of a collecting institution, it undermines any attempt at hypostatization. (Or it did so for a certain time that feels very far away. Crow's normative art history was not yet authoritative when Ryman began but was certainly so by the time he left the museum, as I discuss below.) In being malleable, Barr's idiosyncratic staging of modernism allowed unforeseen practices and inadvertent, sometimes contradictory narratives to develop while the artworks remained grounded in a framework that could accommodate rupture or historical transformations from within.

When Ryman the guard encountered the Museum of Modern Art, he also encountered these laboratory conditions as the collection began to become permanent and installation strategies were being tested. He found works to be unyielding in their materiality, uncompromising in their physical presence, but less than reliable in various people's claims for their significance (or even in the grounds on which the claims were made). The museum installations might have been mounted to secure the autonomy of both the art and the viewer, but for

Ryman they served as practical lessons. They endorsed singular engagements with the literal stuff of art that, while personal, might not prove expressionistic (Ryman understood that signs of uniqueness were redundant as each work is equivalently particularized). According to *Art for the Family,* the artists whose work Ryman scrutinized painted *their* ways, and he was encouraged to find his own. As Ryman suggested thirty years later: "If you can find the focus of your individuality, and you're able to find an approach to it you can work with, then that's the best you can do."[22]

The curatorial staff's assumption of the role traditionally associated with the Education Department precipitated a crisis for D'Amico about the educator's place in the museum. (Two related and inextricable pedagogical trajectories are recounted here—first D'Amico's and then Barr's.) This quandary is evident in an article that D'Amico wrote for the Museum of Modern Art *Bulletin* two years before Ryman's appointment. D'Amico reiterated his mandate but near the otherwise confirmatory text's conclusion questioned his department's efficacy. Never one to equivocate about his moorings in progressive education, D'Amico did worry about whether this pedagogy could operate within the museum of the 1950s. Detailing the museum's commitment to art education under his tenure, from a pilot program conceived as the Educational Project at Barr's behest in 1937 to its current status as a full-fledged department, D'Amico traced a developmental narrative that paralleled the more general history of the museum during these same years.

At the time that D'Amico wrote this article, full-time staff members of the Education Department were reaching fifty New York City public high schools every year with recorded slide-show talks, teaching portfolios, texts, and lending libraries of art reproductions from the museum's collection.[23] The department operated the popular Young People's Gallery and by 1951 had held eighty-three exhibitions of children's art and almost annual Children's Holiday Carnivals. The carnivals drew an average of two thousand participants each year and operated on John Dewey's principle that play could be instructive within an educative environment that stimulated the child through a canny intersection of the visual, the tactile, and the kinesthetic. The carnivals included games to teach topical ideas of abstraction, colored slides of the museum's artworks, "real" paintings, sculptures that could be touched, and a workshop area with art supplies where children could produce their own collages, constructions, and Alexander Calder-inspired mobiles.[24]

The Education Department was also teaching close to five hundred children and three hundred adults a week in seventy-seven different classes at its newly retooled People's Art Center. In addition, it was sponsoring the museum-conceived National Committee on Art Education, which offered monthly seminars, annual conferences (frequently on The Art in Art Education), and forums on the theory and practice of creative art education that drew participants such as Herbert Read, Walter Gropius, Lewis Mumford, Meyer Schapiro, Waldo Frank, and Margaret Mead. Members included national and international students, teachers, and artists as disparate as Stuart Davis and Ad Reinhardt.

Even so, larger questions loomed about the status of the museum's embryonic collection, exhibition program, shows circulating at home and abroad, and educational agenda. D'Amico's attention thus was divided between successively fraught debates on educational reform, which played out largely beyond the institution, and the equally vexed discourses on modern art that were contested within it.[25] Along with a cultural shift to scientism and increasing rationalization, there was a postwar return to basic skills and information-based disciplines that served the defense program. D'Amico frequently worried that the proliferation of utilitarian agendas in a paranoid cold war climate that was marked by a "hysterical rush toward an overweighted science program"[26] would prove detrimental to the arts and liberal education. He wondered "whether there is not a relationship between the growing power of destructiveness on the part of our scientific genius, and that indescribable urge for creation on the part of the general public."[27]

There also was the related concern of whether art museums such as the Museum of Modern Art could provide an education. D'Amico reiterated that the museum was founded on creative education and that the transformative

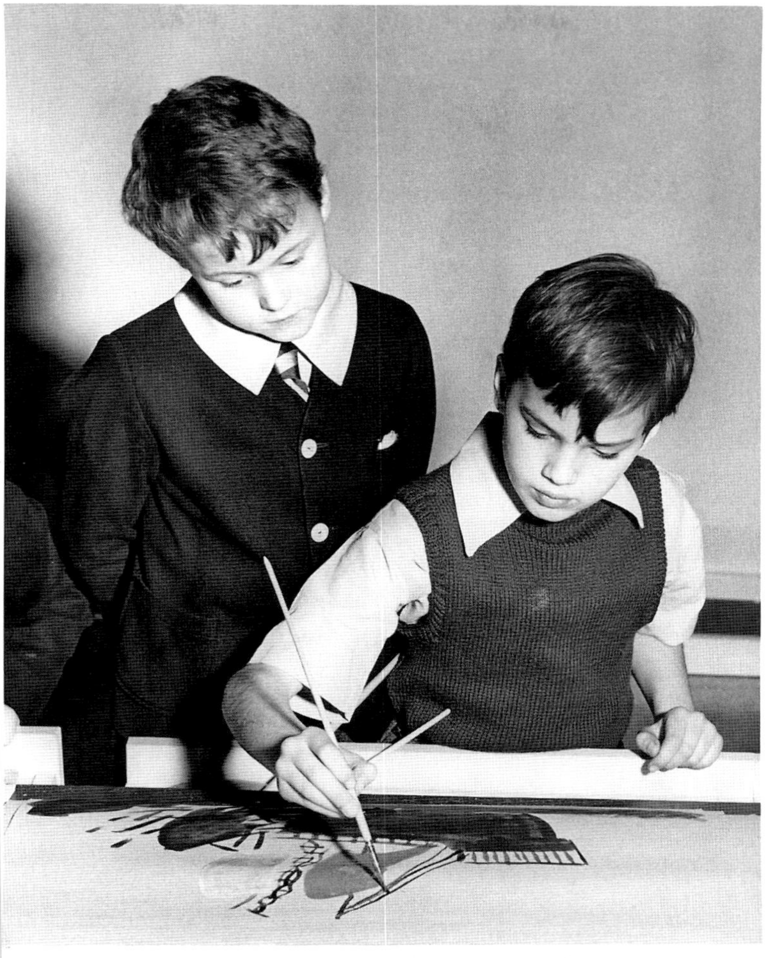

Children's art class of the "Children's Holiday Carnival" (c. 1951–1952), The Museum of Modern Art, New York.

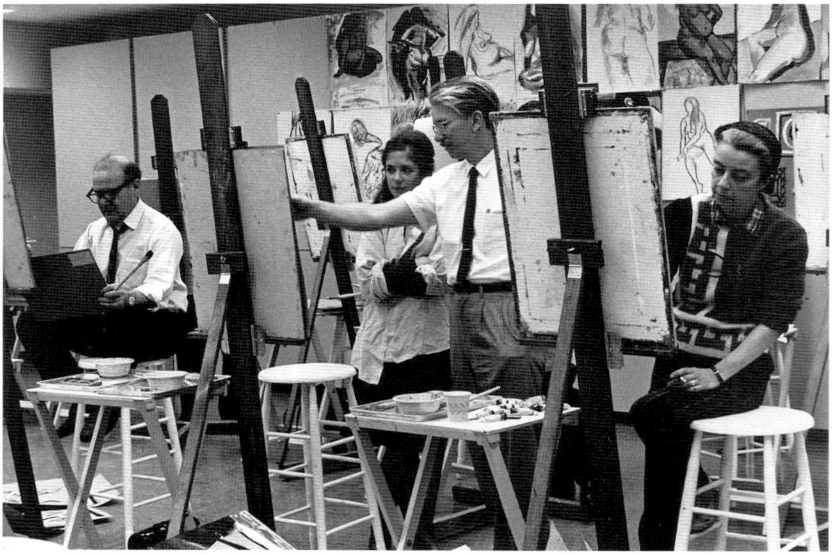

People's Art Center (date unknown), The Museum of Modern Art, New York.

value of the aesthetic must always stand against a backdrop of social and political regimentation:

> The art museum has just begun to recognize its role in education. It is still pioneering as an instrument of education. With the increased production of visual materials by the commercial firms, many of whom are exploiting the child rather than interested in his creative welfare, and with the rise of television as an effective and indelible means of visual communication, the museum, along with other educational institutions, has a tremendous challenge and responsibility to meet. Unless quality in regard to both the esthetic and educational objectives are maintained, the creative education of all youth is jeopardized.[28]

For D'Amico in 1937 and 1951, the Museum of Modern Art was a pedagogical institution—an "instrument of education" that was to be understood as effectively equivalent to other such schools. (As Sybil Kantor quips: "The concept of the museum functioning as an educative tool was democratic in aim and peculiarly American.")[29] But in 1951, these other institutions were neglecting their responsibility for art education such that the museum was forced to compensate for their abdication.

This was D'Amico's primary commitment, and it resounded within the institution that had been founded on a desire to make art culturally intelligible and popularly legible. The museum's 1929 charter from the State of New York's Education Department was specific: it was created "for the purpose of encouraging and developing the study of modern arts and the application of such arts to manufacture and practical life, and furnishing popular instruction."[30] It was to create and educate (or create through educating) an audience for modern art. As Barr wrote in 1944, restating the mission: "The primary purpose of the Museum is to help people enjoy, understand and use the visual arts of our time." In conclusion, he offered: "Obviously, these three activities—enjoying, understanding, using—should be thought of as interdependent. Each confirms, enriches and supports the others. Together they indicate the Museum's primary function, which is educational in the broadest, least academic sense."[31]

Fortunately for D'Amico, although the "why" of the museum was well annotated and even better understood, the "how" of this mission was left intentionally vague and elastic enough to accommodate change. Responsive to the exigencies of development, the Museum's first decades were marked by deliberate experimentation and conscious adaptation at the levels of theory and practice. The museum operated under the provisos that were outlined in Barr's 1933 long-range collection plan and given pictorial form in Barr's now infamous accompanying image of a torpedo advancing through time. The tip of Barr's torpedo would have its nose in the always advancing present, divesting works at specified intervals to allow for the procurement of others in their place. (Barr redrew his icon in 1941 with the tail reaching back only to 1875 instead of 1850 or even earlier, which reflects once again his privileging of inconstancy.) If this museum would have a collection, it would evolve and be subject to continual reinvention and modification.

Barr's plan for the eventual deaccessioning of his hypothetical collection to a more permanent store was modeled on the Musée du Luxembourg's relationship to the Musée du Louvre. The younger museum would be a feeder to a more significant, culturally established collection with a broader purview and longer historical scope. Although a dialogue to this effect had begun with New York's Metropolitan Museum of Art in 1932, an agreement was not reached until 1947 due to prolonged internal deliberation on the matter and curtailed resources during the war.[32] Nevertheless, the Modern soon came to resent the pact and the instrumentalization that its terms exposed. It was abrogated in 1953 through negotiations that revealed the new, postwar balance of power. (One surmises that the arrangement was also problematic in terms of procuring and retaining loyal donors.)

The Museum of Modern Art decided to retain its impressive holdings of "masterworks" from around 1875 on. In the summer of 1951, the museum began to investigate how it could form a permanent collection without violating the terms of the 1947 accord, which stipulated that all MoMA works

9.

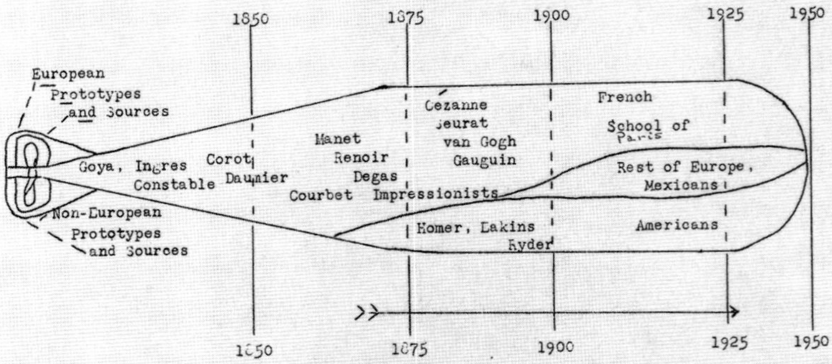

In the past nine years the torpedo has moved a little farther and the Committee would sketch it today in the following form:

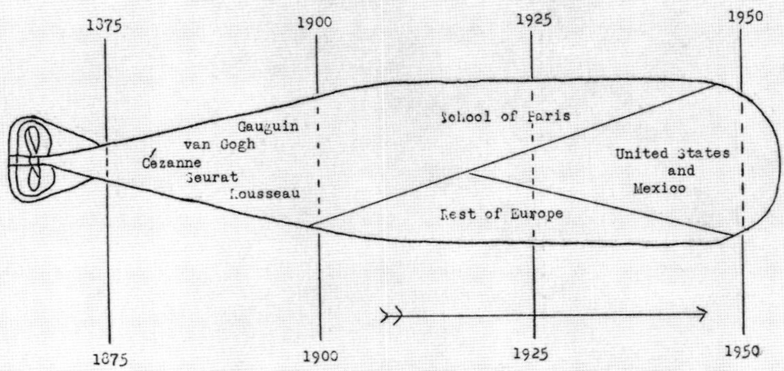

Alfred H. Barr, Jr., "Torpedo" diagrams of the ideal permanent collection of The Museum of Modern Art, as advanced in 1933 (top) and in 1941 (bottom). Prepared by Barr for the "Advisory Committee Report on Museum Collections," 1941.

would eventually end up at the Metropolitan Museum of Art. Legal counsel James W. Husted advised MoMA trustee Nelson Rockefeller on the semantics of such matters: "It is the word *permanent* that creates the difficulty under our agreement with the Metropolitan. . . . [But] there is nothing to prevent us from keeping any painting which is still significant in the contemporary art movement as long as we want and I suppose, therefore, we could maintain a Collection of Masterpieces indefinitely as long as it was not known as a permanent collection."[33]

The new policy, "benefiting the public," was unveiled in 1953, the year that Ryman began working at the museum:

> The Museum has come to believe that its former policy, by which all the works of art in its possession would eventually be transferred to other institutions, did not work out to the benefit of its public. It now believes it essential for the understanding and enjoyment of its entire collection to have permanently on public view masterpieces of the modern movement, beginning with the latter half of the nineteenth century. The Museum plans to set aside special galleries for this purpose and to transfer to them, from its collections, outstanding paintings and sculptures which it considers have passed the test of time, and to acquire additional works of art of equal excellence for permanent retention.[34]

Not coincidentally, this announcement came after a building expansion was completed by Philip Johnson in September 1951 and as preparations for a commemorative twenty-fifth anniversary show were underway. With this document in place, the anniversary show could include 495 examples from the collection as well as loaned or promised works. (Despite the above policy, the details of the "permanent" collection itself were unresolved in 1953 and would be for some time.)

Even in 1957, very few pieces had become "permanent," as Barr confirmed in a response to Hilton Kramer's prodding in *ARTS Magazine:*

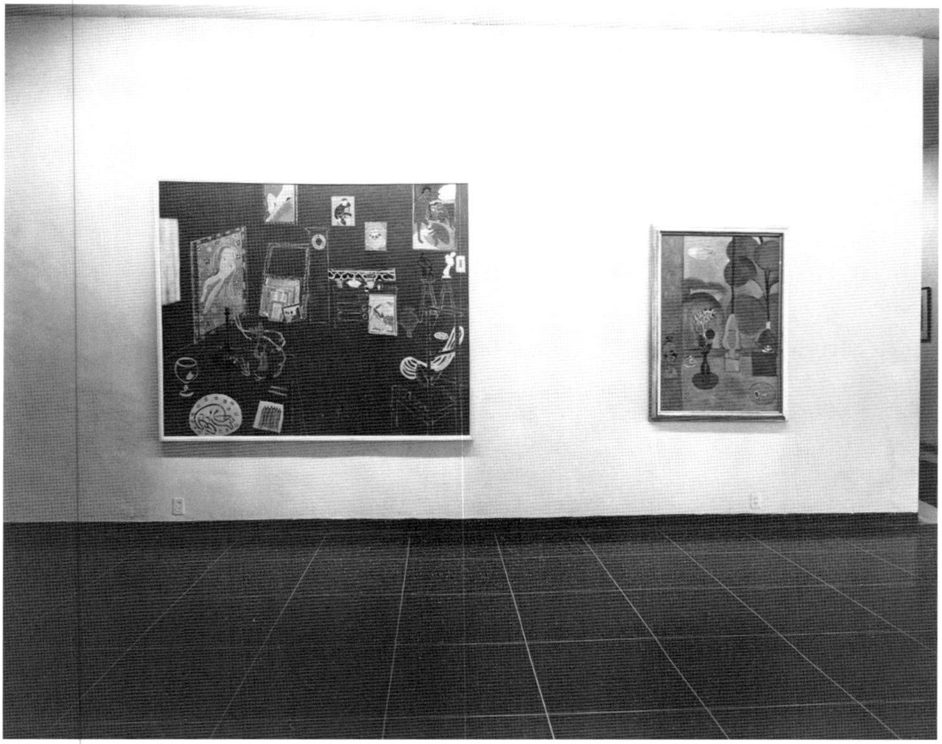

First floor installation view of the exhibition, XXVth Anniversary Exhibitions: Paintings (c. 1954–1955), The Museum of Modern Art, New York.

> As a matter of declared policy, the Museum had no permanent collection until four years ago. At that time, it was announced that an extremely limited number of works of art would be selected as a "Permanent Collection of Masterworks" while the vast bulk of the collection would remain, as before, an active testing ground rather than a repository. Of over 1350 works in the Museum's painting and sculpture collection, only four have so far been accepted for a *permanent* collection. The rest are still on trial and these include all the recent accessions. We have often suggested that of our guesses nine out of ten would eventually prove mistaken.[35]

Everything was open to winnowing and exchange—a stance not unrelated to Barr's admission of the difficulty of prognostication. The practice of calling the Museum of Modern Art an "experimental laboratory"[36] begins with Barr, and this phrase invokes his own educational background and the historical precedents of the Bauhaus and the Soviet avant-garde. A decisive nod to the certainty of contingency, it is telling that by 1964, René D'Harnoncourt could refer back to these halcyon days and wistfully recollect Barr's vision of "the Museum as a laboratory in whose experiments the public is invited to participate."[37]

D'Amico's article in the aforementioned 1951 *Bulletin* allowed him to reaffirm the importance of his work. As well, it linked the Education Department's mission to that of the museum more generally at a pivotal moment of reconsolidation and expansion that saw a full two floors of Johnson's building dedicated to classrooms. This occasion to reflect on accomplishments and to look ahead coincided with the opening of the People's Art Center in new, permanent studios that adjoined the museum. Always adaptive to contemporary pressures and the demands of a relatively young museum, educational services historically had been relinquished when rendered obsolete or assumed by another institution. This was why the museum transformed the War Veterans' Art Center into the People's Art Center in 1948: the "need which motivated the Veterans' Center was being met by other organizations."[38]

Before joining the museum staff, D'Amico directed programs in settlement houses and was head of the Art Department at the progressive Ethical Culture Fieldston Schools in Riverdale, New York. These experiences betray an evident debt to John Dewey, who in 1896 set up a laboratory school through the Department of Pedagogy at the University of Chicago. Dewey's *The School and Society* (1899) propounded ideas about learning by doing that were extended by Jane Addams in her work in Chicago settlements. In her contemporaneous "A Function of the Social Settlement," Addams cites William James's pivotal September 1898 lecture at the University of California, Berkeley, where he first coined the term *pragmatism*.[39] Collapsing abstract reasoning into its material or social consequences, James proposed that "Beliefs, in short, are really rules of action, and the whole function of thinking is but one step in the production of habits of action. . . . [The] ultimate test for us of what a truth means is indeed the conduct it dictates or inspires."[40] James's pragmatism prefigured and helped to formulate Dewey's conception of learning by doing, and it remained a cornerstone of Dewey's subsequent work.

Following James, Dewey maintained that ideas become concrete only in the consequences that result from their application. D'Amico adopted a similar stance and tested Dewey's theories by implementing them in the Museum of Modern Art. He read Dewey's publications and attended Dewey's lectures at Columbia University's Teachers College in New York.[41] Eventually, he was shaped by Dewey's claim that "the work of art has a unique *quality,* but that it is that of clarifying and concentrating meanings contained in scattered and weakened ways in the material of other experiences"[42] and came to understand that art was coterminous with life.

Likewise, D'Amico's technique for instruction was poised between Dewey's "formation from without" and "development from within"—between the rule-and-imitation approach of traditional art education and a laissez-faire abdication where the child learned largely unaided.[43] Yet D'Amico's methodology was less an accommodation or synthesis of these pedagogical styles than an attempt at their productive sublation. Clarifying his model of creative education, D'Amico avowed that "there are two basic extremes of teaching: by rule and imitation or not teaching at all. The solution is not a compromise between the two but a totally new concept of education based on knowledge of the child's creative and psychological growth and on mastery of teaching techniques needed for their development."[44]

This move was more than structural; it was also genealogical. Following Dewey's antipathy for epistemologies of dualism, D'Amico was loath to rely on a binary structure. By framing his argument in this way, D'Amico also replicated Dewey's reaction to the criticism that eventually was levied against his laboratory schools. Almost two decades after his seminal *Democracy and Education* (1916), Dewey clarified his position on education in *Experience and Education* (1938). In his preface to the latter, Dewey chastised his would-be acolytes who, much to the detriment of creative education, had turned his theories into dicta, thereby ossifying his mobile ideas into yet another paltry ideological *-ism* that congealed a set of pedagogical and ultimately social tools into an intractable stance at odds with his intentions.[45]

The cultural threat, as Dewey perceived it, was real. The Progressive Education Association that he inspired dissolved in 1955 (shortly after Dewey's death), mostly because its child-centered approach was criticized heavily for its "lack of discipline and rigor."[46] Even so, Dewey's measured response to critics was not a personal riposte to those who had misappropriated his work. He was suspicious of any idea that became an ideology or of any philosophy that became dogmatic or foundational, most of all his own.

Rather than championing "traditional" education or his vaunted "progressive" education, Dewey suggested that the educator should not "attempt to bring about a compromise between opposed schools of thought, to find a *via media,* nor yet make an eclectic combination of points picked out hither and yon from all schools. It means the necessity of the introduction of a new order of conceptions leading to new modes of practice."[47] He stated further: "For in spite of itself any movement that thinks and acts in terms of an *-ism* becomes so involved in reaction against other *-isms* that it is unwittingly controlled by them. For it then forms its principles by reaction against them instead of by a comprehensive, constructive survey of actual needs, problems, and possibilities."[48]

D'Amico's position owed much to Dewey, but his sense of mounting crisis in 1951 had less to do with national scientism than internal affairs. The museum was an instrument of schooling after all, just not in the terms that D'Amico had envisioned. Barr also had a stake, and by the early 1950s, the museum had so thoroughly become an educative institution that D'Amico's programs became not yet antiquated (he remained at the museum until his retirement in 1969, shortly after which the board of trustees closed the People's Art Center) but nonetheless superfluous.[49]

As introduced in its inaugural exhibition, installations at the Museum of Modern Art became unprecedented scenes for the staging of interactions that underscored the sovereignty of the art and the viewer alike. Barr departed from customary display methods in his hanging of the works on view. While still somewhat reliant on symmetrical pairings of works according to size and shape, Barr exchanged cluttered, salon-style installations and ornamental backdrops for galleries that were lined with pale monk's cloth and paintings that were hung at eye level. So normative did these features become that, as Mary Anne Staniszewski reminds us, by 1959 Barr could tactically revert to "skied" hangs with paintings reaching from floor to ceiling to indicate an institutional crisis (caused by a growing collection and a dearth of exhibition space in which to showcase it).[50]

Similarly, Barr's use of wall text has become almost perfunctory since its debut. Although missing from Barr's inaugural exhibition, it became omnipresent shortly thereafter—a correlative of Barr's educative objectives. Even by the time of the 1935 Vincent van Gogh show, labels were integral. Beaumont Newhall, museum librarian and director of the Photography Department from 1940 to 1947, recollected that "the labels for this show, besides giving title, date, and name of lender, contained excerpts from van Gogh's letters to his brother Theo, often describing the very picture on display. . . . *The Good Samaritan* label included a small mounted photograph of the Delacroix painting upon which van Gogh had based his painting."[51]

Barr's interest in conveying the historical circumstances and art historical contexts for the works on display grew out of his formative training, travels, and teaching experiences in the 1920s. From his time as an undergraduate at Princeton University, he profited from intersecting historical, theoretical, and museological approaches to the study of art that would be transferred wholesale to the institution that he began to shape a decade later. Throughout his career, Barr was forthright about his indebtedness to his professors. Some three decades after beginning his studies, he dedicated his seminal monograph on Henri Matisse (despite its 600 pages, he called it a "far from definitive" "work in progress") to Frank Jewett Mather, Jr., Charles Rufus Morey, and Paul Joseph Sachs, his professors at Princeton and Harvard.[52]

At the time of Barr's matriculation, Princeton began the "separation . . . of archaeology from classics, the introduction of art history as an academic discipline removed from art appreciation, and the marriage of the two in administrative autonomy[, which] became the model and the mold for most institutions of higher learning in America."[53] Started by alumnus Allan P. Marquand, the son of Metropolitan Museum of Art benefactor Henry Marquand, Princeton's Department of Art and Archaeology had flourished in large part due to the eccentric stipulations of William Cowper Prime. In 1882, Prime wished to donate a collection of porcelain and pottery to the fledgling department on the condition that it would be housed in a fireproof building that could be expanded to accommodate future acquisitions in any medium. Prime drafted a fundraising pamphlet with General George B. McClellan (an unsuccessful candidate for U.S. president in 1864 and the governor of New Jersey from 1878 to 1881). Their manifesto, "The Establishment of a Department of Art Instruction," argues for a broad and accessible notion of art that is divested of "a peculiar dialect or jargon of technical terms."[54]

Underwritten by a conviction that objects needed to be studied in the context of a museum and that art education was an ethical imperative, the founding of Princeton's art museum was understood as inextricable from the founding of a department in which art history would be taught:

> Our print factories and dye works, our carpet and tapestry factories, our upholsteries and furniture fabrics, our house fronts and interior adornments, everything which surrounds and beautifies our domestic and public life, bear witness to the fact that if beauty in art were eliminated from modern life, its conditions would be almost

> barbaric, its commerce and industries would come to naught. *Art education is therefore practical education, for practical life.* . . . It is an equal subject of regret and shame, that neglect of instruction in colleges and schools of learning has left so large a portion of the intelligent men and women of our country at the mercy of ignorant teachers, whose profound absurdities, and jargon of technical terms and phrases, have contributed to a prevalent impression that the word *Art* implies a mystery, which can be penetrated by only a few intellects. If the clergy, the lawyers, the educated men in all professions and walks of life, had received in College such instruction as this department proposes to give, they would exercise in the community a power which would overcome these evils, a power for good in all departments of usefulness among their fellows.[55]

This statement assumes the leveling of any medium-based hierarchy. Decorative objects, craft artifacts, and design work are as significant as painting and sculpture and are painting's and sculpture's equivalent manifestations of material culture. Anticipating Dewey's argument, art is not cleaved from quotidian experience but is a form of "practical education, for practical life" (at least so long as one belonged to the appropriate class—another matter entirely and one that Dewey adamantly opposed).

In light of this agenda, the School of Art was founded at Princeton on June 18, 1883, with Prime and Marquand named as full professors. The Department of Art and Archaeology was fully entrenched within a decade, offering many undergraduate courses, boasting a growing museum facility, and operating the first graduate program in art history in the country. By the time that Barr arrived at Princeton in 1918, he found a department intent on modernizing the discipline. Erwin Panofsky would soon contend that "no European scholar . . . could remain blind to the fact that the United States had emerged as a major power in the history of art; and that, conversely, the history of art had assumed a new, distinctive physiognomy in the United States."[56] For Panofksy, this was American art history's "golden age," and it was epitomized, not surprisingly, by the Museum of Modern Art's "meteoric rise" at the end of the decade.[57]

For Barr, the ethos of experimental historicism evidenced at Princeton ceded to connoisseurship at Harvard, where he began his graduate degree in 1924. If Princeton adhered to historiography and iconography, Harvard assumed that art history was an amateur's avocation. Charles Eliot Norton and other professors were notoriously given to hyperbolic oration and florid, Anglophilic prose, often performed in the spirit of John Ruskin. However, this approach changed during the time of Barr's study there with the hiring of Paul Joseph Sachs as the associate director of the Fogg Museum. A lifelong collector, Sachs retired as a financier in his family firm, Goldman Sachs, and decamped to Harvard for a second career. His interest in collecting was redirected to serve the institution to which he had deeply cathected. Typical for this generation (if exceptional in its implications), his private hobby determined his public profession.

At Harvard as at Princeton, a museum was the prerequisite for the instruction of students in the history of art, acting as a primary facility for teaching and training. Sachs insisted that the Fogg was a "laboratory" for instruction and that "everything going on in the building should be 'grist to the mill.'"[58] Sachs and his colleague Edward Forbes conceived of the object-oriented "Fogg method," and in 1915, Forbes started a course called Methods and Process of Italian Painting that surveyed historical techniques by means of hands-on application. In the "egg and plaster course," students were required to replicate oil paintings, frescoes, and tempera panels, to prepare plaster and gesso, and to lay gold leaf. These skills were indispensable for preservation and management. They also were introductions to careers that required practitioners to come to terms with the specificities of an object through its material properties.

In a related move, Sachs, acting in the joint capacity of curator and professor, recognized the growing need for trained museum personnel and in 1922 formulated a course on Museum Work and Museum Problems. Cultivating visual acumen and teaching the skills that produced historical scholarship, the program transmitted standards of academic research into the museum while eschewing interpretation that was not anchored in empirical observation. Sachs routinely queried works' probable origins, possible meanings, states of conservation, and key bibliographic citations; students were also prompted to determine their monetary value.[59] Yet far from pandering to private collectors, instructors taught curatorial skills that were honed for application in public institutions that were—following Sachs—educative and ripe for adopting university standards. Sachs avowed that "in America the Museum is a social instrument—highly useful in any scheme of general education,"[60] and Barr evidently agreed. When made founding director of the Museum of Modern Art in 1929 (a position that was secured by Sachs's recommendation of his student to the museum's board of trustees), Barr put forward this charge.

But even before 1929, Barr had independently substantiated the validity of Sachs's posture. In 1927, Barr was invited to teach a course at Wellesley College and proposed the subject of modernism, making this class the first of its kind in America. Despite the novel subject matter, Barr's theoretical background predisposed him for Wellesley and the "Wellesley method." The Wellesley method offered its students training in "laboratory work"—egg tempera, gesso, gilding—that counted "toward the degree on the same basis as scientific experiments."[61] Following suit, Barr introduced "carefully prepared problems"[62] in each class. Industrial sites and design, decorative objects, architecture, music, film, theater, fine arts, painting, and sculpture became the multidepartmental plan of the museum.

Barr's sense of experimentation might have been extrapolated from scientific methods and their rhetoric, but it was confirmed by his subsequent encounter with the avant-garde. Barr applied for a Sachs fellowship to study contemporary European theater, decorative arts, sculpture, and painting for his proposed thesis, "The Machine in Modern Art." Although his funding proposal was denied, Sachs personally supplied him with the necessary resources to travel and conduct research, and Barr arrived in London in 1927. He studied there before being propelled through Rotterdam, the Hague, Haarlem, and Amsterdam by his interest in de Stijl. Next, he left for Germany to visit the Bauhaus at Dessau. (So profound an impression did this Bauhaus encounter have on Barr that in 1938 he mounted an ambitious Bauhaus exhibition at MoMA, invited Walter Gropius and Herbert Bayer to participate as curators, and allocated nearly half the museum's annual exhibition budget for the exhibit's production.)[63]

Likewise critical was his time in Moscow. About this, Philip Johnson later remarked: "The Constructivists were on [Barr's] mind all the time. Malevich was to him, and later to me, the greatest artist of the period. And you see, the Constructivists were cross disciplinary, and I'm sure that influenced Alfred Barr, both that and the Bauhaus."[64] This is something of an understatement, for Barr's experiences here were of inestimable consequence, even if their terms are contested.[65] "We'd rather be here than any place on earth,"[66] Barr wrote while taking advantage of a privileged position that facilitated his encounters with El Lissitzky, Alexander Rodchenko, and Sergei Eisenstein.

Open to the experiences he was garnering and largely under Eisenstein's magnetic sway, Barr noted that "Rodchenko showed much satisfaction at having delivered the death blow to painting in 1922."[67] Barr stopped seeking out painters and pursued artists who were involved with film montage. By the new year, he was writing: "The essential unimportance of most American films, their vulgarity and trivial sentiment was brought home by *Mat* [Maxim Gorki's *Mother*]. In the kino at least the revolution has produced great art even when more or less infected with propaganda. Here at last is a popular art; why, one wonders, does the Soviet bother with painters? The film in Russia is more artistically, as well as politically, important than the easel picture."[68]

If Barr here championed film above painting, it was a specific contention. The question was why the Soviets bothered with painters, not why painting was no longer possible or even advantageous elsewhere. In Rodchenko's abandonment of painting, Barr recognized the effectible position of art as utilitarian and of the artist as a social agent, but his nonplussed response underscores his reluctance to see the implications of this gesture toward vitiated painting as having any purchase outside of its more immediate circumstances.

Still, Barr's awareness of a legitimately contingent aesthetic or political response to social conditions was elsewhere mitigated by a desire for international stylistic comparisons. Barr bracketed out the pesky importation of "propaganda" and nullified the distinction between Soviets and Americans in his discussion of the aesthetics of national cinemas so that he could contrast Soviet film with its diminutive, vulgar, and "trivial" American counterparts across a seemingly level field that encompassed and even codified national differences. This latter move to compare the forms, qualitative dimensions, and subjective effects of a range of work steered clear of the social content or political ambition manifest therein but enabled him to construct exhibitions and discursive narratives that traipsed the globe, decontextualizing and reunifying much disparate material under the banner of the modern.

It perhaps goes without saying that for Barr, these webs of connections were not capricious. Less obvious, though, is the fact that these connections were neither purely formal nor merely consigned to medium. Motivated by a need to connect modernism to historical art, to link it to a longer trajectory of meaning and form (or meaning in form), and to explain a far-flung grouping of synchronic practices, Barr approached these works as if they were already historical. Only then could they be subjected to the rigorous analysis that abetted their educative function in the present. Objects could be recuperated for art history while, in a sort of sleight of hand, disallowed to have it.

Despite Barr's writing of a history without a history (or at least his curbing of discussions about artworks' sociopolitical emphases), Panofsky recognized his approach not as disinterest but rather as a mode of objective historical analysis without "provincial limitations in time and space" that was aided by "youthful adventurousness" and a measure of Anglo-Saxon positivism. "In the United States," he writes, "such men as Alfred Barr . . . could look upon the contemporary scene with the same mixture of enthusiasm and detachment, and write about it with the same respect for historical method and concern for meticulous documentation, as are required of a study on fourteenth-century ivories or fifteenth-century prints. 'Historical distance' . . . proved to be replaceable by cultural and geographical distance."[69] In this way, the works of art that were deposited at the Museum of Modern Art might not be redeemed by the whims of history and taste but could at least be recuperated for—as D'Amico appreciated and Ryman intuited—a very public form of pedagogy.

2

Paint

In 1958, Robert Ryman participated in his first exhibition, showing a modest casein, graphite, and colored-pencil work on a scrap of paper at a Museum of Modern Art staff exhibition outside the members' dining room. Priced at $70, the untitled work sold to Gertrud Mellon of the Museum's Painting and Sculpture Committee. She later recognized its significance for the artist and returned it to him in 1990, at which time he renamed the work *To Gertrud Mellon*. Unassuming in size, materials, and state (note the roughly cut edges, irregularities of ground, indentations and stains, curlicue corners, and bent bottom right lip), it nonetheless looms large for aesthetic as well as historical reasons. Here are details that matter for this and subsequent works—a preponderance of support peeking out from beneath paint applications; lines drawn on this evident base; overpainting that alternately exposes and occludes the lines; overlapping rectangles that hug the perimeter vertically and horizontally; colors (black, olive, and white) applied in broad swathes or meaty, coinciding strokes; and Ryman's signature and the date, turned on their sides and aligned with the edge of the paper along the lower left, facing out. Built up from the paper, in from the edges and out from the center, *To Gertrud Mellon* reveals how he approached the task of generating a composition with startling clarity.

As the first painting that Ryman ever displayed, *To Gertrud Mellon* is an apt chronological beginning, except that Ryman does not consider it his first

Robert Ryman, *To Gertrud Mellon* (1958). Casein, graphite, and colored pencil on paper.

professional painting. That honor goes to one started in 1955 but not exhumed until 1993 for his retrospective. This work lacks what has been identified as the most salient feature of his paintings—white paint.[1] Yet the earliest painting that Ryman has acknowledged as successful enough to show, *Untitled (Orange Painting)* (1955 and 1959), a medium-size oil on canvas square with impasto sweeps, flaunts reds, dark yellows, and many oranges above black and dark bottle green. Reading "55" on a canvas overlap, a signature and alternate date (1959) exist beneath another layer of paint at lower left, confirming stages of activity in a pair of Manhattan studios (first on Spring Street and then later on 11th Street and Avenue A).

Though *Untitled (Orange Painting)* now is public, Ryman did not expect it to be shown. He gave it to his brother, who took it home to Nashville and hung it over a radiator, where it warped. Paint losses in the upper register became noticeable by the late 1950s.[2] Ryman "fixed" the upper section with a darker burnt-red paint that continues onto the painting's edges over a variety of bright-green incidents and allows the composition to wrap around to the sides with the original orange. The overall surface is heady and roughly marked, with paint tangibly smeared and manipulated. The lower right section evinces an active field of discrete strokes that become all but indistinguishable as they fan out to the bottom corner in a thinner, hazy wash. The liquefied orange, made somehow shallow, overlies an oily black that suffuses the region, granting depth.

Ryman had spent much of the year prior to beginning *Untitled (Orange Painting)* completing black ink drawings in the Museum of Modern Art galleries and painting a few biomorphic and cubist-inflected canvases (discussed below). Many are, at best, productive failures.[3] Seen beside these earlier (and still never exhibited) paintings from 1953 and 1954, *Untitled (Orange Painting)* also announces a transition from multihued ensembles to planes where distinctions between colors—and the natures of their internal relations—become increasingly slight. Finally, there is the somewhat monochromatic field into which increasingly familiar side-bound forms encroach.

Despite *Untitled (Orange Painting)*'s immediate compositional, technical, and likely maintenance-oriented ramifications, notable in numerous works

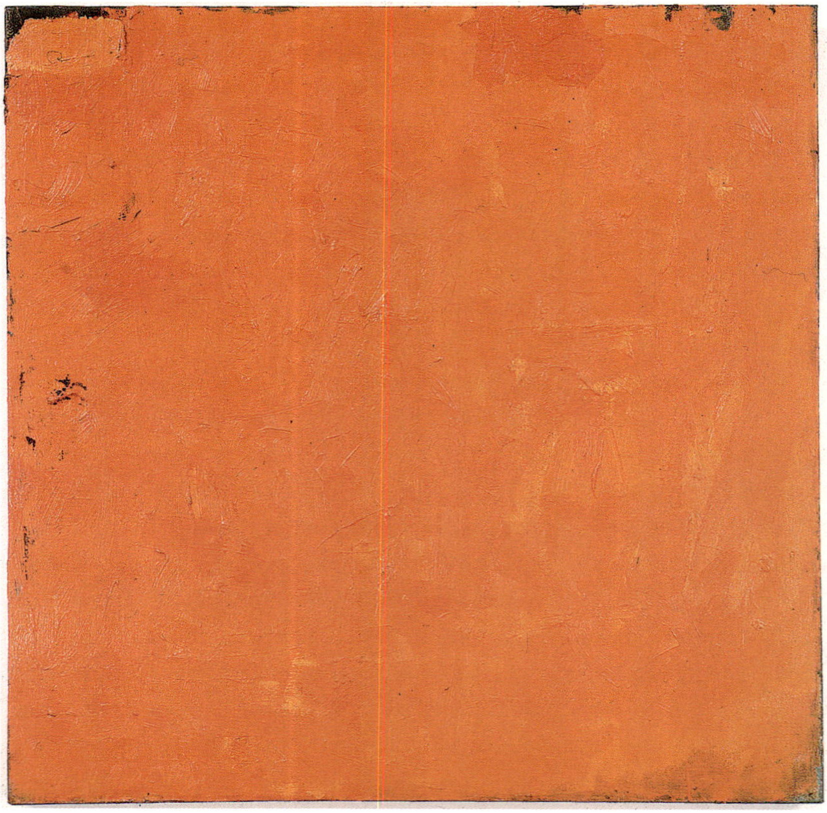

Robert Ryman, *Untitled (Orange Painting)* (1955, 1959). Oil on stretched sized cotton canvas.

including *Untitled* (1959), its implications lay dormant for half a century insofar as white paintings were concerned. Contrary to what Ryman's subsequent employ of white suggests, in 1992 Ryman maintained: "I've always thought that if I ever wanted to paint a white painting it would be in the order of the way this painting was done, because this is definitely an orange painting but there are many nuances and many oranges (and black and green). And if I were doing a white painting I would approach it the same way, and there would be whites and warm-whites and cold areas and then you would have a white painting. As it is, the way I use white it's more as a neutral paint, in order to make other things in the painting visible, color for instance."[4] Improbable as it sounds, Ryman did not paint a "white painting" until 2003, at which time he commenced a series like what he envisions in this citation specifically because he had not attempted it before (see the conclusion for more on these works).

In about 1957, Ryman began to reduce his palette, at which point forms hug the side and then grow toward one another. An *Untitled Study* (c. 1958), for example, flips *To Gertrud Mellon*'s green and black rectangles (the green sits atop the black here) and blows up this intersection to fit the parameters of the entire composition. Within two years, Ryman turned to predominantly white paintings—in the sense of white utilized as a neutral paint—where black recedes and colors dry before white is added.

Robert Storr frames the matter somewhat differently, rendering Ryman a modern primitive: "Like a Bedouin who can make out the subtlest shades of sand or an Inuit who can read with precision a comparably narrow spectrum of snow and ice, Ryman has catalogued white's actual variety, thus ironically demonstrating its latent *non*-neutrality when seen in relation to itself."[5] This point risks upholding the white painting as a Platonic ideal, a telos to which, as Storr would concur, Ryman's practice is not directed, even if Arthur Danto sees the work exactly thus.[6] There is undeniably a tension in Ryman's work and in his comments about it. I think there is a largely unacknowledged idealism underpinning his efforts that nonetheless allows his painting to continue. Ryman's assumption of white's neutrality stems as much from the Museum of Modern Art's naturalized white-box galleries as from its installation ideology

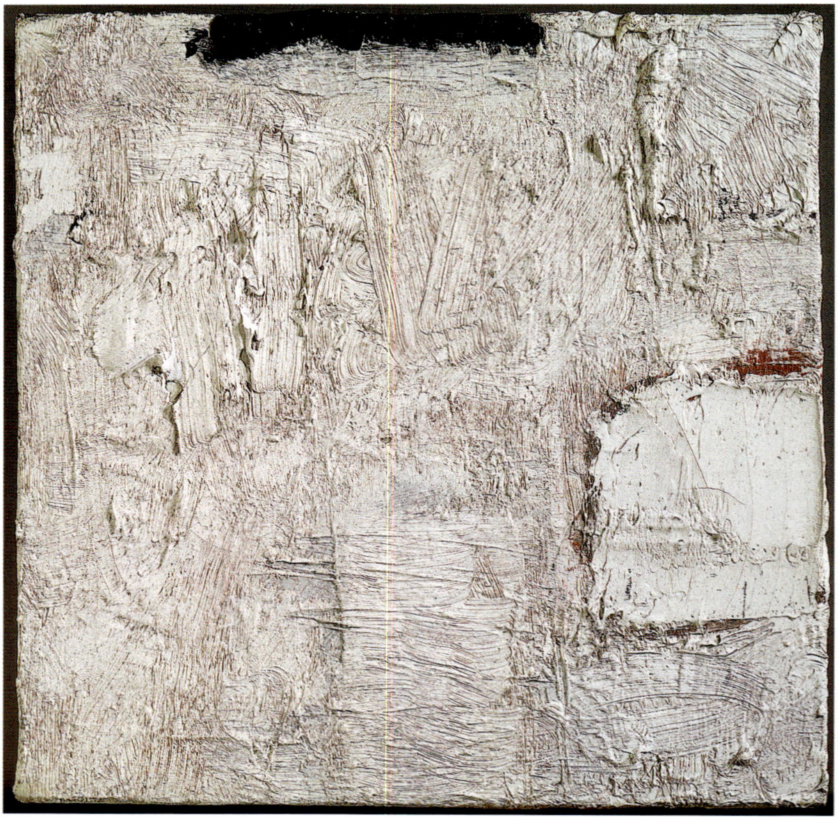

Robert Ryman, *Untitled* (1959). Oil on preprimed stretched cotton canvas.

Robert Ryman, *Untitled Study* (c. 1958). Oil on unstretched sized cotton canvas.

(as ostensibly nonideology). To wit: Architect Yoshio Taniguchi discussed with trustees his 2004 renovation of the museum: "Raise a lot of money for me, I'll give you good architecture. Raise even more money, I'll make the architecture disappear."[7]

Likewise, Ryman's "development" to paintings with a preponderance of white is not absolute. There are isolated instances of largely white fields prior to 1959, as in *Untitled* (c. 1957), with its uniformity relieved only by a visible band of its wallpaper support along its left edge. Many works kept vivid grounds of turquoise, teal, pink, red, and gold for years to come. In fact, Ryman's palette ran the gamut from saturated color (primaries, browns, greens, and oranges are ubiquitous) to dim pastels. Ryman was using richly saturated paint to see what he was doing and to remain alert to the particularities that were yielded by each stroke. An orange mark on an opaque support asserted its presence to render both action and effect clearly perceptible. Progress across the surface could be monitored, and technique could be adapted in response. But by the late 1950s, Ryman was focusing more on the paint and less on the color. The material properties of paint could be better understood without the distraction of overt color relations (as color relations survive in different white paints and sundry supports).

Surveying his work in 1972, Ryman explained that he "kept trying to make it more basic, more simple. I didn't want anything in the paintings that didn't need to be there, because anything that's in a painting that doesn't need to be there, shouldn't be there."[8] The lesson was how to focus on stroke apart from color, which is to say, how to accept color and stroke as indivisible and then somehow mute the interference of the former to study the structure of the latter.[9] This investigation could happen with any paint, but Ryman chose white.

White as a basic constituent, Ryman soon realized, could render its material obdurate while allowing other elements to become more palpable and less prone to the distraction of extrapictorial connotation. And to be rid of the irksome and unsolicited associations of whiteness, Ryman came to insist on the realness of paint (white and otherwise) not as pure color but as a marker of

Robert Ryman, *Untitled* (c. 1957). Casein on printed wallpaper.

its effects. A painting would be an orange painting or a white painting because of the demonstrable behavior and sensible qualities of the paint that was used to actuate it. Color here is not an abstract essence or language game but the physical effect of the paint in which it is suspended. From the *Untitled (Orange Painting)* onward, Ryman learned what he needed (and what he did not need) to make not a white painting but a painting.

Ryman's practice might have one origin point and an unambiguous institutional context within which the origin transpired, but there is neither a dramatic primal scene nor a secure narrative of succession. Instead, small insights based on the internal pressures of his own "problem solving" and the example of other extant models led to different kinds of work. Yve-Alain Bois finds "a tidbit more analytic fervor in Ryman's early works (though it is hard to distinguish between early and late: those concepts do not easily apply to the temporality of the autodidact)."[10] In all cases, the works show a curiosity about paint and the ways that it might move across a support.

Indeed, from his first painting, Ryman consistently shunned figuration in favor of seeing "how the paint worked"[11] apart from representation, never experiencing the crucible of moving from traditional forms of picture making to abstraction. Asked about his early paintings in 1972 by Paul Cummings for the Archives of American Art, Ryman explained why he was never interested in mimesis:

> *PC:* Going back again to the early first paintings, what kinds of things were they? Were you doing figurative things or abstract?
> *RR:* Well, as I say, they were things like all students do. I didn't know what I was doing. I was just painting. I'd just think of doing things with paint. No, I never did any realistic paintings except for these drawings [with a model at the Museum of Modern Art's People's Art Center] as I said. No, they were always abstract. Oh, I worked.
> *PC:* Why was that? Weren't you interested in representational art?

> *RR:* No, never. I knew that I could do it. I mean, I could paint the figure if I wanted to, or I could paint a landscape. I knew I could do that, because it was just a matter of learning the technique. But I knew that, if I could do it, anyone could do it.
>
> *PC:* And it wasn't enough of a challenge.
>
> *RR:* Yeah, that's right. If I was going to do something with the paint and make something happen with it from in me, then that would be much more important and much more of a challenge. And so it was always abstract.[12]

Although Ryman came to understand his painting as realist as opposed to abstract (discussed in chapter 5), at this stage he did not want to replicate nature or someone else's art but wanted to learn by doing things for himself.

So in 1953, as noted in the introduction, he bought canvasboards, oil paint, and brushes and got to work on *Untitled* (1953), a small oil on canvasboard that is an eddy of lurid colors (primarily a mix of red and blue paint on a jarring greenish ground). With paint demonstrably pulled, spread, pushed, and coaxed along the murky surface, often in elongated strokes—which would, in relatively short order, be attenuated and atomized as compositional units—it shows his experimentation with pressure, direction, and viscosity. Taking his cues from the all-pervading biomorphism of Joan Miró, Arshile Gorky, and Willem de Kooning, he floats a yellow-rimmed ovoid at center right next to a vertical red streak. Elsewhere, planar modulations of surface are defined by linear impositions that feel more drawn than painted. Perhaps to conserve resources, Ryman applied the paint so thinly that the board's texture is plain beneath its pellicle. Whether or not the lean coating was born of necessity, its de facto consideration of the support was critical, and it would remain fundamental to Ryman's painting.

With *Untitled* (1954), Ryman made a composition out of the right-angle passage that appears on the left in the earlier picture and preserved the basis of its insight regarding the visible canvas, with pigment scored clean through with a palette knife and a wide, untouched periphery, expressly at the top. Gone,

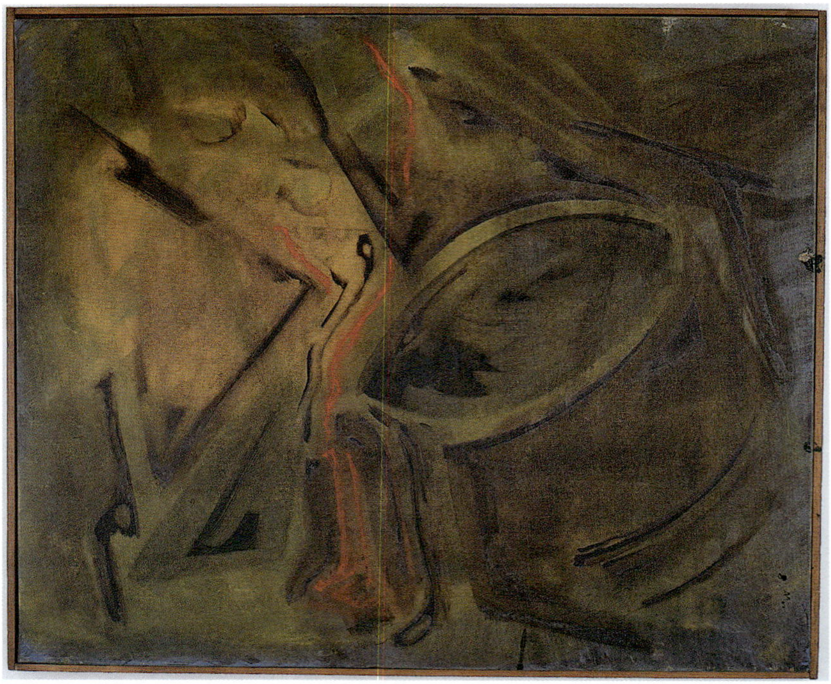

Robert Ryman, *Untitled* (1953). Oil on canvas board set into wooden frame and backing.

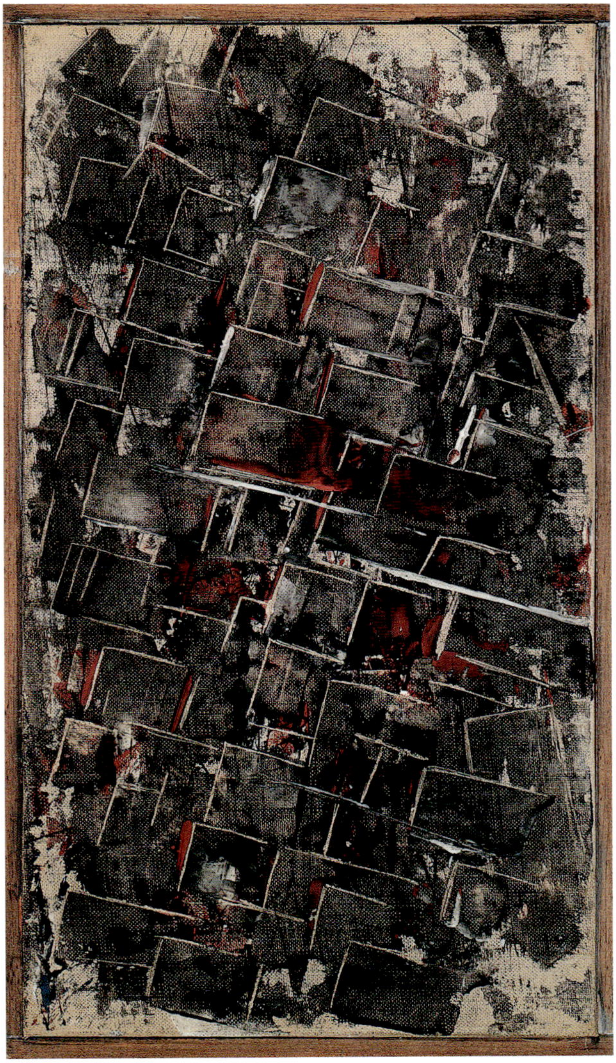

Robert Ryman, *Untitled* (1954). Crayon on canvas board.

though, is the 1953 painting's organicism (which remains notable in an untitled 1954 oil on paper with dark vertical ellipses that come close to reading as leaves or veins). This waxy painting is all tectonics; its form is built on or cut from its amorphous ground. The work renders cubist pictorial fracturing material, and also gives it over to a sort of decorative patterning unmoored from iconic correlates. Ryman seems to be getting the feel for materials, covering and uncovering the surface until there is no room to continue this action. Not unlike a well-traversed page, scripted from top to bottom and from margin to margin, his partitioning of rectangular boxes suggests an enervating repetition that is contained only by the physical parameters of the support. The faceted layers slope downward to the right, belying the arc of the hand and the drift toward the bodily axis that produced it.

On his next attempt, Ryman jettisoned the principle of quantity as quality. A handwriting-derived (and thus unidirectional) composition no longer obtains. Ryman returned to this system of staccato marks applied from left to right and delimited by the size of the backing in the mid-1960s with his *Winsor* series (discussed in chapter 4). In his *Untitled Study* (c. 1954), on paper board, he reworked rectangles within rectangles, this time positioning them adjacently along a shallow horizontal, almost friezelike space and apportioning the composition into discrete sections. At left, a dark-green ground rimmed with a darker halo hangs centered in a square that is defined by bordering boxes. A white box with illegible faux-calligraphic inscriptions crowns an upright brown section filled with black. A sunny column divides the canvas so that between it and a Barnett Newmanesque zip, a red strip of painted masking tape at far right, we find another location with two disks in respective flattened squares above loose patches of facture, twice redoubling the left section in miniature.

Unlike the reiterative code of 1954's *Untitled,* the same year's study is organized around distention. Whether by means of abutting colors of undifferentiated mass, dividing lines, or discrete modes of facture, differentiation is everywhere enforced to uphold a comparative arrangement where each individual element could be seen in relief against another. Relatable to a

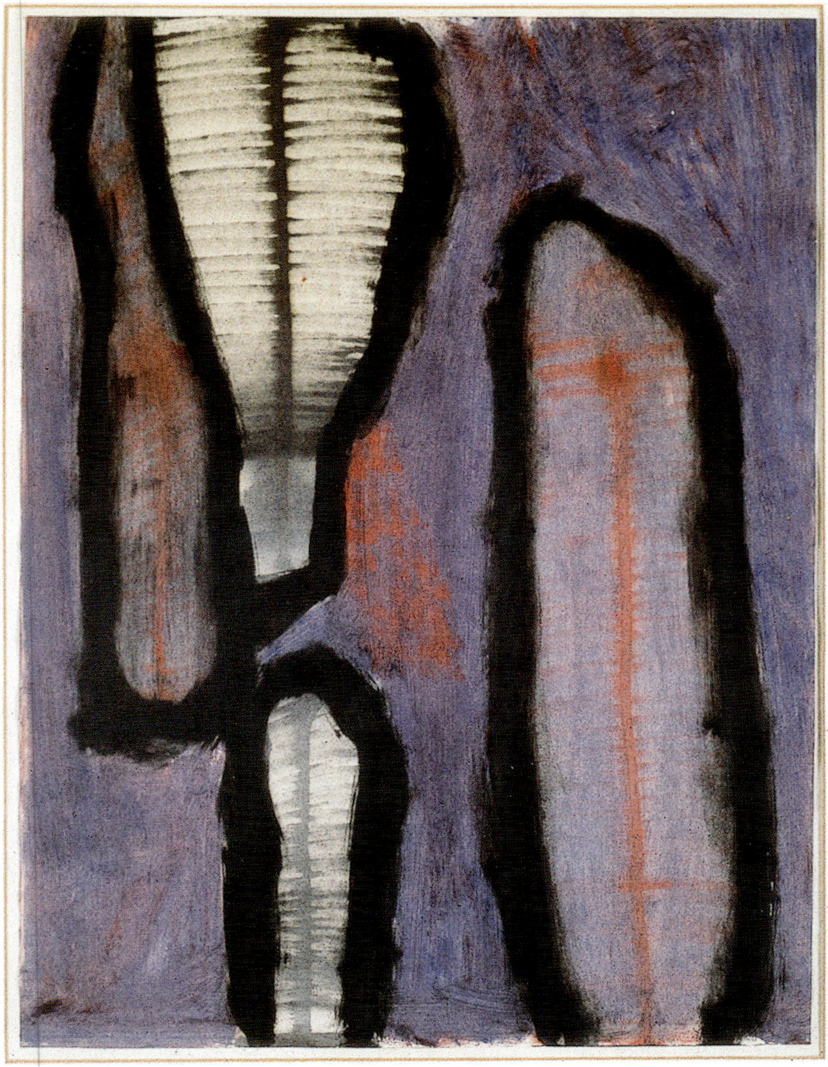

Robert Ryman, *Untitled* (1954). Oil on paper.

needlework sampler, *Untitled Study* demonstrates skill in handling and industry in implementation, archiving the hard-won product as an exemplar, a repertoire for future consultation.

Importantly, Ryman also made the frame for this and related works, including another *Untitled Study* (1954), which was painted as a gift for his mother. Akin to the insight proposed by the thinly covered support discussed above, Ryman's rough and ready attempt to make his work presentable after completion provided a logic of the edge. One sees the connection between Ryman's making of frames and his interest both in the edges of compositions (where they run out of canvas and meet the wall plane) and also in the ways that works manage that transition, whether by means of a frame, a wax frame, no frame, a deep stretcher, no stretcher, or bolts positioned at the painting's quadrants. Elsewhere notable in this regard is *Untitled* (c. 1961), a small, unstretched oil painting with unctuous white strokes above aqua and orange that features six brass grommets, three at the upper edges and three at the lower edges. Its expedient hanging solution predates Ryman's widespread uses of fasteners in the 1970s.

Improvisation that is based on an economy of means persists. The study for Ryman's mother was painted on cardboard backing (anticipating the 1969 corrugated paper works that are discussed in chapter 4), while contemporaneous drawings appropriated free museum stationery, mailers, and cardstock. Further, within the handmade frame of the second *Untitled Study,* material recycling gives way to concept salvage. Repurposed forms from earlier attempts are unmistakable and transmuted to varying degrees. Vertical rectangles survive wholesale, spheres bleed into the background and become small globular dots of white paint, and simulated notations become a string of Xs (what appears to be a flag and a sickle). Even a spontaneous tulip appears out of the juxtaposition of an orange section and its white, U-shaped outline. Although it was not expunged, it did not recur except as the pattern of printed wallpaper remnants—found images that Ryman used throughout the 1950s as variegated, readymade grounds. That the images do emerge in this painting is remarkable mostly for being an

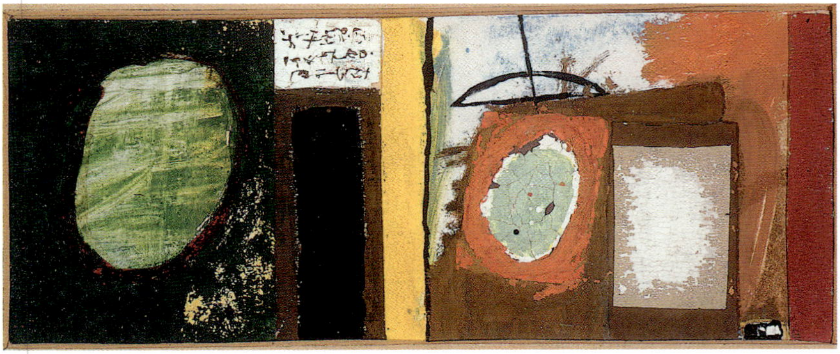

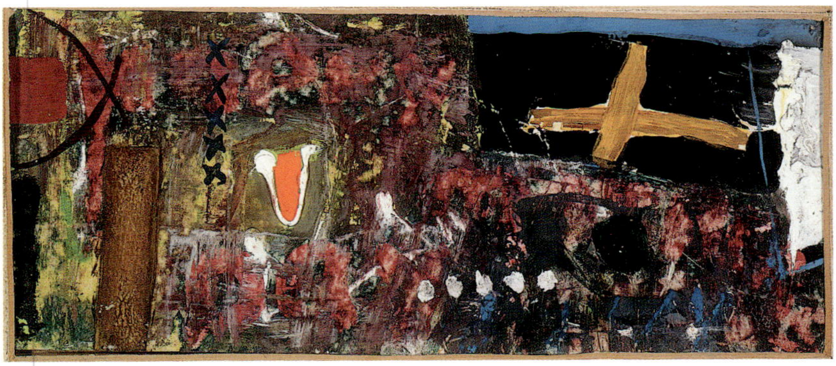

Robert Ryman, *Untitled Study* (c. 1954). Oil and masking tape on paper board.

Robert Ryman, *Untitled Study* (c. 1954). Oil on cardboard backing.

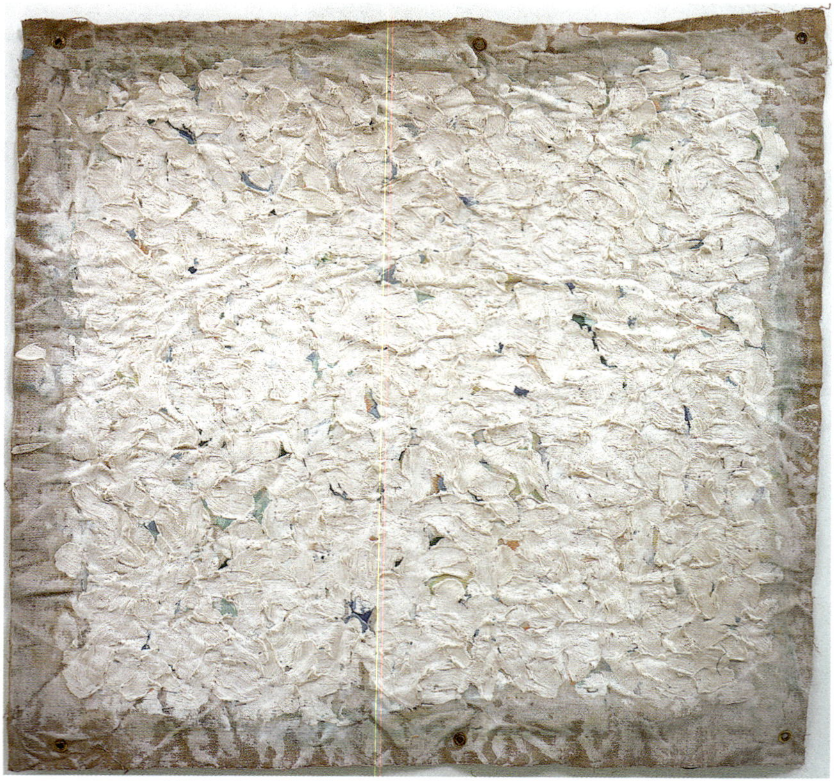

Robert Ryman, *Untitled* (c. 1961). Oil on unstretched partially sized linen canvas with six brass grommets, three each at upper and lower edges, no fixed orientation.

aberration. Similar to the other *Untitled Study,* this one tries on various strokes, colors, and shapes, but in loosening them from a matrix, Ryman ends up with ungirded, nonhierarchical sprawl—an almost entropic leveling that befits the elongated canvas.

As Vittorio Colaizzi puts it, unlike the traditional "good" abstractionist who moves away from the learned skill of representational picture making, Ryman "did not have at his disposal an established vocabulary of structure, color, and value already oriented toward pictorial space that he could then adapt for non-representational purposes."[13] This is especially clear in *Untitled* (c. mid-1950s), where thickly applied, bright color (blue, green, red, ochre) is shaped into quadrilaterals that are disjunctively arrayed within a single, noncompartmentalized area. This work was likely painted in 1955 at around the time of *Untitled (Orange Painting)* because it, too, moves from a horizontal to a square format—a decision that stuck. But in creating its early manifestations, Ryman was not clear about what to do with the set-up. Unlike the stretched contours of the rectangle, which presupposed a horizon or window, a square is uninflected, and Ryman buckled under its arbitrariness, concentrating on application and depositing shapes that occupy zones of the canvas that are free from logical organization. Ryman anchors forms to the edge (seen in *Untitled* at the top and bottom right). They cluster at the boundary between pictorial and physical space and pressure the very distinction that Ryman would shortly cancel.

A related attempt at regrounding can be seen in numerous sketches that were completed almost a decade later, reminding us of the difficulty of positing Ryman's firsts or narrating his developmental arcs as a story of linear progress. In works like *Yellow Drawing #10* (c. 1963) and *Drawing with Numbers* (c. 1963), there are infinite regresses of grids within grids that frame and reframe Ryman's selective foci. Reminiscent of his repeated emphasis on certain shapes—whether reiterated contiguously across a composition or retraced and hence layered on one another—these squares excerpted from their greater environs give form to outlined shape. Ryman would eventually amputate such passages to render them whole compositions. An enamel-painted pattern of superimposed grids (that nonetheless look like a basket-weave from afar) retraces the linen canvas in

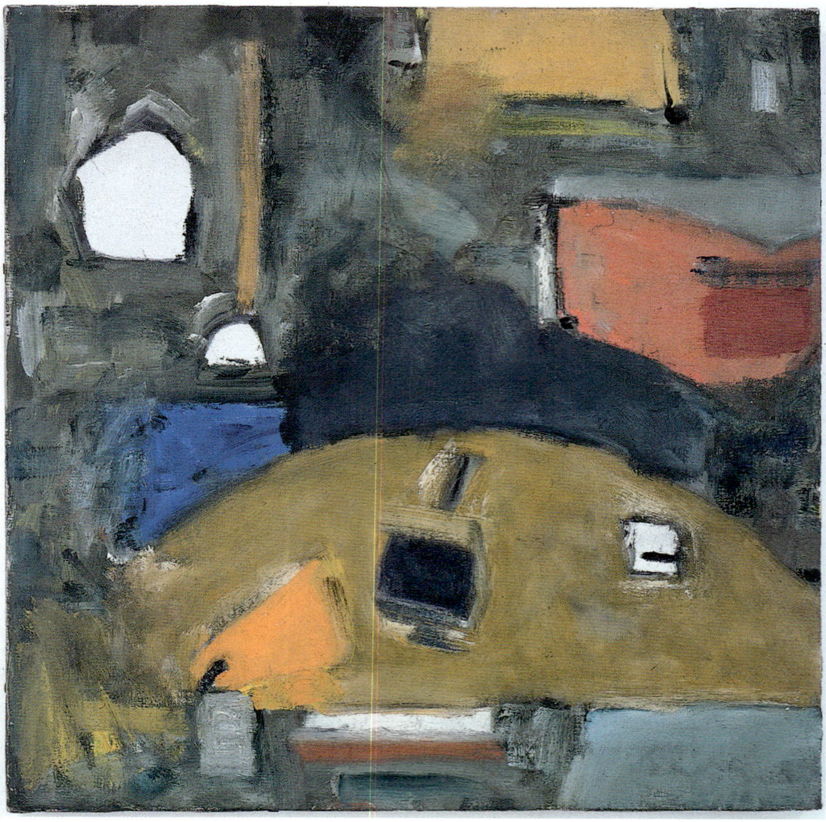

Robert Ryman, *Untitled* (c. mid-1950s). Oil on stretched preprimed canvas.

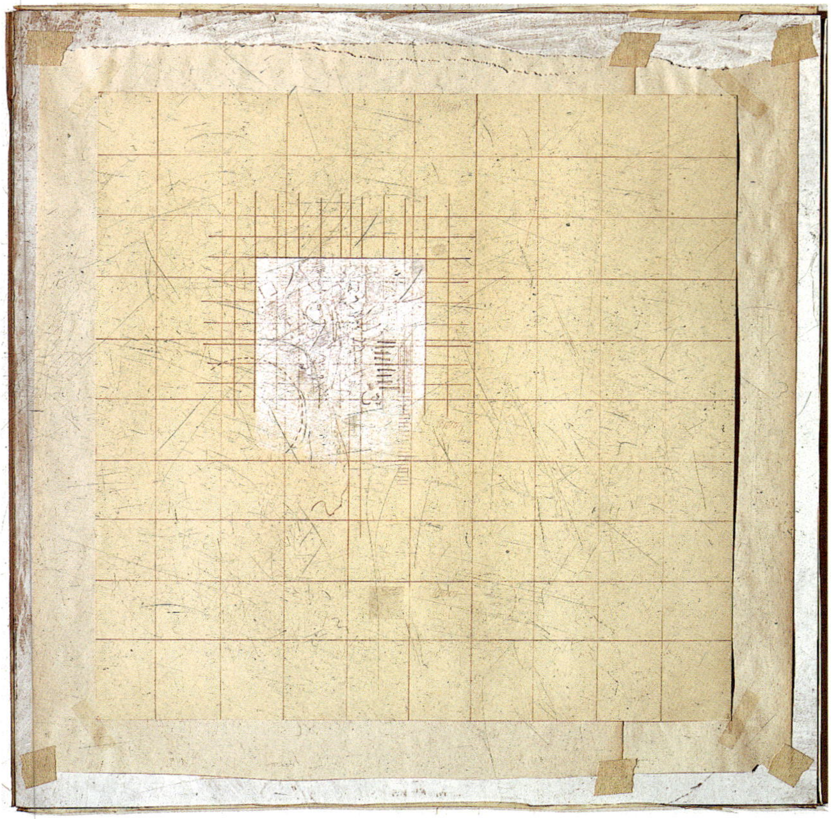

Robert Ryman, *Yellow Drawing #10* (c. 1963). Charcoal, graphite, and pastel on yellow paper.

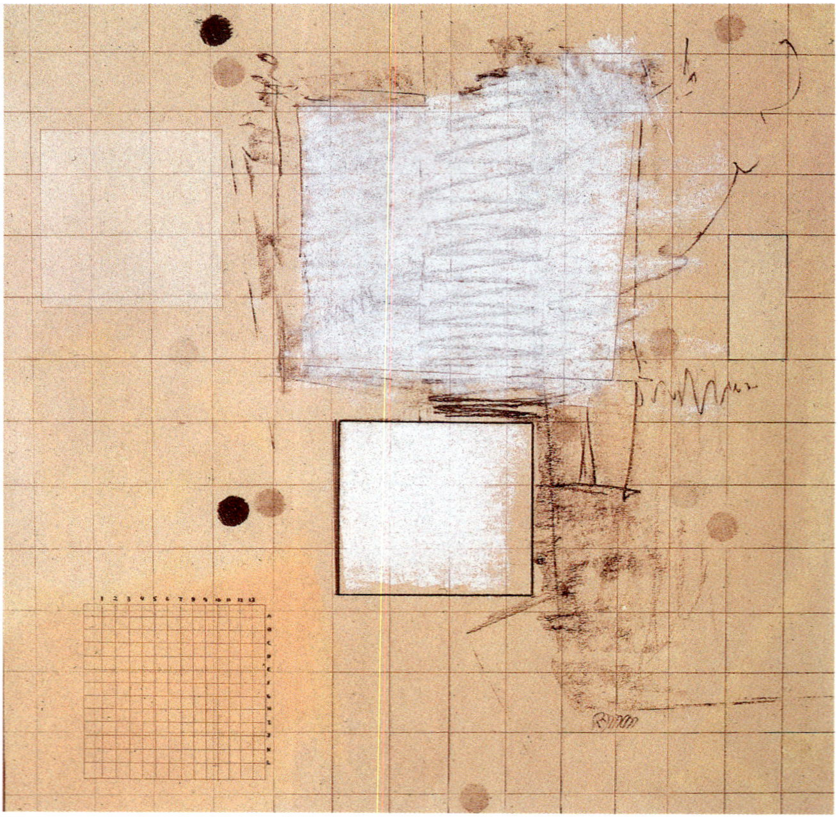

Robert Ryman, *Drawing with Numbers* (c. 1963). Charcoal, graphite, and pastel on yellow paper.

Robert Ryman, *Untitled* (1965). Enamel on stretched sized linen canvas.

Robert Ryman, *(Ever) Since* (1998). Oil and graphite on stretched linen canvas.

Untitled (1965), and a graphite grid is swathed in white strokes, except for a thin linen margin that is visible around the perimeter, in *(Ever) Since* (1998).

From 1954 on, Ryman used his time in the galleries to sketch, and over forty drawings on museum letterhead, stationery, and writing paper (often 8½-by-11-inch sheets that are cut in half) survive out of what must have been many more. They reveal a preoccupation that focuses less on adequacy of transcription (Ryman seems to have heeded Victor D'Amico's advice about not copying other peoples' compositions) and more on materiality of means and fluency with devices. Nothing that survives appears to be anything like the works that Ryman was viewing.

Further abetting his conception that the materials of art making are physically consequential (this material consequence is what Ryman comes to call *realist*), these drawings take into account the properties of paper as a physical object. Many sheets have work on both sides of the paper, as is the case with *Untitled Study* (c. 1954–1955). Colaizzi writes: "Ryman not only made marks on both sides, but employed these marks' bleed-through from one side to the other. This further indicates an absence of pictoriality. Even at this early date the artist conceived of the paper as not simply an empty screen onto which an image could be projected but as a concrete object with qualities of its own: a front, back, determinate thickness, and permeability to ink."[14]

These sketches or trials are unsigned, undated, and untitled, as are other works in various media that have yet to be exhibited. Titles come belatedly for Ryman to differentiate paintings for public identification when the work leaves the studio, and some works are left untitled but are dated. Titles are often derived from the materials of the pieces to which they refer. They can also be unrelated to the work at hand, such as those that were culled from the telephone book (and thus inadvertently related to Robert Morris's *New York Telephone Company Yellow Pages* on view at the 1967 Lannis Gallery show Fifteen People Present Their Favorite Book, mentioned in the introduction) or plucked from commercial usage. They often are even slyly funny (as discussed in chapter 4).

Although these drawings are called studies, they are not preparatory renderings for more resolved work in another medium focused on pedagogic ends.

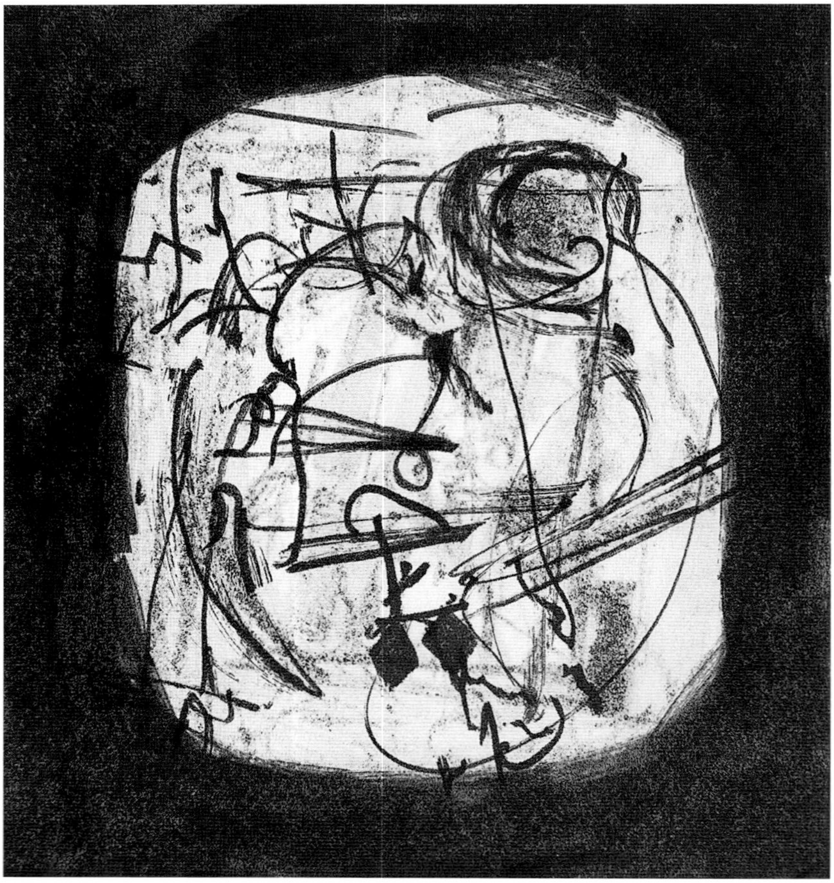

Robert Ryman, *Untitled Study* (c. 1954–1955), front. Ink and brush on both sides of paper with cut upper and left edges, torn right and lower edges.

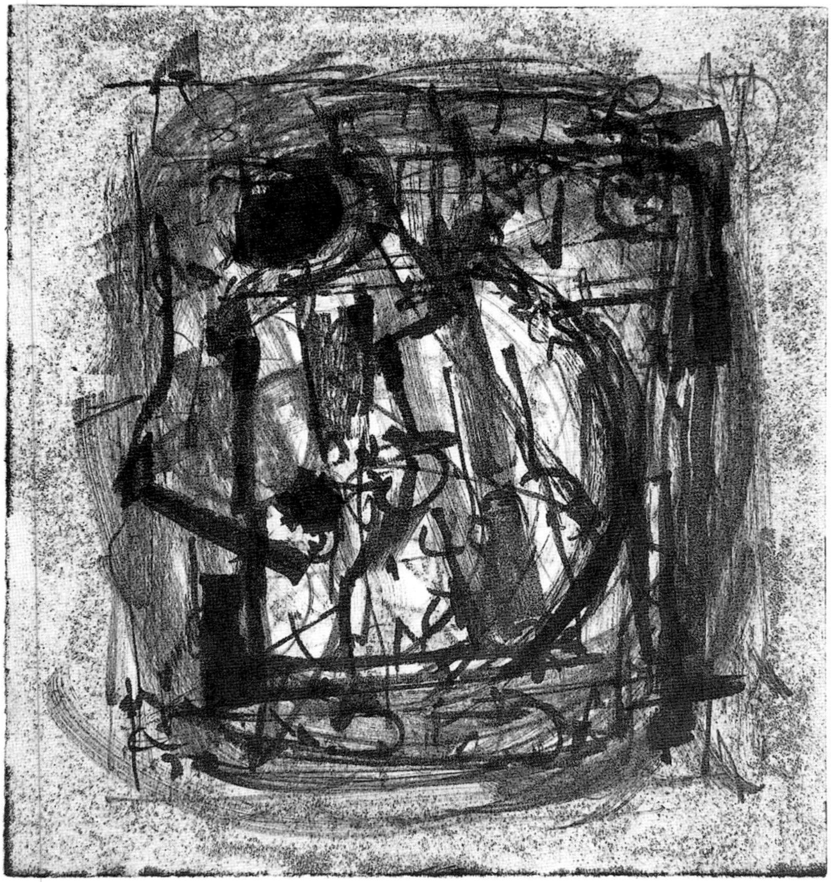

Robert Ryman, *Untitled Study* (c. 1954–1955), back. Ink and brush on both sides of paper with cut upper and left edges, torn right and lower edges.

Indeed, following this period, Ryman only rarely carried out studies, and his use of differently scaled supports or materials does not equate to a qualitative hierarchy.[15] In fact, some paintings done at the same time consist of nearly identical compositions that were executed on different supports. The crossed-stroke blocks of New Masters vinyl polymer acrylic and charcoal on stretched-linen canvas and aluminum in *Untitled* (c. 1964) and *Untitled* (c. 1964), respectively, are examples of this experimental tendency.

Thierry de Duve finds in many of Ryman's canvases from the early 1960s a primacy of touch and a crudeness of materials that imply a hastily made prologue for some other event, an argument that pertains to the MoMA works:

> You get the impression that the painter has haphazardly grabbed offcuts of fabric lying about the studio to test the flexibility and strength of his brush on them, check the smoothness or liquidness of the pigment, and try out his stroke to make sure he's in control of it before seriously getting down to work on a more ambitious canvas, and that some scruple had him hang on to these test bits rather than chuck them out once the real work is complete. This impression is immediately belied by the individualized care with which every scrap of canvas has been chosen, stretched or otherwise, snipped or torn, cut clean or jagged; the care with which the pigment marks on the canvas do or don't impregnate the fabric, stand out on the background, do or don't veil the underlying colors; the care with which the "image" is centered or off-centered, laid down flat or thickly modeled, densely built-up or hemstitched; the care with which the canvas is possibly signed, in some cases several times over. The two impressions are not consecutive, the second gradually replacing the first as we discover that there is no large picture for which these are the test pieces, but that it is they which are the works.[16]

For de Duve, they are simultaneous understandings that point to what he names Ryman's tactful "care" for (and of) painting that is evident elsewhere but concentrated especially in the early works.[17]

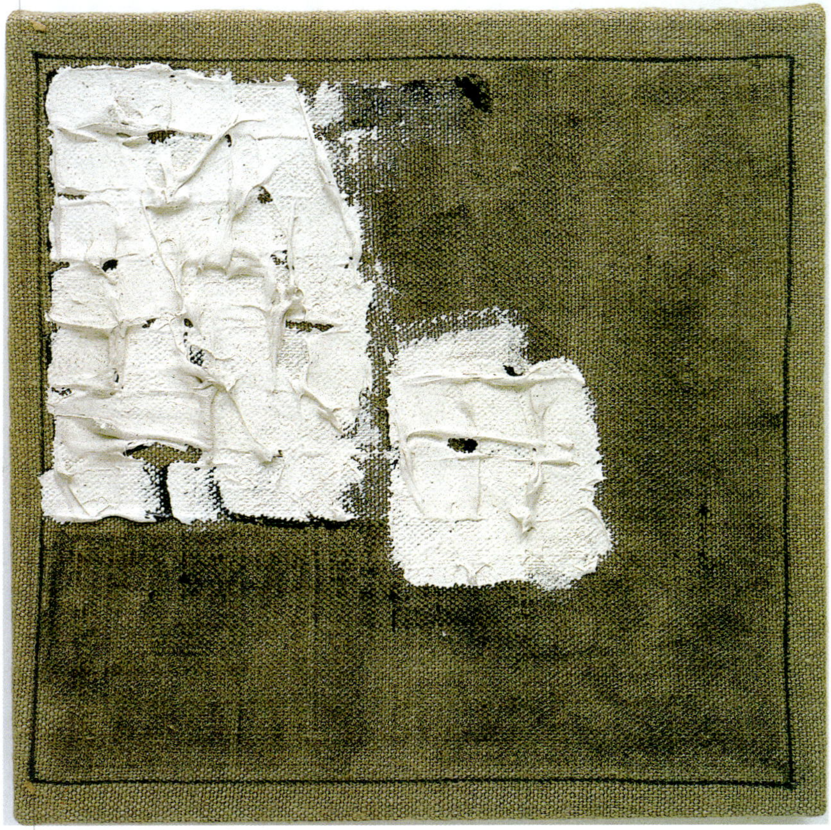

Robert Ryman, *Untitled* (c. 1964). New Masters vinyl polymer acrylic and charcoal on stretched linen canvas.

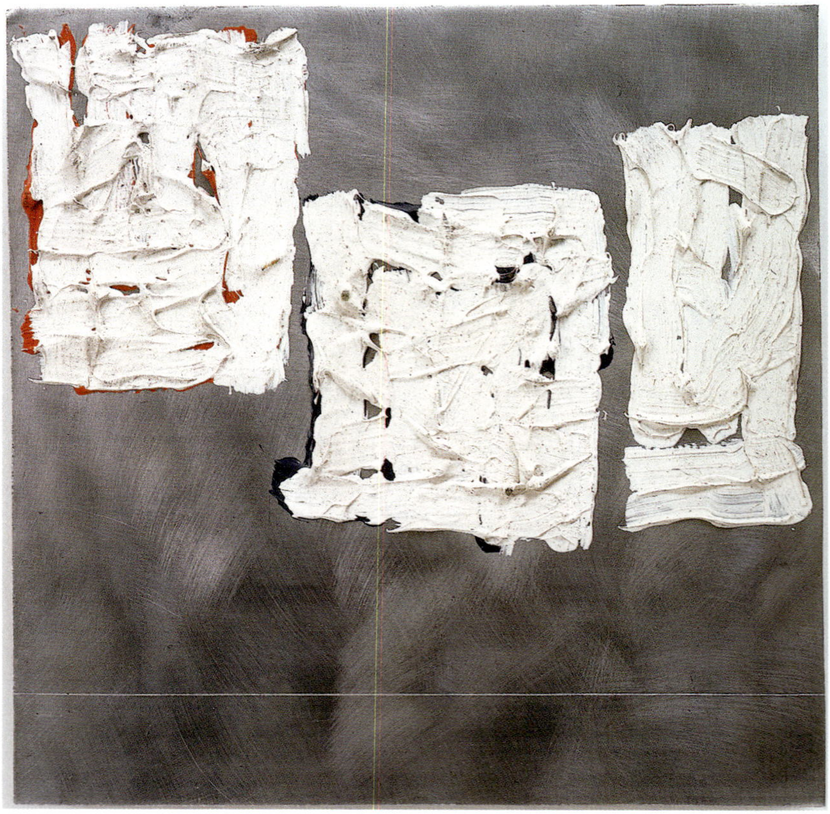

Robert Ryman, *Untitled* (c. 1964). New Masters vinyl polymer acrylic on aluminum.

On the MoMA papers, forms awash in heavy ink transmogrify from drawing to drawing, shifting in contour and emphasis and allowing compositional transformations and accidental insights. Black marker produces everything from wiry filigree passages to heavily clotted compositions with uneven borders and erratic calligraphic lines. Some drawings are elegantly spare to the point of airy expanse within a tightly given, miniature space; others are suffocating in their profusion of insistently hatched marks. One study has only three black lines (one sections a corner, one arcs across a corner, and one bisects its width), although they are enough to create tension. Another on MoMA letterhead, *Untitled Study* (c. 1954–1955), recalls Ryman's sequestering of pictorial information into individual fragments, his having the paper absorb one sketch at a time separated by pauses of paper, or an apparently drawn frame in a lower left corner. These studies make clearer than do the contemporaneous paintings that Ryman was unconcerned with forging or refusing a style in the context of pragmatic adaptation to experience.[18]

This range of techniques and pictorial effects in the early drawings is different from the abstract expressionist emphasis on signature style. Their modest ambition refuses gestural sublimity and libidinal investment. This is partly attributable to the museum's lack of exhibition space that was devoted solely to abstract expressionism. The closest analogues would be the Fifteen Americans exhibit of 1952 (showcasing William Baziotes, Herbert Ferber, Jackson Pollock, Mark Rothko, and Clifford Still, among others) or The New American Painting show of 1958 and 1959 (the latter was planned to tour in eight European countries and, as John Elderfield notes, returned to New York as something of "an afterthought").[19] Only after Pollock's death in August 1956 did the museum give him a single-artist show, a retrospective that was organized by Sam Hunter in December of the same year.

Still, following Harold Rosenberg's 1952 *Art News* publication of "The American Action Painters" and Fifteen Americans, many abstract expressionist canvases were entering the museum, where Ryman noted them. (On a more personal level, he never participated in the Cedar Bar scene or mingled socially, feeling himself to be "too shy" and "out of their league.")[20] But at that time,

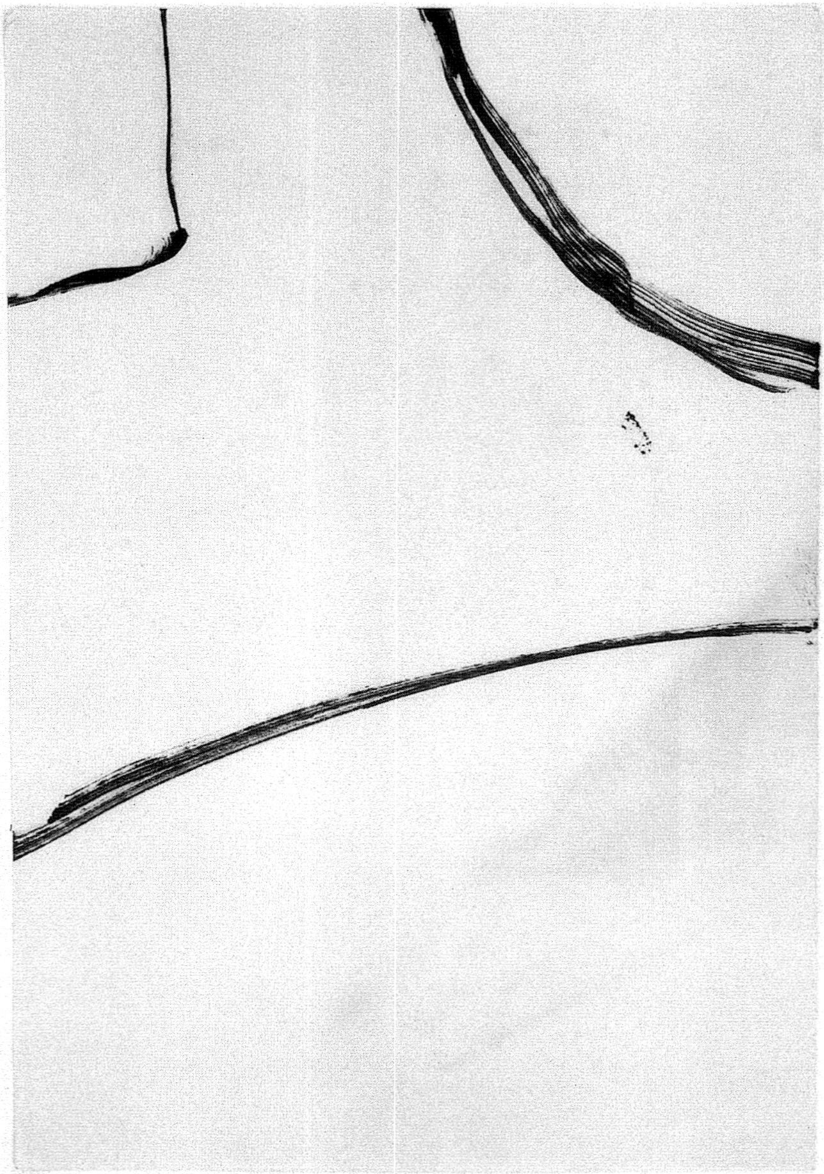

Robert Ryman, *Untitled Study* (c. 1954–1955). Ink and brush on letterhead with Atlantic Mimeo Bond watermark, cut upper, left and lower edges, torn right edge.

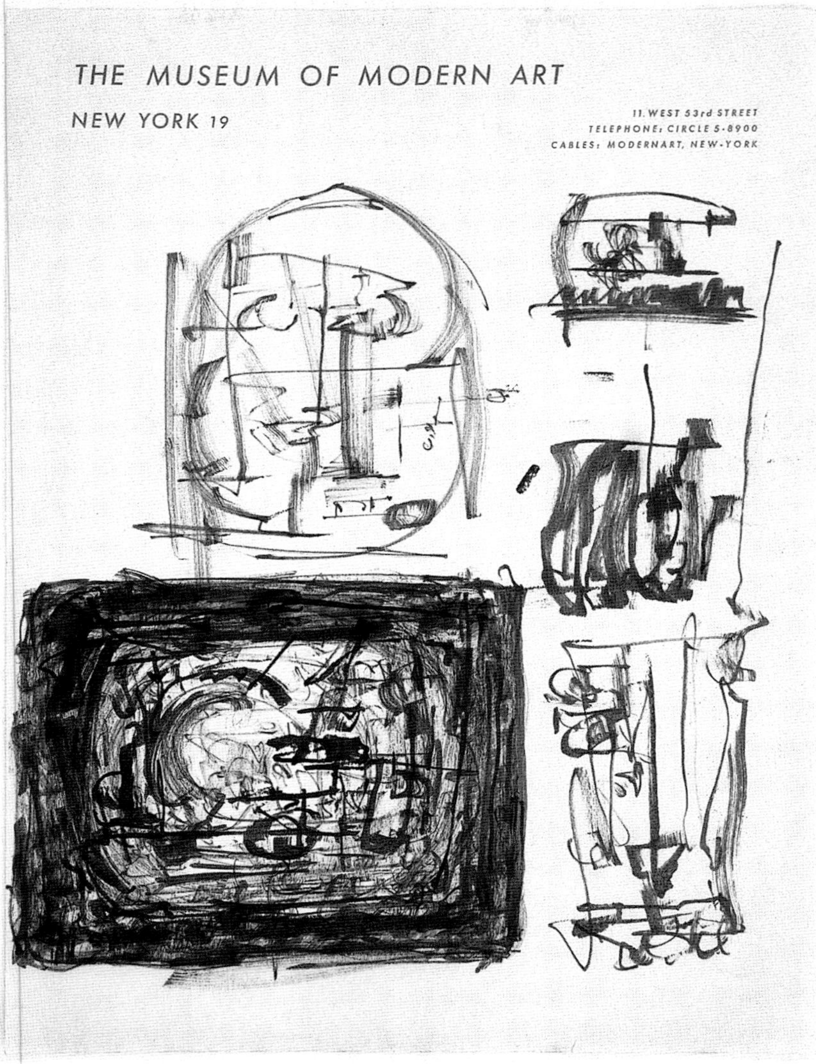

Robert Ryman, *Untitled Study* (c. 1954–1955). Ink on printed The Museum of Modern Art letterhead with Rockledge watermark, cut edges.

there was no one style or movement to which the museum was more beholden than any other. Museum exhibition records from these years show that various historical and contemporary works and schools were vying for public attention. When abstract expressionism was championed and brought into the museum, it was supported across a varied field of abstract and figurative work. Canvases that had entered the collection by 1953 include: Arshile Gorky's *Composition Horse and Figures* (1928), *Argula* (1938), *Garden in Souchi* (c. 1943), and *Agony* (1947); Adolph Gottlieb's *Voyager's Return* (1946); Franz Kline's *Chief* (1950); Willem de Kooning's *Painting* (1948), *Woman I* (1950–1951), and *Woman II* (1952); Robert Motherwell's *Pancho Villa, Dead or Alive* (1943) and *Western Air* (1946–1947); Jackson Pollock's *She Wolf* (1943), *Full Fathom Five* (1947), *Number 1* (1948), and *Number 12* (1949); and Mark Rothko's *Number 10* (1950).

In a certain way, Ryman's sketches show a point of departure from this conceptual territory. For Rosenberg, "action painting" turned on the artist's encounter with the canvas as an arena for physical activity and psychological revelation. The artist as actor needed to be fully present for an encounter with his materials and active in a way that made the paint coextensive with the body unfurling it. Even in the context of a sketch, this encounter held. As Rosenberg writes: "If a painting is an action, the sketch is one action, the painting that follows it another. The second cannot be 'better' or more complete than the first."[21] In this, Ryman's work comes close to Rosenberg's model, but his sketches were not followed by related paintings and were not motivated by the latter-day romanticism (or more topical existentialism) that Rosenberg championed.

In Rosenberg's appeal to a public for this new mode of art making, he provided the criterion on which it could be judged: "A good painting in this mode leaves no doubt concerning its reality as an action and its relation to a transforming process in the artist. The canvas has 'talked back' to the artist not to quiet him with Sibylline murmurs nor to stun him with Dionysian outcries but to provoke him into a dramatic dialogue. Each new stroke had to be a decision and was answered by a new question."[22] Rosenberg's attention to the adaptive engagement between artist and material recalls Dewey's own claims for experience, as does Rosenberg's criticism levied against artists he deemed "insufficiently engaged," since learning for Dewey was active categorically. Inheriting Rosenberg's dialogism, de Duve pushes still further. For de Duve, the canvas not only talks back but becomes fully sexualized.[23] He suggests that "each touch of [Ryman's] brush is a caress addressed to the canvas, as if the canvas were a living body capable of an erotic response. The painter feels the canvas quivering with life, and if he feels that it is dead, he remedies things with the next touch, just as lovers adjust their caresses to their partner's desires. Here he is putting a first brush stroke on the surface, then a second and a third, breaking off now and then to step back and let the canvas address him. . . . [Finally,] he resumes his work, engrossed in his intercourse with the canvas, and always listening to its answer. Clearly, the canvas doesn't answer."[24]

Of the abstract expressionists who were represented in the Museum of Modern Art, Ryman found the works of de Kooning and Rothko to be particularly interesting.[25] As Lucy Lippard recalls: "Bob was mad for Rothko's work and Rothko kept diddling Bob around that he'd have him work for him, he'd be an assistant, but he could never offer enough money for him to live on, or never would, [since] he could have [afforded to hire Ryman] by then."[26] *Untitled* (1958) nonetheless shows the depth of this engagement with Rothko. Its large vertical rectangular canvas is given over to three discrete regions, Rothko's favored format.

In Ryman's hands, Rothko's colored fields become discrete registers of facture. The upper section is covered in dense strokes of white that are interrupted by a black square that continues onto the edge. The middle section is untouched, with a slight discoloration that was left when the cotton canvas was sized. The lower tip is a subtle unsized band bearing the inscription "RRYMAN58" in the same opaque white paint as used above. The composition continues to the sides or edges of the canvas. In this, it stages Rothko's attempts to open a composition out into the space of the viewer, an aim that Ryman saw as chief to Rothko's project and commensurate with his interest in it, misunderstanding the fundamentally pictorial emotionalism that Rothko beseeched as unimpeded materialism. In short, "it was Rothko's form, not his content" that impressed him.[27] Ryman pressed what

Robert Ryman, *Untitled* (1958). Oil on stretched sized cotton canvas.

he saw as Rothko's opening of painting onto space in later works that further emphasized the transition between the painting and the context in which it is sited.

He was also drawn to the "sureness"[28] and immediacy in the deceptively facile work of Henri Matisse, whose presence in the museum was felt in many exhibitions, in hefty catalogue publications (such as Barr's monumental work on the artist, which was published in 1951), and in the publicity surrounding his death in 1954. Rothko found Matisse's *The Red Studio* (1911) to be a singular education,[29] and Ryman also pored over the painting's details. In his homage to Matisse, a painted photograph titled *Studio View* (1959), Ryman looks out the window of his top-floor, 11th Street flat, with its red-flooded interior and oddly rendered perspective. It can be compared with a later, less forthcoming serigraph from the "On the Bowery" (1969–1971) portfolio of prints made by artists who lived near each other. Yet in most instances, he was not trying to produce a painting that looked like a Matisse or even (painted photograph aside) to exploit his palette but to understand how Matisse made a painting.

As Ryman discussed the interest:

> It's hard to describe a painting. You can describe to a certain extent, but it's always more than that. Always. The more is the part that matters. In the *Red Studio,* for instance, Matisse was using an image of the studio in order to make a painting. The studio was the "what," but the "how" was how he did the painting; that's what I am talking about, and that's the important part. The fact that it was his studio is not important at all, or of very little importance. It's how he did it, the flatness of it, the way he put it together: the composition, the color, the way he flattened everything out. That was the "how"; that was what was important. The technical part, maybe how he mixed the colors, that's something else.[30]

In short, the "how" of painting that is posited against Matisse's tactility (juxtaposed with his spatial flattening) is as much Ryman's subject matter as anything

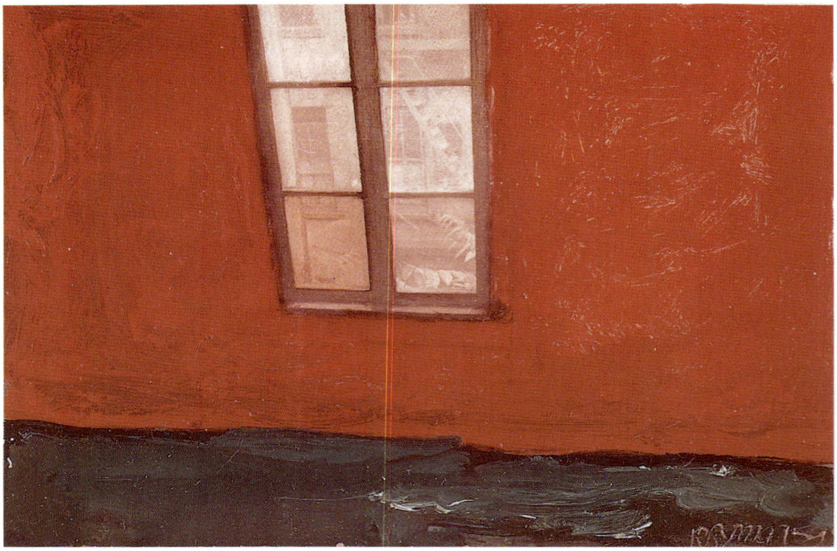

Robert Ryman, *Studio View* (1959). Oil on black and white photograph.

Robert Ryman, *Untitled*, from "On the Bowery" print portfolio (1969–1971). Serigraph on Schoeller-Hammer paper.

else. Following this insight, Ryman came to see that many components of painting—the stroke, the support, the frame, and even the signature—could be afforded primary roles.

In around 1957 (as discussed below), Ryman began using his name as a compositional element in his paintings. This is a traditional device, although he did not put it to use in a traditional fashion. Freed from signification and cleaved from an authorial presence, such inscriptions read first and foremost as lines or curves, visual incidents that are not qualitatively distinct from the surrounding passages of brushwork or graphic incident as in *Unresolved Drawing* (1961). The signature "Ryman"—so akin to a spoken word repeated and nearly voided semantically—is often dissected, truncated, or rendered almost indecipherable, proposing an absurdity and ubiquity that is meant to negate authority. Donald Kuspit inscribes an alternative meaning here, arguing that this is Ryman's "struggle to find his touch," if not explicitly in the wake of Matisse: "In one work the *m* and *n* resemble fingers, a reminder, perhaps, that they were made by hand."[31] Although I am not sure that I endorse this reading, a later work, *Spectrum VIII* (1984) fits this description uncannily—a twist of the screw as this one is on aluminum. Like Matisse's studio as a pretext for a painting, Ryman's name could be drained of symbolic meaning to become the how rather than the what (much less the why) of his paintings and drawings alike.

Many other artists have likewise been cited in accounts of Ryman's work, although in none of these cases did Ryman copy an artist's work or model himself on a specific example. Rather, Ryman found certain artists to be more or less instructive than others. Telling in this regard is a small *Untitled Study* (c. 1956), a gouache on matboard that was done around the time of MoMA's Pollock retrospective. Marked by a dripped line of white paint that circumnavigates the composition, this painting looks like those from a year or two earlier (discussed above) except for the tangled skein. Even if Pollock's utilization of quotidian materials (house paint and cigarette butts) and his play with the edge and all-overness influenced Ryman, *Untitled Study*'s wanton tracery stands as Ryman's sole attempt to think through Pollock in such literal technical terms.

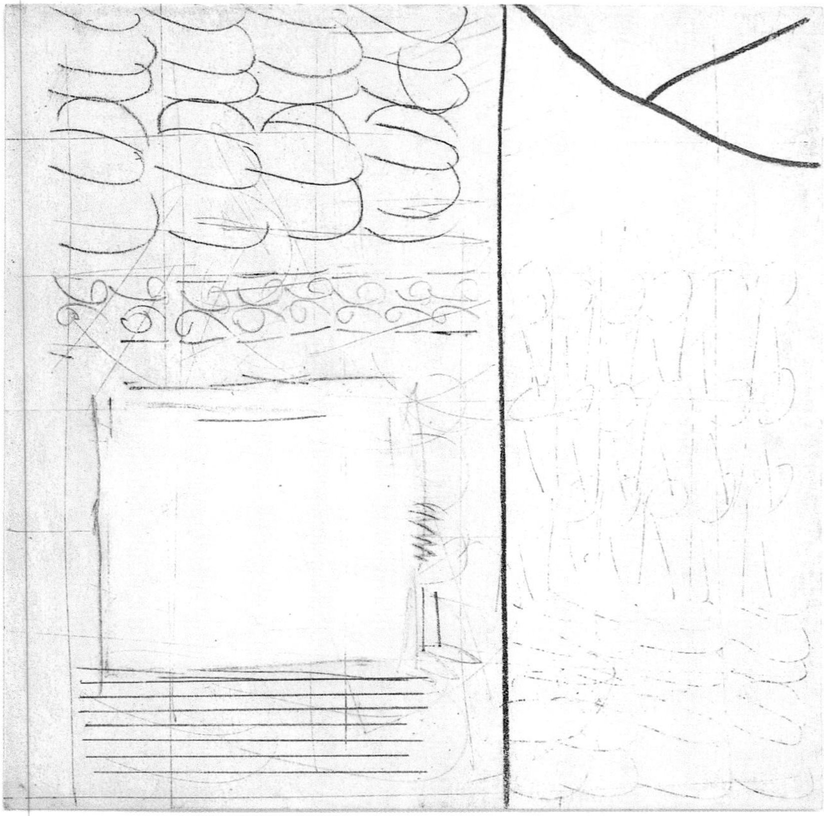

Robert Ryman, *Unresolved Drawing* (1961). Graphite and pastel on gray Rives paper.

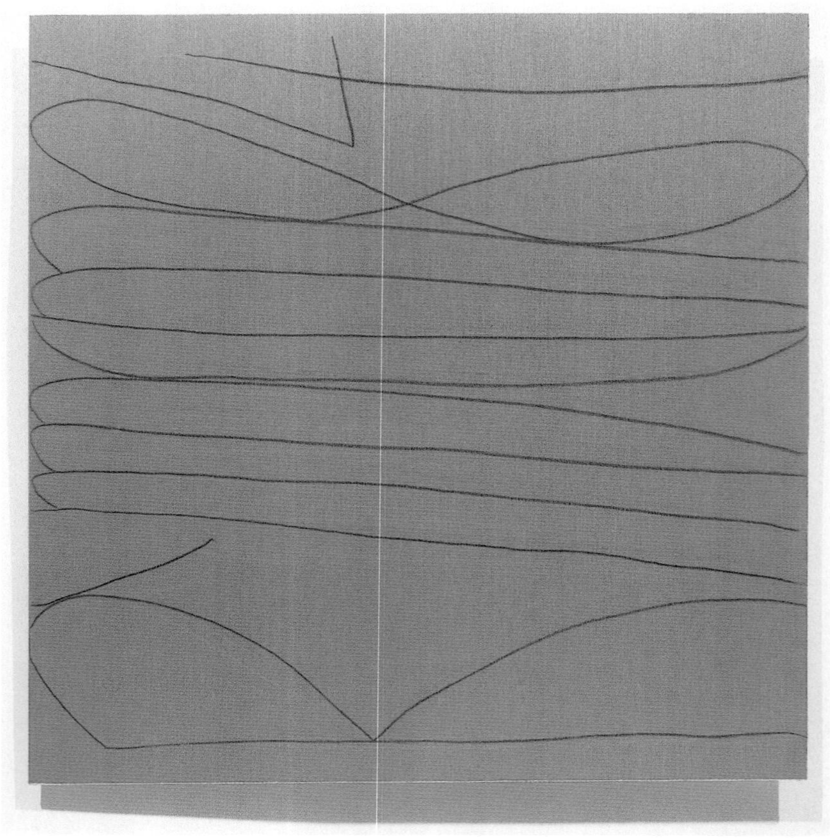

Robert Ryman, *Spectrum VIII* (1984). Graphite on anodized aluminum panel.

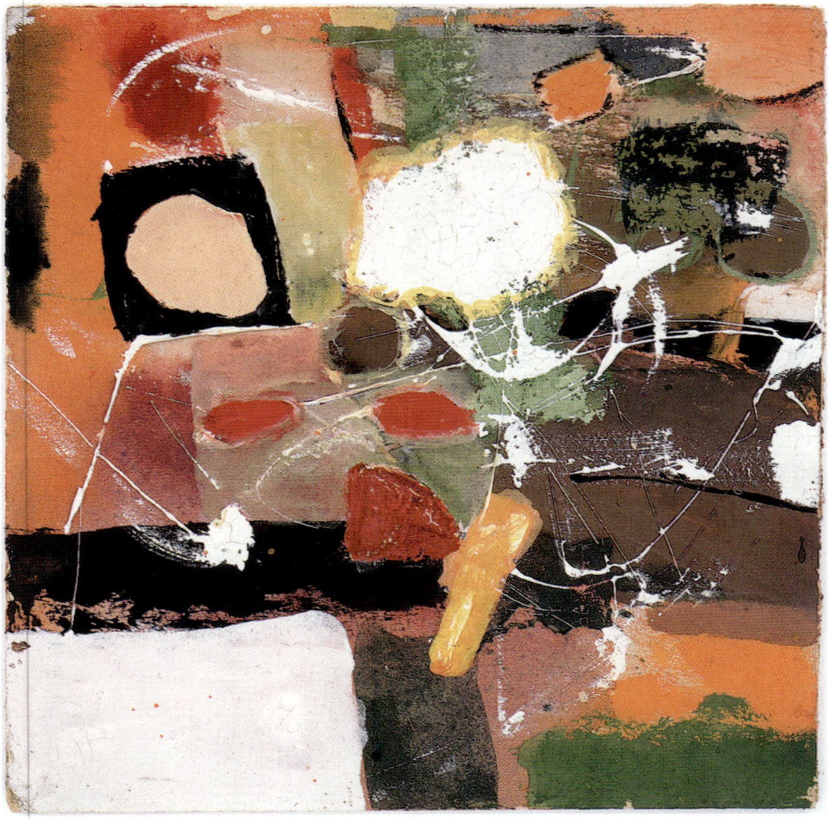

Robert Ryman, *Untitled Study* (c. 1956). Gouache and crayon on matboard, no fixed orientation.

Even so, critics have been quick to posit comparisons on morphological grounds, the most egregious of which is reading Ryman's work not in relation to abstract expressionism but rather in relation to Robert Rauschenberg's *White Paintings*.[32] Shown in 1953 at the Stable Gallery in New York, the *White Paintings* represent Rauschenberg's attempt to move beyond what he understood to be the endpoint of modernism in the form of the monochrome. He categorized his paintings as nonart events that are marked by their durational structures. By giving over their surfaces not to effects of facture but to the plays of light that are cast by a viewing subject or the fields of dust that might collect there (John Cage called these *White Paintings* "airports for the lights, shadows and particles"), Rauschenberg was following the antiauthoritarian and antiexpressionist example of Cage, who, in turn, took Rauschenberg's provocation and ended up with a silent piano composition, *4′33″*.[33]

Although Ryman never saw the *White Paintings* and although Rauschenberg's foundation was antipodal to his own (most explicitly in his positioning of the *White Paintings* against a telos of modernism), the fact remains that they are "white" paintings, presuming an implicit conversation. Arthur Danto tries to get at how Ryman's work differs from the early monochromes of Rauschenberg (who, as Danto explains, "found the white so pristine that he could not bring himself to sully it") by citing an interview with Chuck Close. Close remarked that he would "spend three weeks gessoing and wet-sanding a canvas—ten to twelve coats—getting it all smooth and getting it perfect, and it reminds me of those apartment signs you see on the highway, 'If you lived here you'd be home now.' If I were Robert Ryman, I'd be done."[34]

Traditional modes of composition are supplanted in Ryman's work by tropes from a repertoire of painting's effects that are annexed in a seemingly infinite number of combinations. As Bois writes: "But in work after work the logic of Ryman's testing habit will follow the same pattern: first decompose the synthetic activity of painting into constitutive elements, then alter or redistribute the function of these elements."[35] As with Ryman's sketches from the galleries, an element might shift in placement or orientation from painting to painting, rotating and mutating across discrete sites of activity. Evident within each work are multidirectional and variable strokes that change direction or thickness in the course of their application. A stroke moves upward and suddenly turns sharply to the left or right, or a stroke begins thin at its initial point of contact with the support and broadens out an inch away. Also, these strokes are rarely repainted or executed more than once.

Untitled (1957), a small gouache on paper mounted on board and plywood, is one of a number of related works that play with the introduction of rectangular colored bands into larger white fields that are covered with strokes of various widths and shapes. In this, Ryman is already working from the model of *Untitled (Orange Painting),* with its darker rectangular components bordering another differently colored area. The paint does not reach the bottom of the page: the manila paper is prominently displayed and almost entirely unmarked across the whole bottom edge. In a way, the presence of a black rectangle and a green rectangle formalize the accidents of the prior piece, while new elements, such as the signature, are introduced. "RRyman 57" is painted vertically on the work's right side in the slightest of contours and with the same paint that constituted the field out of which it materializes and literally surfaces. The bas-relief raises and swells above the paint or through it, pushing insistently against itself.

About this, Ryman recalls:

> I don't know if it is the first time I used the signature [incorporated into the painted field]. It is the first time I used it turned on its edge because I felt that I could use the signature as an element in the composition, that it was a traditional device that painters always used; not necessarily as a compositional element, but they generally signed their paintings on the front. And I felt if I turned the signature on its edge it would become more abstract as line in itself, because I rarely use line in my painting. So I could use my signature as line, and that's why I used it on the front and sometimes prominently in white and on the edge because it was more abstract that

> way and could be read more as line, as curves, rather than simply as a signature. At that time, [c.1957–1958] I signed "R Ryman." Later on I just put "Ryman."[36]

Circulating in this passage is a claim for the centrality of the signature—whether small or large, right-side up or upside down, or in reverse—as an aspect of painting and consequently one element that marks it *as* a painting. It does not need to signify anything or to mark an authorial locus per se. It is abstract in this manner, but real in its effects on the painting that, by virtue of the signature's presence, can be categorized as a painting and institutionalized as such.

The composition itself need not have a specific directionality either. In fact, certain of Ryman's paintings from the mid-1950s lack fixed orientations and can be installed rotated in any direction. *Untitled Study* (c. 1956), an oil, casein, and colored-pencil work on unstretched sized cotton canvas, has no signature, date, or top and bottom. Applied with a palette knife in chunks, the surface reveals rose underpainting beneath blocks of white and black. A figure that can best be described as a fin protrudes with a squiggle (a trope repeated in a few other small works from 1957) of nervous activity. *Untitled* (c. 1956) similarly allows hanging on four sides in terms of both its mechanics (Ryman attached wire to its backing to make this structural) and also its composition. Like other free-floating squares in related works, this one's arbitrary placement does not mandate a directionality based on a pictorial ground.

Even when there is a tacit composition, however, closer inspection often reveals this to be a flawed assumption, less fixed or given than contingent on how closely one is looking. In *The Paradoxical Absolute* (1958), Ryman takes the forms from *Untitled* as a starting point and transforms them. He would do something similar in *Untitled* (1958) (where black becomes the dominant color, overtaking the white) and *Untitled* (1959) (where this is reversed back to the all-over whiteness that is interrupted only by a small black square or rectangle, as in *The Paradoxical Absolute*). A black rectangle still hovers at the top edge, but in *The Paradoxical Absolute* it has been shifted farther to the right, while the drab rectangles that line the edges of these *Untitled*s have subsequently been lowered,

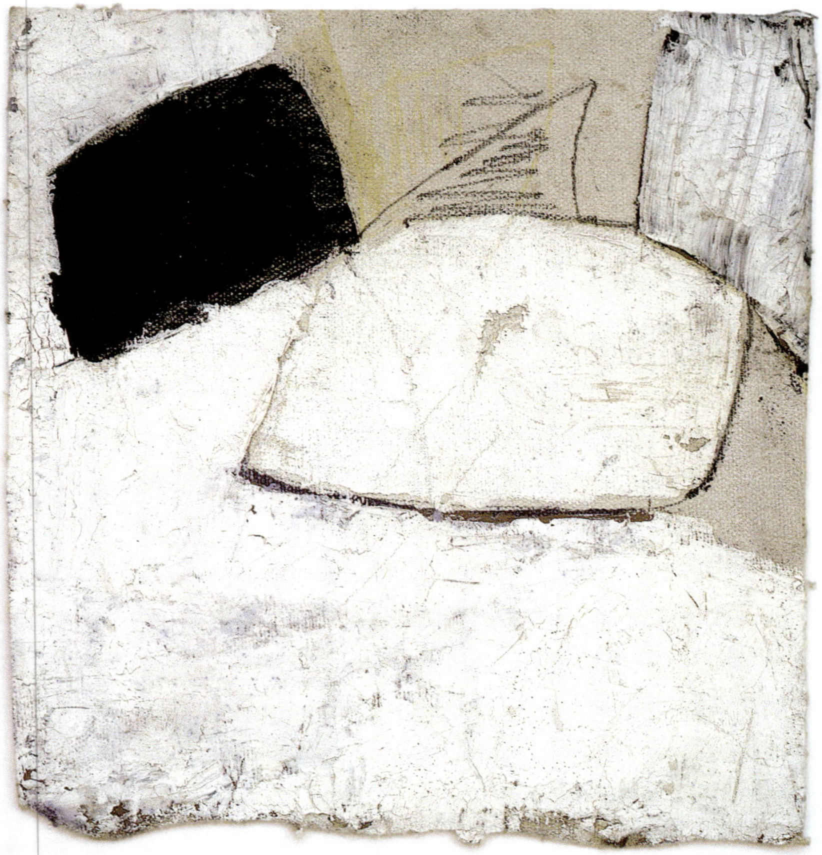

Robert Ryman, *Untitled Study* (c. 1956). Oil, casein, graphite, and colored pencil on unstretched sized cotton canvas, no fixed orientation.

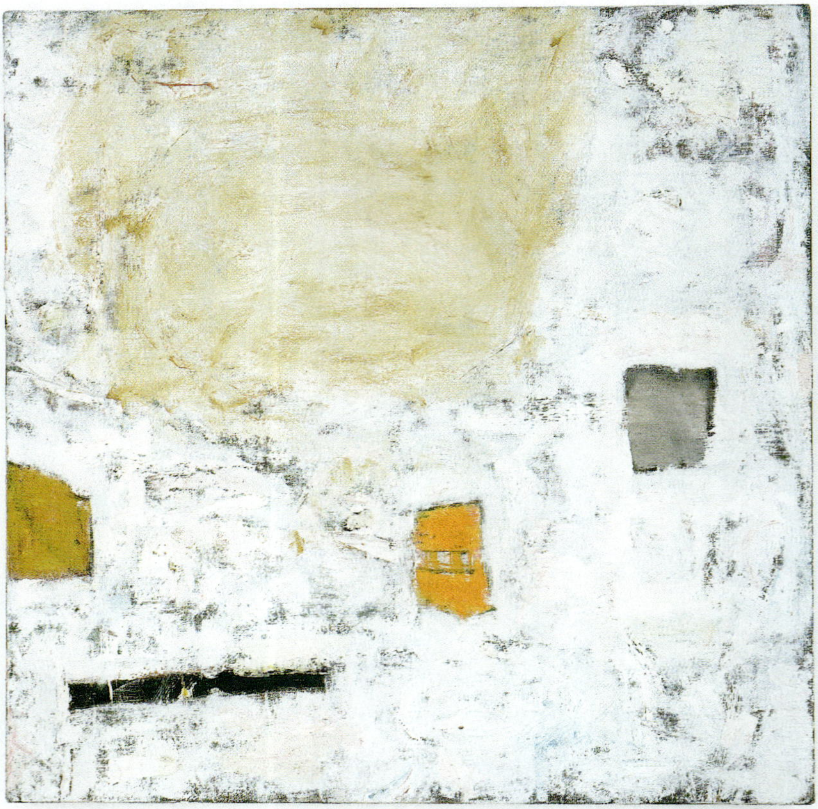

Robert Ryman, *Untitled* (c. 1956). Oil on preprimed stretched canvas, no fixed orientation.

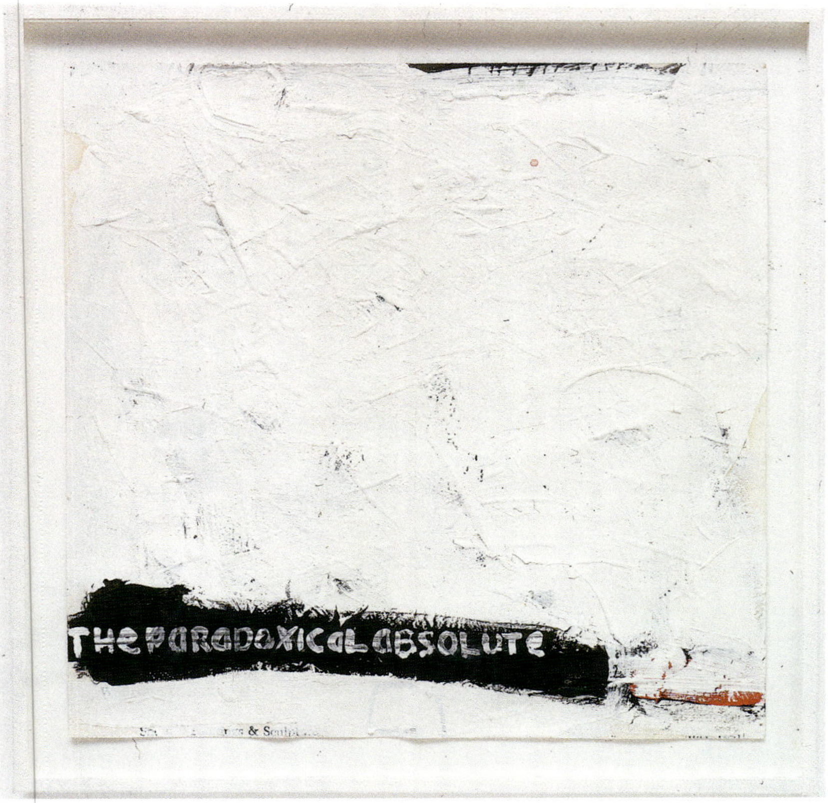

Robert Ryman, *The Paradoxical Absolute* (1958). Oil, casein, and graphite on printed paper.

Robert Ryman, *Untitled* (1958). Casein, gouache, and graphite on newsprint, mounted on board.

Robert Ryman. *Untitled* (1959). Casein on paper.

darkened, and extended to become the ground for the application of text: "The Paradoxical Absolute." This text stands in for a signature, which is another element that can be read; reading as reading-in becomes possible by the pretension to philosophy—even if ironic, nonsensical, or otherwise banal.[37] Perhaps this is why Ryman shunned text other than the signature, from this painting onward, until a 1986 series of five paintings that are inscribed with the word "Test" (see page 22).

Further, *The Paradoxical Absolute* was painted on a found object—a flattened-out folder with gallery listings on the verso, appropriated solely because, like the MoMA letterhead, it was readily available and free—that has text beneath the painted surface. But because the paper was culled from an art mailer, words like "paintings and sculpture," and the dates "May 12–31" can be discerned at the lower edge at left of center. The question becomes whether any of this is meant to be read. In much the way that Pablo Picasso's collages flirt with but ultimately deny a single authorial voice or Jasper Johns's encaustic globs coalesce over their newspaper supports without wholly obfuscating their content, Ryman's mailer raises the specter of linguistic meaning to be parsed at the same time that it disavows that meaning.[38]

In *The Paradoxical Absolute,* a faint "58" is embossed in the white region of the painting with the same white paint that provides its support; it floats upside down if we take the direction of the text to be right-side up. Such an operation can be compared with Picasso's use of newsprint in his collages to both constitute a form and provide the background against which it stands forth in the oscillation between figure and ground. Ryman's understanding of the ground as "something to see" (as opposed to something to cover) undoes clear distinctions between these controls, generating a perceptual parallax between one given and another. Neither figure (painting) nor ground (support) is ultimately privileged, although the viewer's act of engagement with the painting becomes active and self-determined.

The painting might as well be hung with both "texts" on their sides to better literalize their function as markers of the definitional constituents of painting (signature, date, philosophical underpinning) that secure its conventionality as painting. Here is Ryman again: "I used the signature as a line, and

I generally put it up the side or on the end . . . just to make it more abstract so that it would read more as a line and not so much as my name, necessarily. I used my name because that was an accepted element of all painting. . . . If I just used line, . . . it would have been a kind of symbol. . . . It would have been as if I was painting something or trying to say something."[39]

To return to the signature, as Ryman would do after *The Paradoxical Absolute,* is to understand the ways in which the signature is made equivalent to a brush stroke or to a support as part of a lexicon of painting. Naomi Spector writes about this transition in the late 1950s and its implication for Ryman's project more broadly:

> Traditionally it was what was done with the paint that was of interest, not the paint itself. Whether the visual result was representational or abstract, the paint was still used towards certain ends outside itself, whether they were illusional or not. Even "non-objective" pictures used the paint to express emotion, convey ideas, embody theories of art, or achieve a kind of spiritual transendence. But with Ryman, particularly after the early sixties, the paint stood only for itself. It was asked to speak for itself alone, to be itself with its own full complement of inherent qualities. At the same time, the other physical, visual components of the paintings came to be of aesthetic concern in just the same way. Even those elements which usually were kept "behind the scenes," which we habitually do not see—such as the sides of stretchers, the signature, the way canvases are attached to stretchers, and much more—entered the aesthetic arena. Everything visible counts with Ryman, and everything about a work has been made to count visually.[40]

Painting becomes a less static or grounded medium and a more fluid, material site for the continual testing and reworking of conventions and the effects that these conventions or properties produce. What a painting *is* becomes inextricable from what a painting *does.* It all starts with paint, but paint alone is not sufficient to produce a painting; it is necessary but not sufficient. A painting needs paint, a support, a delimitation of that support in the form of an edge, a wall (a viewing context), and someone to see it—to register as a painting (as discussed further in chapter 3). Along such lines, Ryman once argued with Sol LeWitt over a piece that LeWitt was making. The piece had one open box and one covered box that would contain something inside. "Ryman thought it pointless to actually put anything in the closed box since it couldn't be seen. LeWitt maintained that the idea—in which the 'art' ultimately resided—demanded that the piece be completed as conceived."[41]

In the course of a 1978 interview, Barbaralee Diamonstein remarked to Ryman that he does not "make much of a fuss about many things." He replied: "When I'm painting, it should be right the first time. If something has to be struggled over or fussed with, then I think there's something wrong, there's a problem; it never turns out very well and it's best to just abandon it. The approach should be direct and to the point and without anything that doesn't need to be there. So I think maybe that's what you're talking about."[42]

Diamonstein countered that Ryman's rejoinder did not square with his comparison of a painter to a "research scientist." Ryman replied:

> I think that's what painters do. They try and solve problems—aesthetic problems concerning painting—very much in the same way that a scientist goes about solving certain problems. Scientists try to find solutions, and they pick one problem out of thousands to explore and work on. It's a similar thing, I think, that painters do. You can't work on everything, so you take what interests you most and you explore it, and you find what solutions are possible, what can happen with this, and where it will lead to, and one solution will set off a new problem that enables you to see something that you weren't able to see before, because you didn't know about it. Then you compare your solutions with other solutions in the same

> field, and see that someone else has solved a certain thing, so you take that into consideration, and that's where the exchange of information is important.[43]

We could chalk up to nervous irresolution the seeming inconsistencies that Diamonstein pressed and render this inadmissible; however, a suspicion lingers that Ryman did not view these positions as antagonistic.

Indeed, this involuntary juxtaposition cuts to the core of Ryman's understanding of his painting. A concern for Matisse-inspired simplification—manifest in formal terms and the process that self-consciously gives rise to them—is checked by an equally pronounced interest in laboratory-derived problem solving (a position that gains in significance relative to Victor D'Amico's Deweyan pedagogy and Alfred Barr's institutionally sanctioned rhetoric of experimentation, as explored in chapter 1). A dual imperative, it advances a practice that is characterized by an engagement with materials as options to be tested and reworked against their results—their fineness, complementarity, viability with other chosen implements, and so on. Ryman controls the test each time to reach provisional "solutions" that are free of extraneous diversions and residual indirections.

Ryman excises variables to allow for subtle modulations and shifts of emphasis—as given, for instance, by the choice of matte or glossy paint, a flat or rounded brush, a canvas or a linen support of differing weight, grain, tooth, and absorbency—and fosters innovations from work to work within an overarching series or even across the zones of a single painting. He proposes that work need not be motivated by a dissatisfaction with tradition but can instead be inspired by the inclination to see how forms might retain relevance in new circumstances ("Painters do make you see things in a different way; for example, Matisse").[44] Ryman believes painting to be in its infancy, and sees as—if only—potential substantiation of this his own ability to effect limitless variations with a minimum of tools. Even if suggested in part by what has been, the outcome of each painting is not presupposed, as ideas are productive hypotheses to be tested and

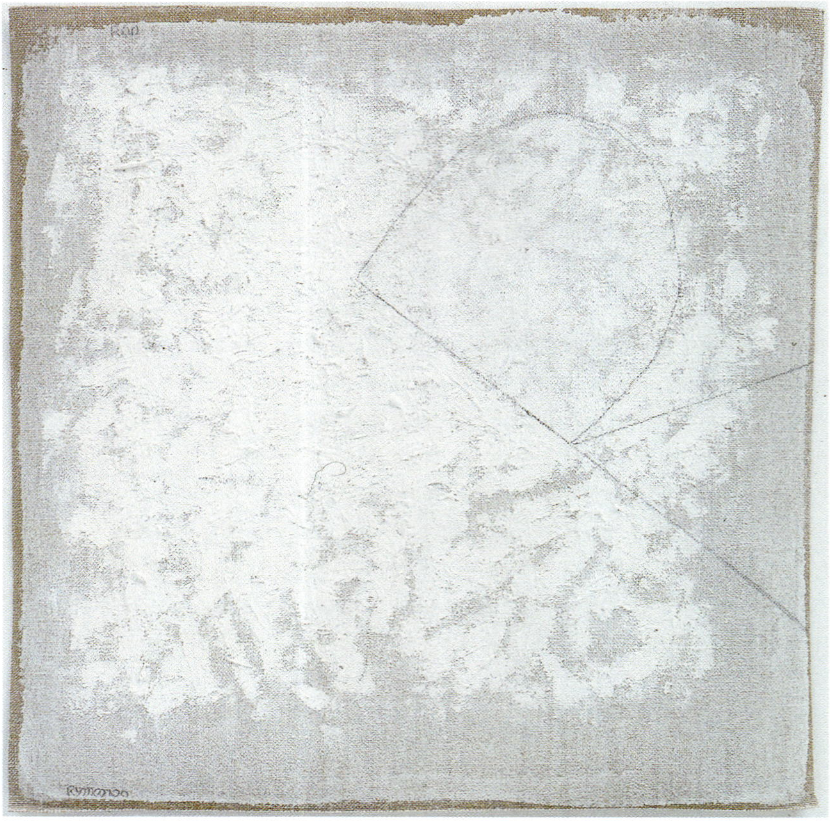

Robert Ryman, *Untitled* (2000). Oil and graphite on sized linen canvas.

revised against their consequences. Derived from a series of encounters through which actions unfold out of and against a discrete set of options and concerns, Ryman's painting is both the byproduct of an experiment and the evidence of its material instantiation—a process that continues to the present, as *Untitled* (2000) demonstrates.

His ingenuousness about the unforeseen difficulties of this process is hard to ignore. As Carter Ratcliff writes, Ryman's "surfaces show themselves being decided upon as they appear, deciding to occupy vision in one way and not another; and taking into consideration nothing but the nature of paint, brush, surface and the act of painting. This is an emphasis on gestural texture, and sometimes it changes partway through a painting: the surface will cohere by achieving a new texture, just as the first is somehow getting beyond the painter's reach."[45] One might conclude that this bluntness is related to his being an autodidact, although Ryman's candor has outlived his early education—unless we take the whole of his production to be reducible to it. This is not to trivialize, but to insist on the hesitancy with which he has continued to approach each act, knowing, from Matisse, how nearly impossible it is to do something well enough to make it look easy.

3

Support

Of the many definitions of *support* that appear in the *Oxford English Dictionary,* the most pertinent for a discussion of Robert Ryman's paintings happens to be the most physical: "The solid substance or material on which a painting is executed." Other entries include "spiritual help," "mental comfort," and the deftly operational, as in "the action of keeping from failing, exhaustion or perishing." In all cases, however, the active and the passive are mutable, and "the action or fact of holding up, keeping from falling" becomes "the condition of being so supported." The definitions characterize relationships between actions and conditions—between the doing and the being done—such that the support is both a circumstance of engagement and a registration of that action's consequence.

Taken in relation to painting, the support's "solid substance or material" proves less fixed or given than might otherwise be assumed. If painting is the action of the verb *to paint* as well as the medium through which it is effected, then the support is its ground, though one that provides resistance more than comfort, "mental" or otherwise. For a definition of *painting*—participle, gerund, and noun—to be functional for Ryman, the fractured linguistic terrains that hold what something *is* apart from what something *does* (or even who does something or to whom or what something is done) must be consolidated.

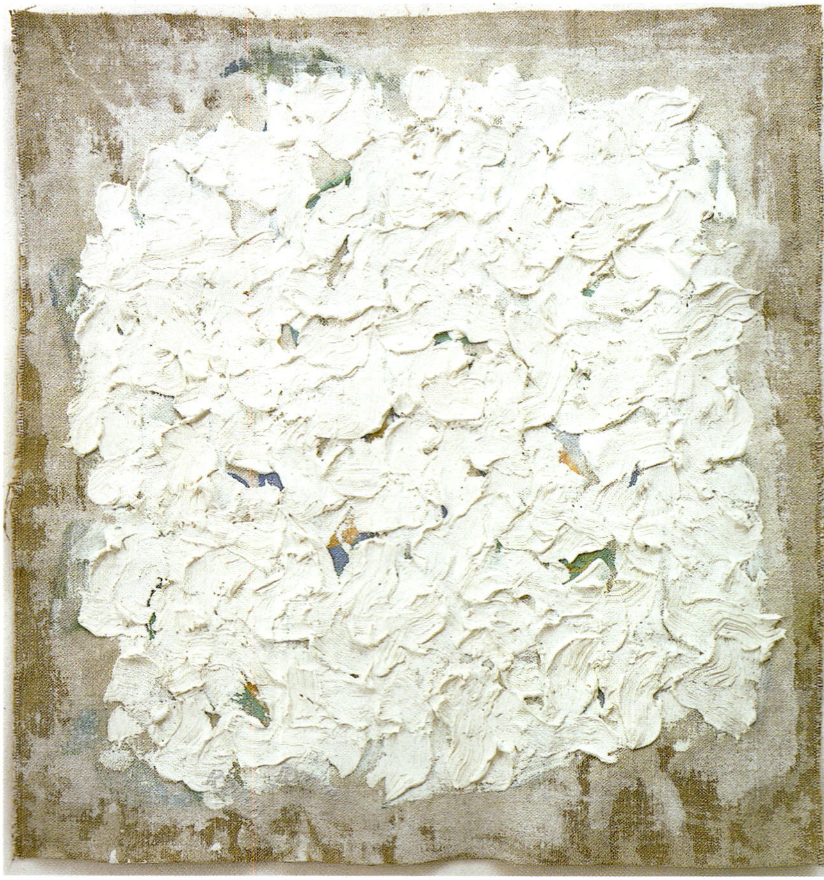

Robert Ryman, *Untitled #1004* (c. 1960–1961). Oil and gesso on unstretched sized linen canvas.

The question of "what is a painting?" opens onto the effects that might, even provisionally, constitute it.

In September 1971, Ryman composed a relevant statement about his work:

> In the Fall of 1968 I did my first show at Konrad Fischer's gallery in Dusseldorf. The exhibition consisted of six paintings on paper panels, nine panels to a painting [the *Classico* paintings on paper, discussed in chapter 5]. The panels were crated and shipped to Dusseldorf. In the process of getting them though customs (in order to avoid the duty that is to be paid on "Art" arriving in the country), Konrad had listed them as "paper" and not as paintings. But the customs official said "But? It is expensive paper (handmade) so you will have to pay so much!" "Yes, it is expensive paper," Konrad said, "but it has been used." The customs official agreed that it had indeed been used. So the paintings arrived designated as "Used Paper." Since that time I have wondered about the possibility of paintings being defined as "Used Paint." Then there could be "Used Bronze," "Used Canvas," "Used Steel," "Used Lead . . ."[1]

In Ryman's work, the generic idea of painting is tested against its specificity as material consequences so that the question of what a painting is can be answered only by, in, and as painting. However, whether for drawings on fabric, paintings on paper, pencil drawings on paper, or oil paintings on linen, there is also a chance that a painting is no more than used paint. This chapter seeks to understand Ryman's conception of what constitutes a painting.

Painting is the support for Ryman's production. Indeed, painting delimits its field stroke by stroke and painting by painting, it defines and tests it, and it plainly acts on it. Paint and support together produce painting. They are motivated not to secure a composition but to designate its effects as painting within a social and institutional sphere of signification and apprehension. In this way, his approach is at odds with Clement Greenberg's contemporary medium theorizations and Ellsworth Kelly's acompositional paintings that seek to disable composition. Both projects are instructive contrasts to Ryman's pragmatic testing of materials as constitutive of painting (and composition) and are explored below.

A painting is made a painting for Ryman through his interplay of paint and support. In illusionistic painting (or, indeed, Greenberg's construction of optical painting), the support is specified only to be, in a sense, disavowed—insistently covered over and hence dematerialized into a picture plane that recedes into the transparent perspectival depth of an image in comprehensibly deep space. In contrast to this type of painting, Ryman's work insistently stays on the surface to affirm it as a ground for practice. Ryman explains:

> The painter is concerned with putting the paint on the surface and making the paint into an image. But I approach a painting in a different way. I approach painting beginning with the material. The traditional painter would say that the canvas was empty, and they would put the paint on it and make an image with the paint. When I approach a painting, I say the surface that I'm using, whether it's canvas or whatever it is, isn't empty; it's something in itself. It's up to the paint to clarify it, in a sense . . . to make the surface or the structure something to see.[2]

Rarely does Ryman uniformly cover the support *as* surface, and the only transparency on offer is a material clarity. To the extent that it remains less than wholly visible, the support is often veiled beneath the thinnest scrim of paint, obviating distinctions between paint and primer and frustrating attempts to pry figure apart from its ground. Yve-Alain Bois writes:

> The main reason why [Ryman] never considered painting images was because he wanted above all to avoid any kind of a priori projection which could be applied with any material to any surface and

> which would therefore immediately define the ground as neutral: no two materials reflect light or receive paint the same way, he insists, and it would have been against his empirical ethic to ignore such a determining factor.[3]

The support frequently flaunts its presence and becomes, as Ryman says, "something to see." It is integral to the painting and acts with the paint. Whether the support is stretched or unstretched canvas, cotton duck, linen, jute, Bristol board, corrugated board, feather board, fiberglass, newsprint, paper, tracing paper, wax paper, the front and back of wallpaper, Chemex coffee filter paper, wood, steel, or copper, it does not unify through all-over facture but instead calls attention to the ground on and against which it flourishes.

Clement Greenberg reasoned that the transposition of three dimensions into two survived in even the most abstract paintings. Vestiges of pictorialism and illusionism could, for Greenberg, be found within the geometry of a Piet Mondrian. In his "Modernist Painting," Greenberg maintains that "the first mark made on a canvas destroys its literal and utter flatness, and the result of the marks made on it by an artist like Mondrian is still a kind of illusion that suggests a kind of third dimension. Only now it is a strictly pictorial, strictly optical third dimension."[4] In an essay where Greenberg argued for modernism's logic of self-criticism (he claimed that the "characteristic methods of a discipline . . . entrench it more firmly in its area of competence"[5] and preserved its autonomy and its correlative "experience"[6] within a larger cultural domain that presumably threatened it), what surprises is Greenberg's insistence on the persistence of tradition in the face of its apparent disenfranchisement.[7] At issue for Greenberg is not modernism's specificity but its perpetual renovation—a reformation of what had always been inherent to painting, whether "the flat surface, the shape of the support, [or] the properties of the pigment."[8] With modernism, Greenberg contends, these factors became overt. The strategy was not to create a new medium but to transvalue the terms that were already implicit within it—to call attention to art rather than to "dissemble" it and to render a picture first and foremost a picture.

Robert Ryman, *Untitled* (c. 1957). Colored pencil, gouache, casein, and oil on verso of printed wallpaper.

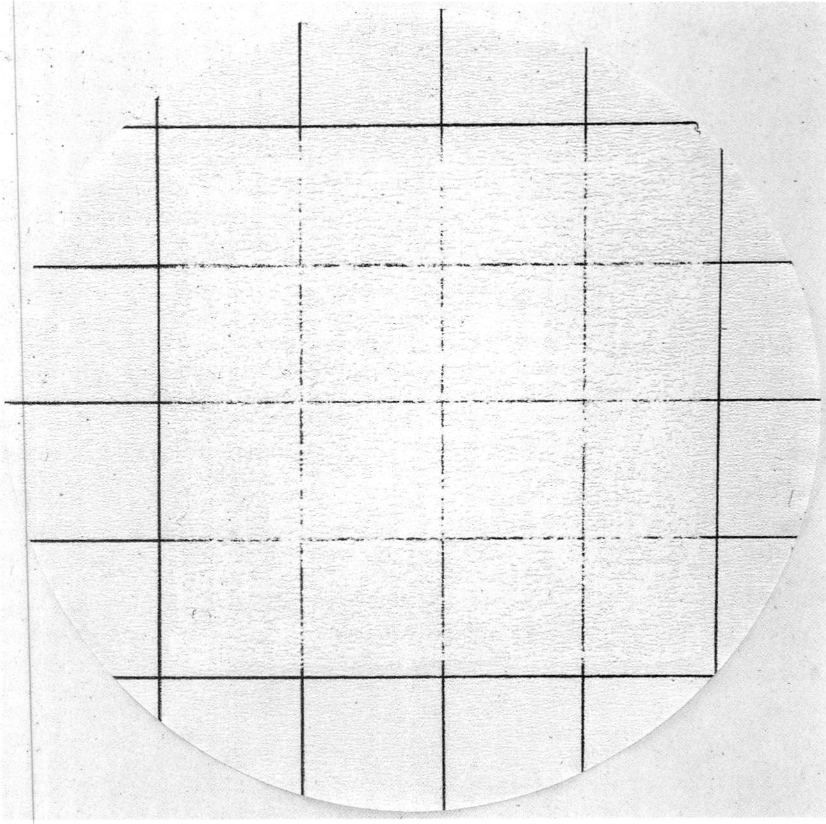

Robert Ryman. *Untitled* (c. 1964). Pastel and charcoal on Chemex coffee filter paper.

In this drive for self-criticism, the logic of which (under Greenberg's watch, at least) stressed the flatness of the support, modernism could profitably jettison representational space in favor of an "opticality" that can be traversed only "with the eye"[9] (unlike sculpture, which is safely lodged in the three dimensions of "real" space that can be physically circumnavigated and somatically registered). But this slippery move from flatness to opticality unsuspectingly and perhaps against Greenberg's better judgment introduced a porous demarcation between a picture and an arbitrary object.[10] Even if opticality was still connected, if inversely, to traditional perspective, it opened up the pictorial plane beyond and in excess of its material support while rendering its decipherability newly contingent on modes of convention and address.[11]

This aperture likewise had implications for the stability of the medium, which was made uncontrollably subject to the ambitions of wildly disparate practices. While Greenberg is often read as legislating the diminution of painting to its essentials, in his reading of illusionistic space as nascent opticality Greenberg inadvertently invites claims for an art that is born not of materials but of concepts and conventions. His most explicit critical consolidation betrayed the complexities of such a predicament. Greenberg's emergent anxiety about what of painting remained securely intact and hence categorical in the wake of abstract expressionism led him only two years later to retool these theories in an essay appropriately entitled "After Abstract Expressionism."

Here, Greenberg reaffirms his earlier mandate by arguing for the sustained relevance of the medium while shifting its terms in the face of an expanded aesthetic (and extra-aesthetic) field:

> Elsewhere I have written of the kind of self-critical process which I think provides the infra-logic of modernist art ("Modernist Painting"). The aim of self-criticism, which is entirely empirical and not at all an affair of theory, is to determine the irreducible working essence of art and the separate arts. Under the testing of modernism, more and more of the conventions of the art of painting have shown themselves to be dispensable, unessential. By now it has been

> established, it would seem, that the irreducible essence of pictorial art consists in but two constitutive conventions or norms: flatness and the delimitation of flatness; and that the observance of merely these two norms is enough to create an object which can be experienced as a picture; thus a stretched or tacked-up canvas already exists as a picture—though not necessarily as a successful one. (The paradoxical outcome of this reduction has been not to contract, but actually to expand the possibilities of the pictorial: much more than before lends itself now to being experienced pictorially or in meaningful relation to the pictorial: all sorts of large and small items that used to belong entirely to the realm of the arbitrary and the visually meaningless.)[12]

Greenberg still points to the self-critical underpinnings of advanced modernist art, reaffirming his own privileging of flatness as crucial to this enterprise. But he obliquely admits that such matters are legible only through the discourse that can attend to minute and yet consequential discrepancies between the pictorial and the meaningless.

Even as Greenberg insists that self-criticism is "entirely empirical and not at all an affair of theory," he concedes that pictures have become interchangeable objects that are marked by readymade cues and by perceptual givens that must be addressed by qualitative discriminations rather than categorical mediumistic imperatives. This is what Thierry de Duve reads as Greenberg's foray into "formalism" at the expense of modernism, which is defined by de Duve as follows: "I shall reserve the name 'modernism' to designate modernism as specific self-criticism and I shall use the name 'formalism' to designate modernism as generic quality (art as art). As far as painting is concerned, 'modernism' thus refers to its specific tendency to assert the flatness of its medium, and 'formalism' refers to its tropism toward aesthetic value as such."[13] The question became not whether any of this new art was art but whether it was good art. Yet this theory, like any other, is only as good as the art that it can explicate.

As contraction becomes expansion, definitions become harder to secure, even by means of the very terms that Greenberg has set in play. In the above passage, Greenberg conspicuously abandons high "Modernism" for its generic correlate, lowercase *m* modernism, while leaving synthetic cubism and abstract expressionism capitalized—conceptually and stylistically intact. The inference is that this appellation is no longer salient. For Greenberg, the old distinctions among mediums—which held painting as painting apart from sculpture as sculpture and which held both painting and sculpture apart from kitsch, nonart, or eventually design—were no longer stable (if they ever were).

The arbitrary was, perhaps unexpectedly, not countered by a return to a fetishization of materials but through a canny displacement of painting into word. If something is taken as a given (for instance, "that a stretched or tacked-up canvas already exists as a picture"), its meaning resides less in its assumption of being a painting than its qualitative refinement—that is, the ways in which it is made significant (as a "successful" painting) in writing, among other things. In this sleight of hand, Greenberg supplants materials (and the vaunted medium-specificity for which he was lionized and ultimately damned) with the conventions that are productive of painting; consequently, he approaches what could be called a pragmatic position. This ploy to rescue art from its obverse bristles uncomfortably against the openness (or pluralism, a term that is not customarily used in relation to this period) that such a position should seemingly encourage. Greenberg's parenthetical explanation of the expansion of the "possibilities of the pictorial" was nowhere, for him at least, liberatory.

Although for Greenberg the opening up of painting and its attendant sloughing off of superficial or inessential conventions inaugurated its regrettable descent into a world of mundane objects and categorical instability, for Ryman the willful reduction to paint and support that was evacuated of illusion was the fruitful ground on which painting could be made tenable for his practice. Ryman's great intuitions were that painting was painting by virtue of its conventions and effects, that these conventions were not indissoluble, and that their effects (as much as their processes of which their results were the manifest residue) were not immaterial. That a "stretched or tacked-up canvas already exists as a picture" was not assumed by Ryman as much as it was taken as the ground—indeed, the support—for his practice, which then could gainfully be tested through such terms. Maybe it would stand as a painting, and maybe it would not. But for Ryman, the acts of querying its status and observing its effects could happen only in painting (and not in representational painting, whose potential Ryman seems to have disregarded) and not in philosophy, criticism, or theory applied to painting from without.

Christopher Wood writes that "the great difference between Ryman's analytic tinkering and a written treatise or handbook is that it is conducted in the medium of paint. It enacts the effects of paint even as it describes them. . . . Ryman's paintings show and tell at the same time. In each case, the real presence of the sign doubles back and corroborates the very message it signifies."[14] As Greenberg was preparing to write "After Abstract Expressionism," Ryman was painting *A Painting of Twelve Strokes Measuring 11 ¼″ × 11 ¼″ Signed at the Bottom Right Hand Corner* (1961). One of several small unstretched linen canvases that Ryman completed around this time, this painting is comprised of a small square within which a hazily uniform patch of pigment shades into a lighter rectangular field to its right. On this painted ground and on the ground of the uncovered support, Ryman applied twelve modular bars of paint in neat, thick, stark white strokes. This vertical band fills the entirety of the right section of the canvas, starting from top to bottom, where, as space is dwindling, Ryman exchanges a painted bar for a signature of the exact same size and proportions. This signature continues the pacing and spacing of the above marks while it redirects their energy, as the "RYMAN61" slightly arcs or arches upward to counter the downward thrust of the stack.

An All White Painting Measuring 9 ½″ × 10″ and Signed Twice on the Left Side in Umber (1961) displays layered white oil in vertical and horizontal strokes. This elongated cross-hatching produces a densely and tightly woven surface that reconstitutes the support on which it is painted. Here, too, as in many of these works, like *a painting on canvas measuring 9-¾″ × 10″ and signed in green at lower center and twice in neutral green at the bottom right corner* (1961), Ryman has let the threads of the support unravel. He calls attention to the linen as loose, untacked up, and raw.

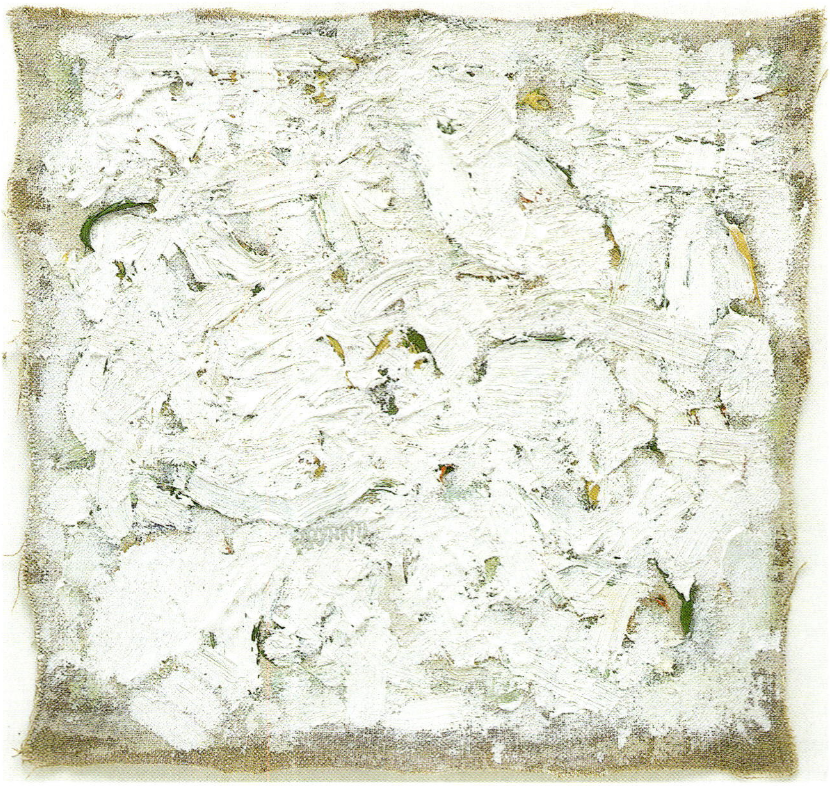

Robert Ryman, *a painting on canvas measuring 9-¾″ × 10″ and signed in green at lower center and twice in neutral green at the bottom right corner* (1961). Oil on unstretched sized linen canvas.

In *Untitled # 1005* (1962), Ryman worked in oil on yet another unstretched linen support. In this case, though, there is overt irregularity in the support, which remains both ragged and scalloped. Frays of untethered and bluntly cut threads emerge at all angles from the painting's sides, and the bottom edge is marked by a selvage strip that is interwoven with linear red thread (which Naomi Spector describes as being simultaneously "an honest part of the material and . . . like a 'found image'").[15] Materials and their procedural history are prominently displayed. The support is uneven but not erratic. Scallops show where the canvas had been stretched and stapled flat for sizing before it was laid flat, unhinged from its backing. These material cues are part of the painting and are as constitutive of its "image" or "composition" as is the overwhelmingly active painted field of furrowed and wormy strokes above a vibrant blue-green that comes to be marked on it. Through his testing of the possibilities of the unstretched canvas in the early 1960s in works such as this, Ryman decided to exploit the dynamics of stretching itself.

Indeed, these works suggest that the support could affect the painted mark, which could, in turn, be adapted to its demands. With them, Ryman perceived the means for another series—the *Stretched Drawings*—that culminated in the slide from painting to drawing with doubly stretched canvases. Even earlier, Ryman's *Untitled* (c. 1962–1963) implied a heterogeneous space of drawing and painting through the repercussions and potentialities of the unstretched support. Irregular and unprimed linen canvas is marked with a grid of wavering pencil lines that continue unabated off the edges. Conventions are layered and suspended, remaining visible as an additive sequence. The drawing becomes a painting through the application of paint. First comes a blanket of diluted grayish white. Then a sunny cornflower blue cedes to a milky, frosty white that covers what had come before, allowing the formative, underlying matrix to remain integral as index and origin for what follows.

In this play of conventions against one another—of paint versus support, drawing versus painting, material fact versus pictorial illusion—Ryman shows the medium to be internally fractured and thereby left constructively ajar. Bois writes that "the major difference between the space of drawing and that of

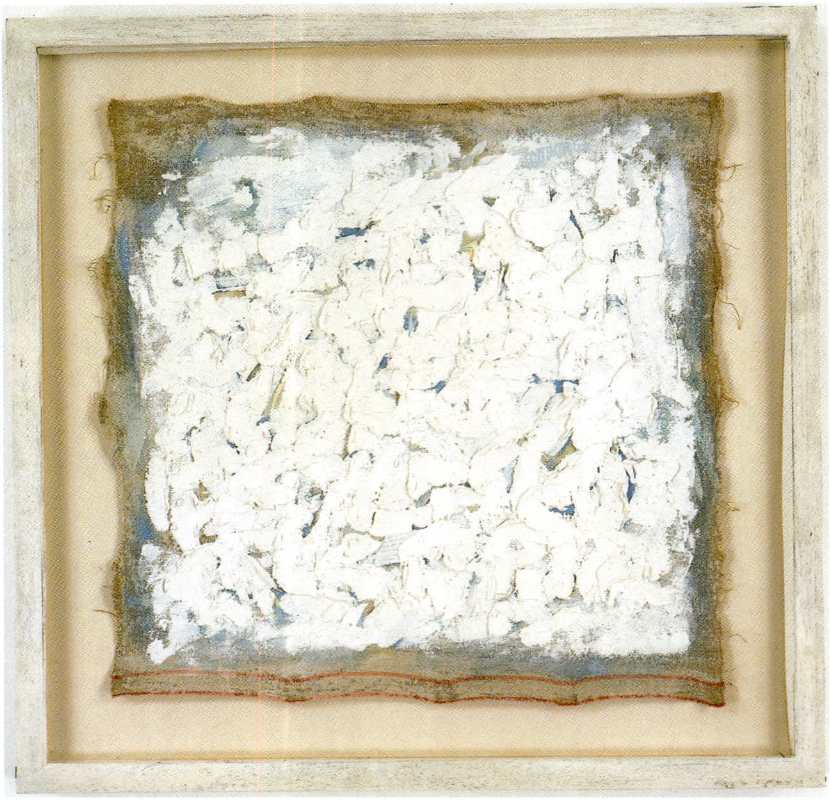

Robert Ryman, *Untitled #1005* (1962). Oil on unstretched sized linen canvas.

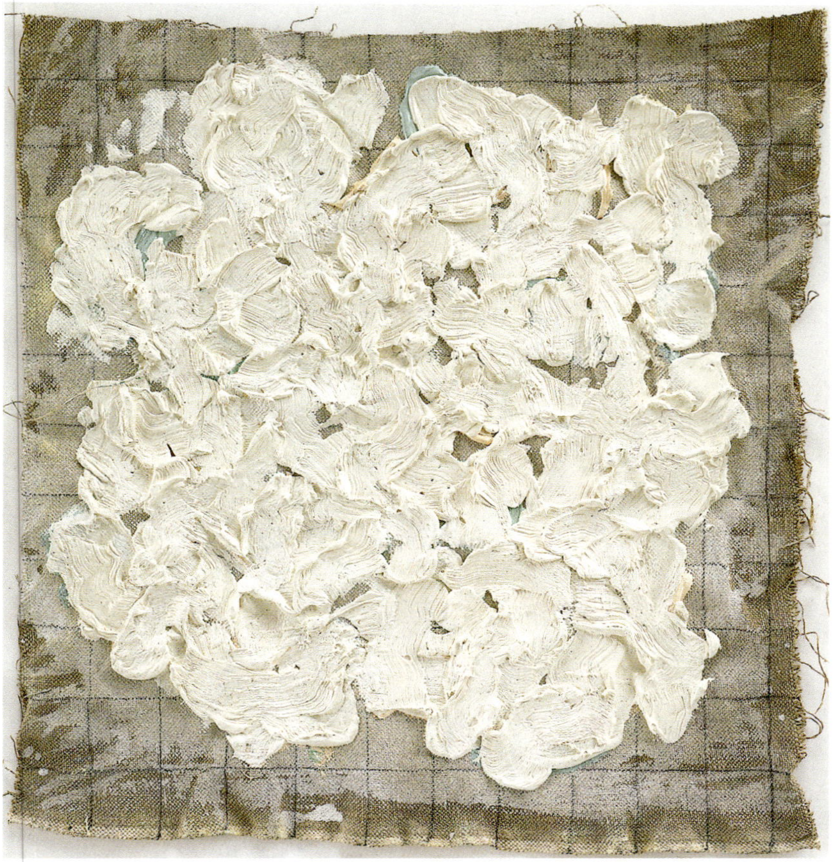

Robert Ryman, *Untitled* (c. 1962–1963). Oil, gesso, and graphite on unstretched sized linen canvas.

painting concerns the nature of the support. Since the time of [Leon Battista] Alberti, the picture plane is assumed as transparent in painting, but the condition sine qua non of this transparency is that the supporting ground be covered over without reserve."[16] Bois follows this by citing Walter Benjamin on drawing: "The graphic line can exist only against this background, so that a drawing that completely covered its background would cease to be a drawing."[17] Noting that Benjamin came to this conclusion in 1917 after seeing a show of Picasso's cubist paintings that presumably troubled this opposition, Bois goes on to remark that Picasso and especially Cézanne had canceled this "constitutive difference."

But for Ryman, such distinctions between a painting that is constituted as covering and a drawing that is known by the differentiation of the mark were yet another boon.[18] Were a drawing made on canvas or even made by canvas, would it remain a drawing? And what of the status of the support, rethought as part of the mark-making system and not as its passive ground? In his aforementioned *Stretched Drawings,* a series of methodologically constant works ranging in size and materials executed around 1963, this question of the neutrality of the support was raised. After drawing a charcoal grid on a stretched cotton canvas, Ryman unstretched and restretched the canvas to see how this newly wrought tension would transform the assumedly rigid lattice.[19] The result, *Stretched Drawing* (1963), is a pliable, slightly wavering web, a framework yielding to the tension of the support, which, as Barbara Reise notes, was "sized to 'fit' the grid so it bent around the three-dimensionality of its stretcher while presenting an almost square 'outline' barely within the square of its frontal surface."[20] This interplay of materials and registrations of actions—what is done to the support and what the support does to what is put on it—consolidates Ryman's preceding investigations and thwarts the distinctiveness of the mantles of drawing and painting.

The slightly later *Bent Line Drawing* (c. 1970) is the result of a drawn square that was precise on loose fabric but warped when the elastic polyester was stretched. In contrast to the charcoal and pencils that were employed for the earlier stretched works, for this drawing Ryman used a ballpoint pen that was capable of withstanding the multidirectional pull of the stretchy support.

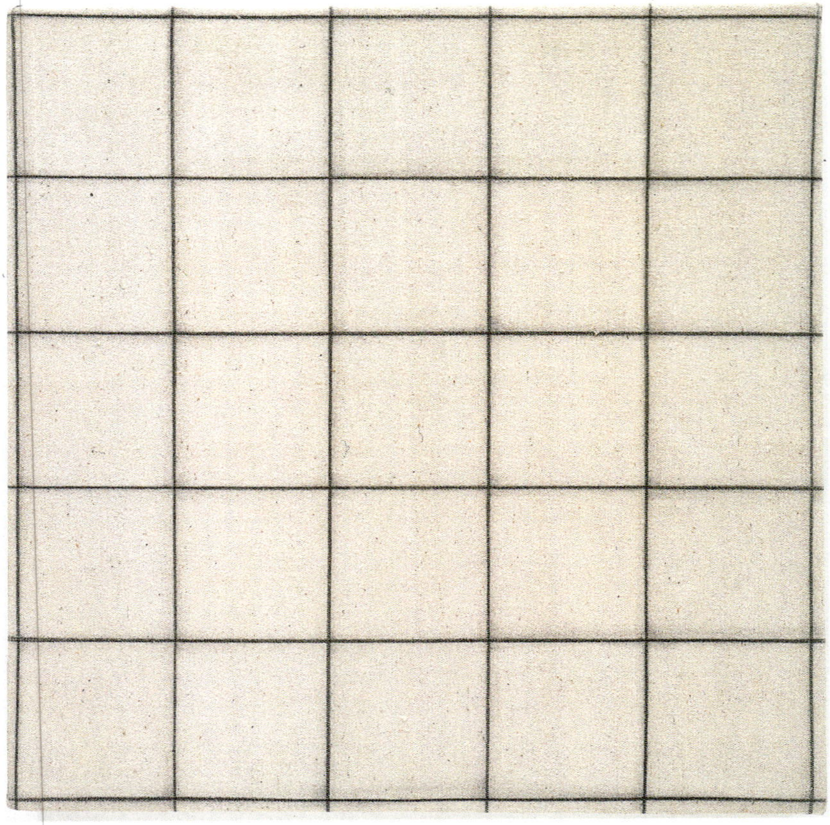

Robert Ryman, *Stretched Drawing* [5 × 5 grid] (1963). Charcoal on stretched sized cotton canvas.

For Reise, these works "have a congruity of materials and the procedures of their usage which is particularly strong and fine. For even charcoal pencil might disappear during the manipulations of the polyester material; the oily ink of ballpoint pen is more adhesive to that fabric and also more flexibly tensile in itself." In terms of categorizations, she continues, "it is a 'drawing,' not a 'painting,' for dried paint—even on cotton canvas—cracks into non-adhesion during an accentuated stretching and re-stretching process. If Ryman were *only* 'into process' he might have used paint and accepted its disappearance: but assuring direct evidence of his procedure in the 'final work' is part of his important integration of conceptions and their realizations into potential permanence."[21]

Although I agree with Reise's description of the work and of the "potential permanence" of its materials and their usage, I am not sure that the *Bent Line Drawing* is "not a painting" simply because it does not involve paint. If anything, the unstretched paintings and stretched drawings offer sites through which to think about these divisions and the grounds on which we make them. In Ryman's work, materials are critical, but the specificity of their use is not sufficient to confirm medium. The *Bent Line Drawing* is a drawing that consists of lines made on a surface that is not covered "without reserve," and it proposes a legible figure and ground relationship. At the same time, a stretched canvas might exist as a picture without a single mark of paint adhering to its surface. It becomes a drawing through nods to convention, even while it flirts with registration as painting through competing, contradictory nods to convention—in its evocation of the frame and the space of illusion as much as its nonpaper ground, rejection of paint, and so on.

Because the lines of the *Stretched Drawing* and the *Bent Line Drawing* demarcate squares, painterly composition (following Alberti, discussed below) is also in play. Yet as was the case with Ryman's earlier works from the 1950s that could be rotated and multiply displayed, these works lack conventional orientation. The squares are symmetrical, balanced, and composed seemingly without Ryman's help, leading Robert Storr to remark that "the obvious focal point implied by the coordinates running between the four equal sides or four equal corners, allowed him to operate around and especially off the center without ever requiring him to fix it in any explicit way."[22]

Robert Ryman, *Bent Line Drawing* (c. 1970). Ball-point pen on polyester fabric over foamcore.

As a corollary, the use of a square support heightened the effect of this format and survived in most of Ryman's successive works irrespective of medium (actually, the square had already become a mainstay of Ryman's practice by this time). Ryman had been predisposed to utilize the square for its so-dubbed neutrality and its plain departure from Alberti's rectangular and perspectival "window" of easel painting. In his treatise on painting, Alberti made clear that optical geometry was external to the eye. He sought to understand its workings and translate its structures to the surfaces of paintings that could then be seen as pictorial equivalents or visual descriptions of the natural world.

To this end, Alberti described ways to compose a painting that would mark out illusionistic space and demonstrate how bodies and objects rendered therein could be understood relationally in a referential interaction. Schematically, he began by drawing a rectangle on the surface he was to paint and regarded it as an "open window through which the subject to be painted is seen."[23] After framing the scene, he suggested establishing a vanishing point in the center of the composition where receding lines would converge, establishing parameters for foreground and background and their interrelated and mutually determining scale where "men depicted standing in the parallel furthest away are a great deal smaller than those in the nearer ones."[24] Through this system of one-point perspective, the grid of the flattened support would be torqued to reflect the "veil" through which the scene or objects to be transcribed were first apprehended, which would then be redrawn as the parallels of the picture's "pavement" as its foundation and newly optical, if essentially mathematical, support.

Ryman clearly exhibits a distaste for conventional perspective, but his *Stretched Drawing* and *Bent Line Drawing* admit an interest in composition and ways to reimagine it through the properties of materials. Ryman arrives at composition almost by default. There is no a priori. There are only the contingent consequences of materials as born out of their interactions and mutual adaptations. Spector writes: "Ryman's convictions have come from the experience of making paintings, and not vice-versa. He is not concerned with 'shoulds,' with aimed-for results, with theories. For him the crux of art is in the making. With every work he knows beforehand what materials he will use and he knows what he is going to do with them. There is no question that there is a considerable investment of thought and intention at the start. But the way every decision is carried out, each touch of the paint to the surface, and the whole visual result, are still unpredictable."[25]

If this implies or results in composition or even an image, then it is still a world away from Greenberg's Mondrian, who trafficked in illusion, or Ellsworth Kelly, who concurrently with Ryman was smuggling illusionism into his most abstract works.[26] Back from six years in France on the GI Bill and newly repatriated in New York in 1954, Kelly was working on the problem of composition or, more precisely, the lack of composition in painting. While in Paris, Kelly had made clear his own opinion of Alberti's mandate for illusionistic painting in his *Window, Museum of Modern Art, Paris* (1949), a constructed relief that took its proportional and compositional directives from a window casement at the Musée National d'Art Moderne at the Palais de Tokyo. Like a "real" window, Kelly's window is comprised of two panels. The lower panel is nothing more than a stretched, blank canvas turned to abut the wall. Unlike the stark white upper section, it is painted gray and is bisected by two wooden rods that, along with the frame, are painted black. Here is an immovable window that obscures vision beyond itself, tautologically referring to its opaque materiality as the only vista on offer. As Kelly recalled in 1971:

> In October of 1949 at the Museum of Modern Art in Paris I noticed the large windows between the paintings interested me more than the art exhibited. I made a drawing of the window and later in my studio I made what I considered my first object, *Window, Museum of Modern Art, Paris.* From then on, painting as I had known it was finished for me. The new works were to be paintings/objects, unsigned, anonymous. Everywhere I looked, everything I saw became something to be made, and it had to be made exactly as it was, with nothing added. It was a new freedom: there was no longer the need to compose. The subject was there already made, and I

> could take from everything; it all belonged to me: a glass roof of a factory with its broken and patched panes, lines of a roadmap, the shape of a scarf on a woman's head, a fragment of Le Corbusier's Swiss Pavilion, a corner of a Braque painting, paper fragments in the street. It was all the same, *anything goes*.[27]

With that "anything goes," Kelly contended that his new aesthetic was to be located in and predicated on the appropriation of something—anything—from the world at large. Imported into art, an already made or given composition could be traced and newly counted as a picture. Despite Kelly's permissive posturing, however, anything did not really go. Kelly refused to relinquish the aesthetic: his work would still be made (and meticulously so, with brushes not rollers, no less), markedly unlike a Duchampian readymade, and it would still somehow stand apart from the world of objects out of which it was appropriated.[28] Kelly was therefore reluctant to show the *Window,* even though it was then referenced as *276. Tableau. Objet* in the context of the Salon des Réalités Nouvelles in the West Wing of the Palais de Tokyo, for fear that the proximity of the work to its compositional source would have been too obvious. (Despite his reservations, he did show it there, and, according to Kelly, "no one recognized the connection." By 1951, the work was known as *Construction: Relief en blanc, gris et noir, November 1949.*)[29]

The point was to cull meaning and form from the world without having its locus register in or as representation. The referential link was to be severed so that a one-to-one correlation between object and image could not be exhumed. For what Kelly meant by "anything goes" was that any referent could generate a so-called painting/object that then could harbor its indexical link without actually picturing it in a naturalistic or mimetic way. The referent was to go missing as the image appeared as a wholly manifest given—an already made pattern that existed in advance of the artist's sight of it and was subsequently transcribed by the artist in the materials of art. As Bois puts it: "There's no smoke without fire, as the saying goes; Kelly does not deny this, but he is solely interested in the smoke, and couldn't care less about the fire, as he prospects this illogical object,

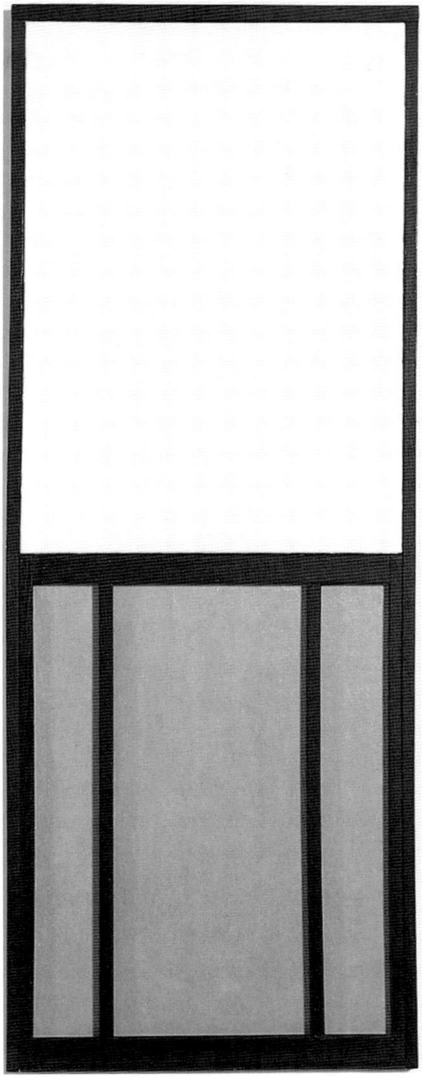

Ellsworth Kelly, *Window, Museum of Modern Art, Paris* (1949). Oil on wood and canvas, two joined panels.

an index without a referent."[30] This strategy of a recognition that supplants and supersedes invention was employed by Kelly over and again in his systematic efforts to dismantle composition.

In addition to the already-made in such works as the *Window, La Combe, 1* (1950), *Awnings, Avenue Matignon* (1950), *Cité* (1951), or *Meschers* (1951), Kelly had recourse to the aleatory in the monumental *Colors for a Large Wall* (1951) and *Spectrum Colors Arranged According to the Laws of Chance* (1952–1953), to the grid in *Colors for a Large Wall, Spectrum Colors Arranged According to the Laws of Chance,* or *Méditerranée* (1952), and to the serial, "additive elementarization" in many of the grids listed above.[31] Regardless of the acompositional strategy, the common denominator seems to be that the more Kelly worked to undo composition, the greater the vengeance with which it returned. Kelly recognized that composition was not easily abandoned, and even a composition arrived at by chance bore the unsavory mark of authorial engagement and choice. So Kelly took another route that led him right back to the foundations of pictorialism—namely, an investigation of the cognitive dissonance that was wrought by the primordial separation of figure and ground within a reduced planar scheme of two or three colors.

From about 1958 to 1965, Kelly executed paintings of red, green, and blue. These colors were separated into broad, matte swaths that were demarcated not by lines but through the imposing solidity of flat, elemental forms abutting one another. Drawing was excised from painting. (In this, too, Kelly is antithetical to Ryman, who does not draw in advance of painting or conduct preparatory formal investigations. Instead, he resolves issues of form by virtue of materials in the course of working with and through them.) Since the late 1940s, however, Kelly has drawn on whatever was at hand, and since the 1950s, he has preserved these images haphazardly in multiple containers.

Some of Kelly's designs eventually made their way into sketchbooks (where they might be refined over time and across multiple iterations, as patterns were repeated, colors switched, and sizes altered) or even onto a discrete canvas. Most sketches were nonetheless deemed unusable, mere "first drafts" that were subject to accumulation *en masse.* In 1973, Kelly sorted through over eight hundred loose pieces of paper scraps and archived them in so-called tablets. Years after their inception and disposal, forms emerged and were reconceptualized in relation to one another and more recent work. For ready access, Kelly mounted these fragments on 15 1/2- by 21-inch sheets in, more often than not, a random order to maximize heterogeneity and suggest infinite configurations out of the new juxtapositions.[32]

Sequestered in preparatory work (whether on paper, newsprint, envelopes, postcards, or whatever else was nearby when an idea struck), drawing remained contained so that the paintings stood apart from the drawings, which were still sites of autographic marking and authorial presence. (Many of the tablets are exceedingly personal: drawings were made on the back of a Pan Am menu, a telegraph from Kelly's mother, a ticket stub, and a shabby paper napkin.) Even with this segregation securely in place, subjective choice nonetheless remained at issue. It was perhaps Kelly's Sisyphean effort to roll composition back—even as he inevitably collapsed under its weight—that led, in these years, to his ensuing resignation and defection into prismatic color gestalts that were born of formal invention and pictorial spatiality. The perfect stasis registered in Kelly's counterpoise of elegant and often surprisingly sensuous forms enact composition at its most foundational—primary forms and structures, if not always primary colors.[33]

Like Kelly's earlier Parisian works, the first pieces of this series were derived, abstracted as already made from the world at large only to be somehow severed from incipient referentiality. *Mask* (1958) was the first work to combine red, green, and blue into a single painting, and it plays this game of the missing referent for all it is worth. The title pictorializes the colored sections, assembling them into a figure in profile and naming it as such, while it too cloaks and distracts from the initial, "real" subject from which it was drawn. (It was originally a representation of the shadows cast on the page of a book that Kelly was reading on a bus and was first conceived in black and white.) Were it not for its title, this source would have remained at the level of abstraction. Title aside, the colors aid in this as well. The blue triangular slash at the upper right is legible as an eye, and the lower red rectangle stands in for a mouth. Hereafter, associations again become less pronounced, and colors do not mimetically relate to their pictorial "equivalents," despite a continued utilization of the already made. When Kelly remade *Mask* on a less modest scale, he called its gargantuan counterpart *Blue Green Red* (1963) and distorted its identifiable facial features into saturated masses of elongated shapes.[34]

When he worked from new source material, as opposed to already made forms that were taken from his own previous work, Kelly overtly tampered with pretensions to reality. In the same year's *Red Blue Green,* Kelly referenced a photograph of trapeze swings, additionally building on *Green Blue Red* (1963). But he inverted much in the translation from photograph to painting (he never works directly from explicit sources). Kelly excised the lines that carve out space in the photograph and filled his painting with abutting forms of differentiated colors that now bear no resemblance to their referents. The rectilinear and the curvilinear sections are also reversed from their position in the photograph. The ground that is given in the title—the last color listed, as is customary for these works—is green. It is not the blue sky of the image. The angle that is intimated in this displacement is exaggerated by the intense cropping and effective change in perspective so that the photograph's point of view (looking up at its object) becomes the painting's straight-on, deadpan view, centered and all-encompassing. Through a series of reversals of illusionistic devices that were once called on to render convincing pictorial representations—where transparency cedes to opacity, shading becomes the play of hue, and space gestures toward arbitrary, flattened colored planes—Kelly found a new way to approach painting that was not about negation but that sought renovation from within.

This, finally, is where this series' connection to the earlier works really ends. For in this transformation of perspective, Kelly intuited that perspective alone could be the foundation for painting stripped of extrapictorial allusions or subjects. By 1964, Kelly was painting *Red Green Blue,* a work that is built on a perspectival scheme that is both subverted and turned inside out. Vertical rectangles of varying scales are nestled within the bounds of the canvas. Pictorial conventions become the key to abstraction, and the work invokes Alberti only to once again disenfranchise his mode of picture making as world making.

Kelly has actuated a play of perspectival space that is complicated by his choice of colors and their placement. He uses a hot, advancing red at what should be the picture's vanishing point and a cool, receding blue at its perimeter. These colors stymie any attempt at optically engaging with this painting as a window even as it depends on this reference to do its work.[35]

Here the referent does not go missing so much as it stays—awkwardly, even ambivalently—in place to show what the artist has done to it and how he has transvalued that history. Composition is part and parcel of the work's constitution and reference. The history of art history is the reference because it is being acted on and remotivated from within. Kelly's work thus manipulates fundaments of illusion and representation for a new mode of abstraction that presents as already made not tiles or shadows or awnings but the conventions of painting from the Renaissance forward as one perspectival system—the history of painting—that can be manifested and newly activated. This framework is capable of supporting practice and sustaining criticism alongside it. It is a default system when other modes of composition or acomposition have failed to produce their desired effects, which acknowledges and disavows that referent's sustained applicability in a single informed gesture.

If Kelly was motivating his work by connecting it to tradition so that illusion and representation could become the support for a mode of historicist abstraction, Ryman was relating differently, if no less palpably, to that same material past. One work presents itself as a striking comparison—*Untitled* (1965). In this work, ten horizontal and nine vertical oil strokes huddle on stretched cotton like the *L*s in Kelly's painting, a sequence of two stroke registers forming right angles from the upper right corner. But as with the *Winsors* (discussed in chapter 4) and dramatically distinct from *Red Green Blue,* here there is no recession into a picture plane. Instead, there is a parsing of space relative to the physical edge of the support.

For Ryman, an abstraction of the conventions of painting—paint, the support structure, the signature, and otherwise—produced effects that made a painting a painting. As Christopher Wood writes:

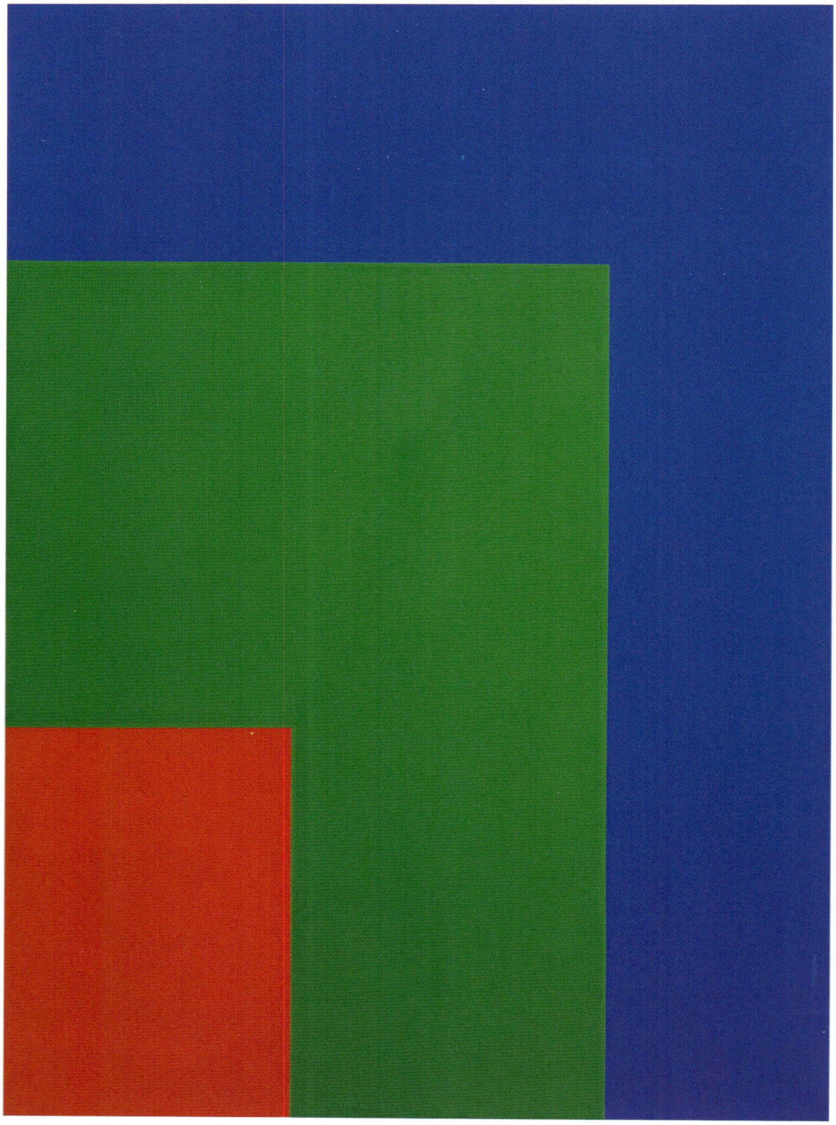

Ellsworth Kelly, *Red Green Blue* (1964). Oil on canvas.

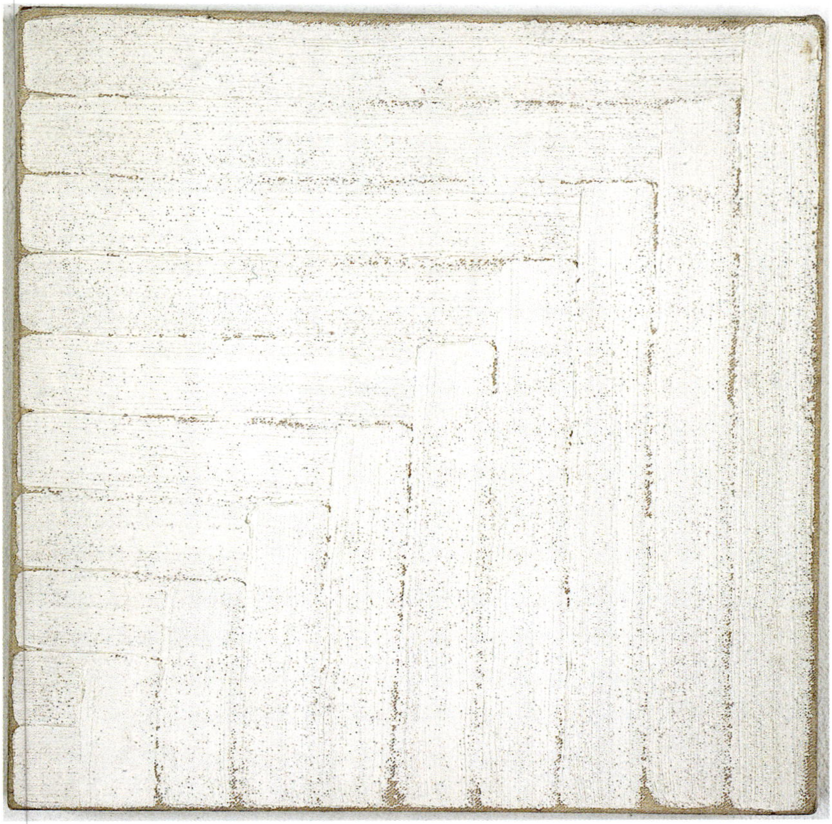

Robert Ryman, *Untitled* (1965). Oil on stretched cotton canvas.

> Abstraction implores us to look at the rest of painting *as if* it were abstract. In Meyer Schapiro's paradoxical formulation, realism itself re-created the world by a "series of abstract calculations of perspective and gradations of color." Ryman's paintings are asking the opposite: they are suggesting that we collapse abstraction back into the rest of painting. Abstraction, it appears, was never anything more than a refinement or a mannered distortion of the components of painted art, totally consistent with the previous history of painting, and capable of very many of its effects.[36]

Wood articulates the stakes of Ryman's adherence to an economy of painting, which by being contracted actually becomes an expansive reconsideration of painting by means of its effects. Ryman's work, as Wood rightly suggests, opens onto conceptions about painting and its history that are at once deconstructive and flexible. His responses are provisional and are adaptable rather than immutable.

Ryman's connection to a material history of painting as support for practice is tacitly understood without being made literal as a way of making instead of representing. Never becoming the subject or composition of his work, the history of painting does, however, inform his beliefs as to the possible effects of the medium, based on what has worked for other artists in the past. Ryman eschews trajectories or narrative retellings in favor of an atemporal yet conditional mode of presentness in which the whole of painting can be abstracted to abet his investigations into its continuing relevance and viability.

Ryman's pragmatism comes dramatically to the fore in that his painting, while based on "painting," offers no guarantees for future success any more than it argues against such a potentiality. His works are neither gauges nor summations. Nor are they "already made" or already otherwise determined. They are, if anything, bets on an uncertain future and ways, in the meantime, of keeping painting, or drawing for that matter, fluid.

In Ryman's insistence on painting in the present tense, his distance from Kelly becomes all the more telling. Ryman's is a practical relation to both the past and future in which the present replaces the historical. Kelly's reliance on a *history* of painting introduces a different sort of temporality that is, almost against itself, resonant with modernist criticism. For all of Kelly's efforts to undo composition and transgress the bounds and demands of illusionism, his work is still intelligible in relation to a formalist critical position. Conversely, Ryman was never taken up by this tradition, even as a negative example.

Kelly's work thereby exposes a risk that was posed by Rosalind Krauss in 1972 in relation to Frank Stella, Kelly's peer from the Museum of Modern Art's seminal 1959 Sixteen Americans show. Although Kelly's sacrifice of autonomy to the referent is distinct from Stella's differently envisaged compositional dictates, I think Krauss's point nevertheless obtains:

> The flatness that modernist criticism reveres may have expunged spatial perspective, but it has substituted a temporal one—i.e. history. It is this history that the modernist critic contemplates looking into the vortex of, say, Stella's concentric stripes: a perspective view that opens backward into that receding vista of past doors and rooms, which because they are not re-enterable, can only manifest themselves in the present by means of diagrammatic flatness.[37]

This is the heart of the problem with Greenbergian modernism as Krauss then understood it. It would also help to formulate her ensuing resistance against it, through a turn to structure in opposition to history (a move that is homologous to Ryman's approach).

Greenberg's telos of modernist self-criticism and painting's reduction to flatness and the properties of the support would be unthinkable, Krauss surmised, without a compensatory temporality that connected seemingly disparate objects in a great historical, interpretive sweep. She recapitulates this position through an anecdote involving Michael Fried. In the galleries of the Fogg Museum during the 1965 exhibition Three American Painters, Krauss watched Fried respond to a skeptical student who wondered what was so great about Stella's striped works: "'Look,' he said slowly, 'there are days when Stella goes to the Metropolitan Museum. And he sits for hours looking at the Velázquezes, utterly knocked out by them and then he goes back to his studio. What he would like more than anything else is to paint like Velázquez. But what he knows is that that is an option that is not open to him. So he paints stripes.' Fried's voice had risen. 'He wants to be Velázquez *so he paints stripes.*'"[38] For Krauss, Fried's ellipsis connected modernism to three centuries worth of picture making, the logic of which insisted on an unbroken continuum of content and engagement that was beholden to the art of the past—a trajectory that was assumed to be moving in only one direction.

Tradition was at issue still. In response to modernist criticism's (Greenberg's) assumption of an aesthetic positivism, Krauss herself revisited perspective as a way to visualize or spatially analogize causality—"one thing follows the next in space according to rule"[39]—as a conventional plot with a recognizable temporal succession. Meaning relied on an existing narrative to flesh out its flatness. For all the antipathy to Greenbergian doctrine, though, Krauss's critique did not dismantle it but maintained it on other terms. She had little patience for formalist criticism's self-indulgence or, as she puts it, its "innocence." This was an indictment that she saw bearing on three counts: "it refuses to see the temporality which it never tires of invoking—'the entire history of painting since Manet'—as that perspectival armature on which it structures the art in question (and on which that art has increasingly tended to structure itself); it thinks of that history as 'objective'—beyond the dictates of sensibility, beyond ideology; and it is unself-critically prescriptive."[40] This reading supposes a unified "modernist criticism" that grants it more coherence than it arguably warrants. Even Greenberg was faltering by the late 1960s, if not before.[41] In art, such a hegemonic notion was questioned by the 1950s (hence the seeming necessity of Greenberg's "After Abstract Expressionism"). Things seemed not too prescriptive but not determined enough.

In a public debate in 1987, Greenberg came clean on the matter of ontology in a manner that few would have expected. Pressed by a discussion of quality versus definitions, haunted through and through by the specter of nominalism and the looming figure of Marcel Duchamp, Greenberg showed his hand, effectively silencing the line of inquiry that had pushed him into this exchange. Thierry de Duve, functioning as moderator, voiced the opinion that "art cannot be defined. There is no such thing as an ontology of art, I believe," to which Greenberg emphatically replied, "I agree, I agree."[42]

Definitions inevitably fail, but elsewhere work continues unabated for different audiences and under different conditions. Following this charge, Greenberg emphasized that an assignment of value is not an act of description or prescription, as even he upheld flatness as a "condition" rather than a value. Further, Greenberg contended that such an assessment makes no claim for what is *to be* in the future or what *should be* made in its stead.[43] This is Greenberg at the limits of his doctrine, a Greenberg to whom Ryman might have had much to say, although "to say" is wrong because Ryman's response would have come in paint.

Ryman's work similarly questions what of painting remains, and in acting on painting by continuing to paint, his work becomes both an action and a condition, both support and the medium through which it is supported. Here a very different implication of the problem of definition surfaces once more in relation to effect rather than essence. These definitions circumscribe and delimit relationships and actively establish parameters of intelligibility. Ryman's is not a game of substitutions. In his paintings, the contingent coming together of paint and support forms a makeshift response to the questions of what is painting and what makes it good. Possibilities within a radically reduced set plot out the points that constellate around painting without collapsing that same classification into one of hypostatized medium.

For *medium,* in one of its definitions in the *OED,* is the middle term of a syllogism and "hence, a ground of proof or inference"—a way station leading to something or somewhere else. But it is equally a registration of atmosphere or background as a pervading or enveloping substance—"any intervening substance through which a force acts on objects at a distance or through which impressions are conveyed to the senses: applied, e.g., to the air, the ether, or any substance considered with regard to its properties as a vehicle of light or speed." Rendered figuratively, it is thus "one's environment, [the] conditions of life." It is also a vehicle of communication. This is the description that tallies best with Ryman's practice and that links it to yet another definition, this time of support.

In relation to mathematics in the *OED,* the support is "the smallest closed set of elements [in terms of Ryman's painting, this would be paint and support] outside which a given function or mapping is zero." Support is a property of the map and a registration of the extent and contours of its possible field, a key to and representation of the values (or inputs) that cover the full range of the system's potential outputs. The point becomes how to label an abstract conceptual structure so that its results are positive—how not to get nothing. The support spans the set of all possible outcomes of applying paint to a material ground, changeable inputs that give a nonzero output, where there are as many achievable variations as there are chances to actuate them.

The support for a particular function is a property of the function or the mapping itself. Ryman's painting is a mapping from paint and support onto paintings. *Painting* is the noun and verb—what it is and what it does. It stands as the condition and its constitutive act, which takes all possible combinations of paint on support and produces paintings as the product of those interactions. The range of outputs for that function is the region of possibility for this given domain. Such a system is predicated on the desire to achieve something (to get a nonzero output) through a cumulative process that refers back to the set out of which it is composed. This effectively maps that set back onto itself as a recursive gesture that need not be constrictive as there is always another surface, another support onto which more paint can be applied and another painting made. Thus, the support is generative; it is not an end any less than a beginning.

My point here is direct: Ryman shores up the notion of the possible without making claims for—or attempting to exert control over—what will result. On the most basic level, how could he? Antilinear, antireductionist, antiontological, and antidiscursive (or arhetorical, as I claim in chapter 4), Ryman opens the material and conventional dimensions of painting to a different kind of medium-specificity that involves a narrow-band infinitude of provisional answers to questions of what makes a painting, how it is made, with which materials, and why. Ryman's tactile works show meaning to be formed in strokes of paint apart from the obligations of representation. Foreclosure becomes anticipation, and prospects displace retrospection. What will come next? Accepting that there is, for the moment at least, something else to try, why not do so? But for Ryman as much as for anyone else, this implies not a teleology—an obvious, necessary, or otherwise prescribed next step—but a zone of uncertainty to be explored.

When Robert Storr asked him whether he believed that "abstract painting requires a sense of overall historical or aesthetic direction," Ryman replied: "I don't know. I think maybe it doesn't. It does from time to time and it does in small ways. There are problems that you work on and there is an awareness of what has been done[,] what others have worked on[,] and how they've approached painting and the solutions that they've come to. . . . It isn't a blanket kind of historical thing that everyone is involved with. I think everyone has to take little bites, little pieces of it and work on that. . . . But I don't know that there is any big philosophy that encompasses it all."[44] Such is Ryman's distrust of irrevocable claims and the unspoken positivism that justifies making them. In Ryman's language, even "taking little bites" offers much to eat. On the other hand, coincident with there being no big claims is the certainty that there are no assurances, either. He investigates a paradoxically liberal terrain of opportunity between zero and one, even if (as critics, customs officials, and savvy dealers made clear) it is still hard to see.

4

Edge

From 1942 to 1963, the Museum of Modern Art mounted a series of contemporary American painting and sculpture exhibitions that were expediently titled according to the number of contributors (Fourteen Americans in 1946) or the year (Americans 1963). These Americans shows were curated by Dorothy Miller and presented a heterogeneous array of work by established and emerging artists. This is not to suggest that there were never moments of congruity, as in 1952, when Fifteen Americans showcased New York School stalwarts (as they would be canonized), and in 1963, when a pop sensibility was hard to ignore in the work of Robert Indiana, Marisol, Claes Oldenburg, and James Rosenquist. But Miller meant to expose the often incommensurable nature of simultaneous practice.

Gallery by gallery, visitors could confront the contradictions and ambiguities of the present in artworks that were assembled less as a coherent narrative than as so many abutting rooms—really a series of solo shows—vying for attention. Given Miller's privileging of "marked individuality,"[1] synchronicity ceded to claims for autonomy. As she wrote on the occasion of the Sixteen Americans exhibit (consisting of Jay de Feo, Wally Hedrick, James Jarvaise, Jasper Johns, Ellsworth Kelly, Alfred Leslie, Landès Lewitin, Richard Lytle, Robert Mallary, Louise Nevelson, Robert Rauschenberg, Julius Schmidt, Richard Stankiewicz, Frank Stella, Albert Urban, and Jack Youngerman): "Differences rather than similarities in point of view, as well as in age, experience and fame, have been emphasized in these exhibitions at the Museum. . . . Sixteen Americans continues the pattern by bringing together distinct and widely varying personalities, contrasting these personalities sharply rather than attempting to unite them within any given movement or trend."[2]

Such a catholic purview aroused criticism, and Miller took this in stride. She commented on the 1952 installment: "That show made, I think, the biggest splash of any of them. . . . Oh, it made no splash with the critics. It was beyond them. That's one way I knew it was a success."[3] If a success for Miller was tied up with discourse or the lack thereof, failure was a badge of avant-garde credentials. Reticence or even hostility (as two sides of the same coin) was interpreted affirmatively as a sign of the prescience of the art that Miller championed, and she consistently adopted this self-protective gambit. In relation to Sixteen Americans, defensiveness was warranted. Some critics—like Katharine Kuh, Thomas Hess, and Stuart Preston—celebrated the exhibition, but most found it difficult to accept.[4] The *New York Times* critic John Canaday attacked the show four times, lest his opinion be overlooked. (This despite the conspicuous fact that Canaday did not like much else: He denounced abstract expressionism as repetitious art-for-profit, warned younger artists about the perils of "suicide by auto-cannibalism," chided Hess for *Art News*'s overpromotion of Pollock, and maligned Alfred Barr for his lumbering influence as a "tastemaker").[5]

Still grappling with the Sixteen Americans exhibition well into 1960, Canaday wrote that it was "a show that continues to haunt me because it was such a disastrous exhibition of painting yet such an 'exciting' one to talk about."[6] For Canaday, this "excitement" was synonymous with, and the symptomatic byproduct of, contemporary art, where what "sound[s] good" is "what counts."[7] According to Canaday, "The crux of the problem of contemporary art, and I don't mean only for the critic who has to find things to say . . . [was that] contemporary art is first of all something to talk about, not something to look at. Once it stops supplying material for verbalizing, it dies as painting. . . . The saying is that one picture is worth a thousand words. We might vary that today by saying that one painting is worth about a thousand words, more or

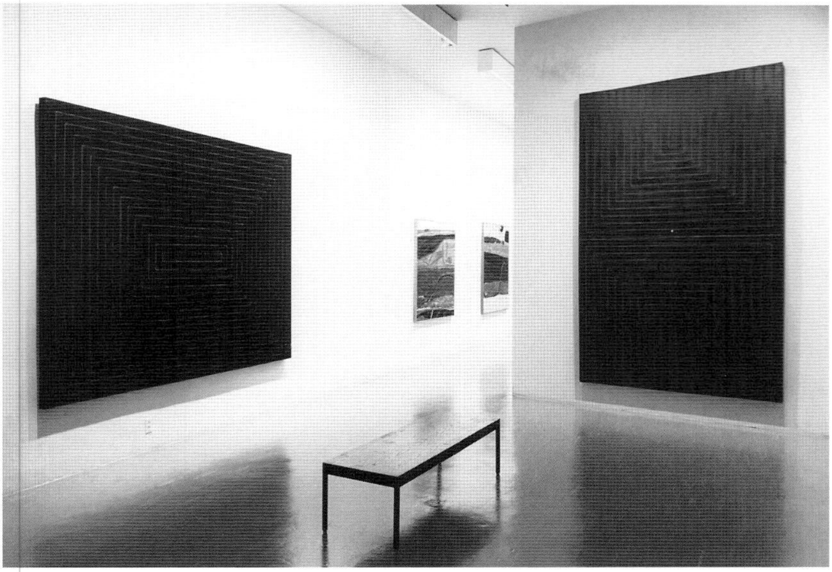

Installation view from the exhibition 16 Americans (1959–1960). The Museum of Modern Art, New York.

less, and after that not worth much of anything else."[8] Canaday also felt that MoMA should institute a moratorium on the exhibition of works less than ten years old. The excision of just topical and readily exhaustible work would mean, as a gratuitous effect, that the museum would not need to expand. It could just hang its collection in "the space normally allotted to such breath-takers as last year's Sixteen Americans."[9]

Sixteen Americans elicited an outpouring of similar commentary that was not unprecedented but emphatic, as Canaday's repeated remarks make clear. For Robert Coates, it was "chaotic but stylish,"[10] a charge that deftly transvalued Miller's terms, negatively invoking the damning moniker of style. Against the respectability of historical importance or legitimate and assumedly lasting significance, the derision of the show on the grounds of taste would be one of the first—if by no means the last in these years—to deflate formal invention into mere fashion with passing, seasonal interest.[11] Coates focused on the assembled artists as a would-be and thus deficient group, but others were quick to air their grievances about specific artists. In 1959, this most commonly meant Frank Stella with his curious paintings and his fresh-out-of-college back story.

Bad press did not deter the museum from supporting Stella or from acquiring the lynchpin *The Marriage of Reason and Squalor* (1959) out of the show.[12] Museum staff—artists, above all—remained polarized. Robert Ryman resigned from his job at the museum in May 1960, just a few months after Sixteen Americans. But before he left, he had ample time to study the offerings and hear the gossip that they provoked. In particular, Ryman recalled liking Stella's *Black Paintings:* "A lot of the artists didn't like those at all. They thought 'This is ridiculous.' I thought they were good paintings. I didn't really know exactly what it was about, but I thought they were okay."[13] In fact, he has since revealed that he "liked them, a lot" and wanted to buy one at "six hundred dollars, but that, even that amount for me was out of the question at that time."[14]

If Ryman had perused the Sixteen Americans catalogue, he would have seen a twenty-three-year-old Stella smartly dressed in a dark suit, as photographed by Hollis Frampton against a white studio backdrop. He could have

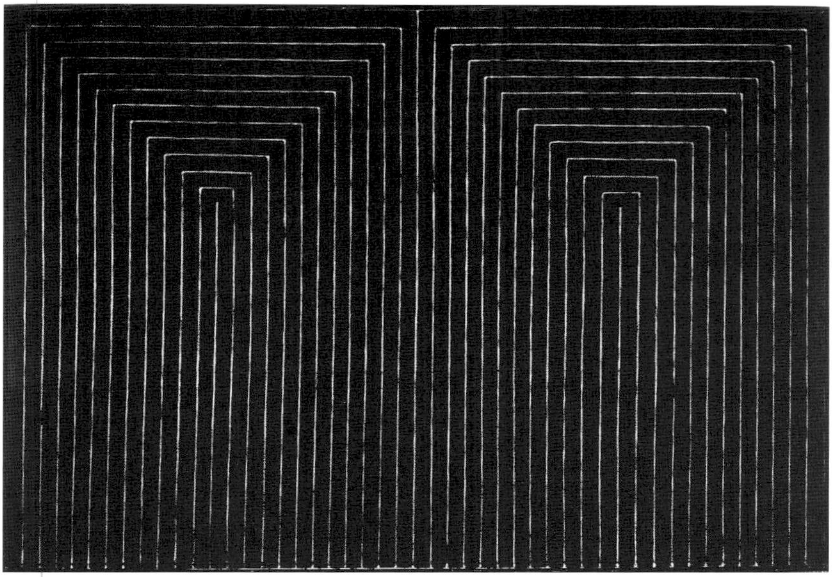

Frank Stella, *The Marriage of Reason and Squalor, second version* (1959). Enamel on canvas.

read Carl Andre's text on Stella as well.[15] Amid self-penned artist statements (such as those by Jasper Johns) and routine commendations (E. C. Goossen writing for Ellsworth Kelly), Andre's gnomic contribution stood out: "*Preface to Stripe Painting / Art* excludes the unnecessary. Frank Stella has found it necessary to paint stripes. There is nothing else in his painting. Frank Stella is not interested in expression or sensitivity. He is interested in the necessities of painting. Symbols are counters passed among people. Frank Stella's painting is not symbolic. His stripes are the paths of brush on canvas. These paths lead only into painting."[16] Andre claimed Stella as a practitioner of a new mode of painting wherein metaphor was stunted and symbolism disabled. As Stella himself put it in a 1964 attempt to foreground the implicitly formal nature of his paintings-cum-objects: "What you see is what you see."[17]

But as Stella quickly discovered (hence the obligatory 1964 corrective), his stripes' paths more often led out of than into the paintings. Unable to resist the associative possibilities that were born of Stella's *The Marriage of Reason and Squalor,* critic Tom Donnelly (who wrote in Washington, D.C., before seeing the show) countered Andre's interpretation with his own. The stripes were "the sort of material a gangster might have made into a suit to be buried in: discreet, but snappy."[18] He also addressed Andre directly:

> Ah well, we don't have to worry about what the symbolic content of Mr. Stella's painting might be. Unless Mr. Andre has goofed in his preface. Mr. Andre just MIGHT have. After all, Mr. Stella calls one of his compositions *The Marriage of Reason and Squalor.* (I can see the reason in this; there's something very reasonable about stripes. But the squalor? Possibly that refers to the condition of the studio where Mr. Stella found it necessary to execute this insensitive composition.)[19]

Given Donnelly's desire to locate meaning physically (just not in the painting itself), Andre's ventriloquism assumes a questionable efficacy. In painting stripes and in having Andre insist on the futility of looking for something beyond or beneath them, Stella was attempting to forestall precisely the kinds of comments that Donnelly voiced. Yet his "non message," as Donnelly called it, was precisely what enabled compensatory articulation. At cross-purposes with both Andre and Donnelly, Stella eventually engaged the press (although he had been engaging it all along). However salacious the readings as readings-in, his statements chiefly aimed to set the record straight on process, sidestepping the squalor of the studio to reiterate the way in which the painting was made.

Although Ryman's relation to this horizon is elaborated in what follows, Stella's move foreshadows Ryman's approach to such matters. As Yve-Alain Bois has commented about Ryman: "Ask him *why,* he'll always answer *how.*"[20] A decade after Stella, Ryman began to participate in the construction of his own discourse after he was besieged by readings of his work as representational—or mystical or metaphysical. In short, white was as easy to make mean as black.

Reviewing Ryman's Fischbach Gallery show in 1969, Grace Glueck highlighted his paintings' "'gestural' quality that puts them slightly at crosscurrents with the big Cool wind. . . . Viewed individually, they could be skyscapes or studies of mist, but that is not their intention. In fact, as has been critically noted, Ryman is one systemist painter who manages to have his cake and eat it too, producing, within a series format, works that assert themselves in individual terms."[21] Phyllis Tuchman interviewed Ryman three years later and, without naming names, asked about Glueck's review: "When someone looks at the paintings, say, on corrugated paper, do you think they should just see white gestures on a tan surface rather than skyscapes or studies of mist?" He responded:

> You mean like clouds? That I have no control over, what someone sees. You can fantasy [*sic*] about things. You can look at clouds and see faces in the clouds, that kind of thing. That's not really there; it's just the imagination of the viewer. I don't intend that. What the painting is, is exactly what they see: the paint on the corrugated and the color of the corrugated and the way it's done and the way it feels. That's what's there. Of course, you can listen to some music

> and think of a waterfall or this or that. But that's up to that person. You can't tell anyone how to look at something.[22]

Still, Dan Cameron writes:

> Suddenly, [Ryman's] paintings weren't really paintings anymore: they were more like pictures in the magnified sense of representing an ideal about painting which simply cannot be realized in any other way. . . . It may seem simplistic, but I have always imagined that Ryman chose the format of the white painting in part because he knew that it would draw out the viewer's inclinations to project one's desires across its surface. . . . It is almost as if the artist is proffering us the vessel in which signification can be conveyed, while asking us to go and fill it ourselves.[23]

For one critic in 2004, Ryman's "atmospheric paintings . . . make you feel you are walking inside a cloud, a quiet place where spirit and matter intertwine."[24]

While Ryman discourages this sort of interpretive fallacy, neither does he contradict it. "Ryman's move to verbal communication did not come about through an awakening of theoretical interest," Christel Sauer insists, "but through the simple realization that the unconventional character of his work was frequently misunderstood, and in consequence the exceptional elements in his painting were not given due consideration. Ryman became aware that part of an artist's practical responsibility is to avoid possible misconceptions about his oeuvre."[25]

The case of Stella is instructive. In a *Herald Tribune* review, Emily Genauer had written that Stella's black canvases "carefully lined with white pin-stripes" were "unspeakably boring."[26] She added that the artist "calls the results, very accurately, 'stripe painting.'"[27] This passing construal rather than anything more speculative prompted Stella to write a letter to the editor. Contrite, he explained that he "did not invent the term 'stripe paintings,' but rather the paintings themselves. . . . I concede it is sufficiently accurate. My paintings are what I do, not what I omit. In fact, I paint *black stripes* about 2 ½ inches wide. Therefore the unpainted white spaces between them are not the stripes, but what you call the 'background.'"[28] An exasperated Genauer stood corrected, but the contest was more than semantic.

Stella's relation of his stripes and their support involuntarily invoked representational tenets. His designating of the ground as the "background" as if this were the space of illusionism seemed to make it so. Coming full circle, it newly emboldened critics to find in that representation something—anything—represented. To explain the confusion away, the *Herald Tribune* editors included Andre's writing after Stella's letter. Reproduced in full, it concluded the piece without commentary. Sensing in this exchange a provocative case of art-world-insider nonsense, *Time* ran a little dig on the disagreement shortly thereafter, synopsizing how Genauer, the "veteran art critic," misread Stella and how Stella had replied to her in print. As its final conceit, *Time* reproduced Stella's *Tomlinson Court Park* (1959) with the caption, "Mostly nothing."[29]

For being mostly nothing, Stella's *Black Paintings* resulted in a lot of spilled ink—a circumstance that gains in irony given Stella's criticism of art writing. Even before the Sixteen Americans exhibit, Stella and Darby Bannard had charted a three-year progression of an everyman artist through the pages of *Art News:*

> Darby and I used to play a game which was to decide what the paintings were really like on the basis of what the people wrote about them, . . . and how you were supposed to look at something. . . . (Name) showed at the Stable, and all of a sudden (Name) who was commonly reviewed in *Art News* about 2 or 3 pages from the beginning . . . is suddenly in the first pages of the reviews, and there's a photograph, and now (Name) has a "breakthrough" of the overall battle, collage, and it becomes "very complicated," "very expert," "very well done.' . . . I began to feel very strongly about finding a way of working that . . . you couldn't write about . . . something that didn't lend itself easily to being blown up, to being

> quickly overpromoted, something that was stable in a sense . . . that wasn't constantly a record of your sensitivity, a record of flux.[30]

For Stella, finding a way of working "that you couldn't write about" became a path of resistance, but it also became a way to fold discourse into its very object. Hence, his stripes led only into painting and away from the words around it.

As illusionism metamorphosed into objecthood, there was a critical faltering. Criticism was coming to a place beyond which words would fail to disambiguate artworks—and they were being made to fail by artists like Stella and Ryman. Since the time of his debut, much has been made of Stella's position as a crux of modernism whose pure painting culminated Greenbergian formalism (for Michael Fried) or led to minimalism and the production of objects (for Andre and Donald Judd).[31] Fried claimed that he and Andre were "fighting for [Stella's] soul."[32] Upping the melodramatic ante, Fried later recalled that "I was sure that what I was doing mattered—in fact, I thought that nothing less than the future of Western civilization was at stake in 'Art and Objecthood' and the other essays of 1966–67. I'm being ironic, but only up to a point."[33] Fried's imperative was to wrench art from a realm of mundane presence—the space of mere things and the dispiriting temporality of the workaday world—and thereby to salvage its possibility for presentness. It was a claim for the perpetuation of modernism and its self-determining subject. In Hal Foster's words, art here becomes a "secret [or not so secret] substitute for religion."[34] For Foster, Fried's anxiety about minimalism was that it was not good art and, more important, that it "may corrupt belief in art, that it may sap its conviction value."[35]

As a surfeit of words (certainly more than Canaday's thousand) compensated for lost presence and attempted to reground it by other means, much criticism further estranged art and viewer, rarifying the art under discussion. An equivocating self-consciousness about limits haunts much writing on Ryman, as critics all too often saw his work as frustrating their attempts to appraise it. Attention to discursive edges, as opposed to what material those frames delimit or contain, additionally marks out the territory of minimalism into which Ryman was absorbed (and from which he was somewhat unevenly disqualified). A move from essences to boundaries—or from autonomy to phenomenology, ontology to epistemology—provided and challenged its contradictory language.

Rosalind Krauss has noted that minimalism opened up illusionism to part-by-part associations and interactions in real rather than pictorial space. The dialogue of 1960s aesthetics "had been focused on justifying or legitimating the internal structure of a given work—a structure made visible by the articulations of a surface by drawing or of a three-dimensional object by the separation of its parts—by means other than those of mimesis or illusion."[36] This telos was evinced in the minimalist engagement with the literal, "with the purging of illusion from the work of art by making everything about it external. . . . Literalism was an attempt to make the work, whether sculpture or painting, stop at its surface. In order to do this, all divisions of the surface had to be experienced as the actual separations of the material of the surface."[37] Thus, "more than anything else," Krauss formulates, "minimalism was focused on surface, and where the surface stops, which is edge."[38]

One surmises that it was Ryman's focus on the edge that entertained claims for connections to minimalism. On the other hand, it is extraordinary that neither Greenberg nor Fried wrote about him. As Thierry de Duve charges: "In the 1960s, in New York, there were abstract painters who, without further ado, took up a stance elsewhere than in the thick of the crossfire between Greenbergian modernists and minimalists. Not one of them, not even Frank Stella, has had the good fortune to find favor with Greenberg, not to mention Brice Marden and Robert Ryman, who have never even been entitled to a line on his part."[39]

Less accusatorily if no less directly, Willis Domingo noted in 1970 that

> the creation of a blank surface is the logical conclusion of a search for the essence of painting under the terms defined by the late fifties and early sixties. When it became necessary to point out a few years ago that even an empty canvas may be considered a painting although not necessarily a good one, the suspicion became prevalent

> that perhaps it was, at that point in history, the only kind of painting possible. Although no artist has seen fit to test this thesis, Robert Ryman's *Delta* paintings of 1966 [three almost 9-foot-square paintings of broad horizontal strokes on cotton canvas with deep stretcher bars] began to explore the area between illusion and an unresponsive blankness. While there is activity on the surface, it seems forever to be in the process of being dissolved.[40]

For Domingo, Ryman's paintings were connected to formalist critical mandates, even if somewhat involuntarily. Accounting for his *Delta* paintings at the same time, Carter Ratcliff wrote that Ryman's

> works have sometimes seemed to be just barely classifiable as paintings. The canvases in his 1966 *Delta Series* are blank, but they are well within the limits of "painting." In fact, they are near the center of the definition. Mounted on thick (3 inch) stretchers, their surfaces are all white—these are all-over paintings—with a fine horizontal texture which spreads the light across itself in an unpredictable, almost (but not quite) illusionary manner. Ryman even raises the issue of "the edge": the paint is spread toward it but usually not right up to it; this means that his white (his non-color) may be more than a surface—it may be a depicted shape.[41]

Ryman's insistence on the support in tandem with his emphasis on the aesthetic could have been seen in modernist terms. However, a work like *Untitled* (1962) also points to Ryman's tampering with these codes and the tactility (familiar from the unstretched works discussed in chapters 2 and 3) that Greenberg often repressed. (De Duve, too, finds in Ryman an "amorous tactility of the stroke.")[42] In *Untitled,* Ryman triggers a wormy expanse of white strokes above a frenetic ground of rust reds and greens that is in no way contained. Instead of stretching the canvas and securing it on all four sides, Ryman left the right edge untethered. It creeps outward across the plane of the wall so

Robert Ryman, *Delta II* (1966). Oil on stretched cotton canvas.

that the support is both reduced to literal flatness and implicated in a world of things. As Ratcliff saw, this emphasis on the edge and the implication that the painting may well exceed it undo boundedness and frontality (that is, pictorial autonomy) even while the lush, performative facture would annul charges for opticality as much as deadpan mechanism.

In 1972, the *Generals* (1970), fifteen artworks that were named for a lumber company, were shown at Fischbach and the Guggenheim. Their dimensions vary in half-inch increments (the smallest measures 48 inches and the largest measures 55 inches), and they are organized on the basis of their perimeters. All panels have a solid central square of glossy white enamel that is applied in multiple layers and bordered by a cotton primed with Enamelac. The stretcher determines the width of the margin so that the edge assumes a central role. *Untitled* (1973) is double-baked porcelain enamel on copper panels with thin peripheries. As is customary in many early works, rectangles are clustered at compositions' boundaries and subsequently proliferate in heterodox guises. Signatures, dates, colors, or hardware fasteners persist on the edging, and stretcher bars remain thick, thin, or absent. Ryman's tactical play with the edge continues to this day. The no longer extant *No Title Required* (2006), for one, consisted of ten panels painted with enamel on cherry, maple, and oak.[43] All slightly different sizes, like the *Generals,* the wood rims further warped comparative perceptions of scale, a sensation that was helped by the fact that the multiple panels comprised a single painting installed across a corner on two walls. From almost any station, the work would be seen obliquely.

Ryman made so literal the condition of the edge that he stood beyond the lines of formalism, a blind spot in this criticism and a refutation of it. This is partly practical. Ryman was coming into visibility as Greenberg was retreating (Greenberg showed his hand in relation to minimalism in 1967 at about the time that he bemoaned in *Vogue* magazine the loss of the avant-garde),[44] and Fried was conceptually elsewhere. Ryman all too often was claimed as a minimalist in those years anyhow (see the introduction), obscuring the ambition of his work. Despite Greenberg's injurious claim for minimalism as a "feat of ideation,"[45] the point that Greenberg never conceded is that painting, too, is

Robert Ryman, *General 49 × 49* (1970). Enamel and Enamelac on stretched cotton canvas.

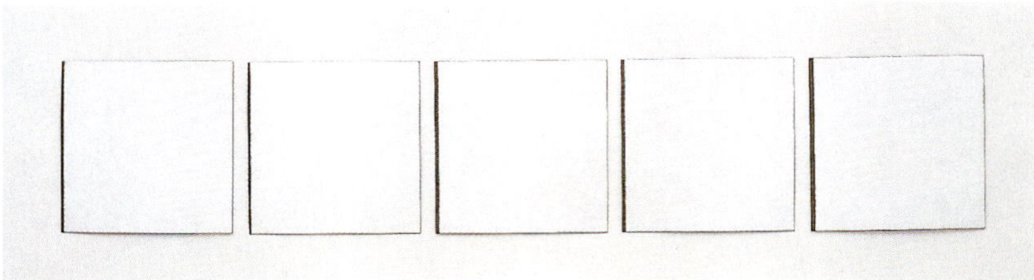

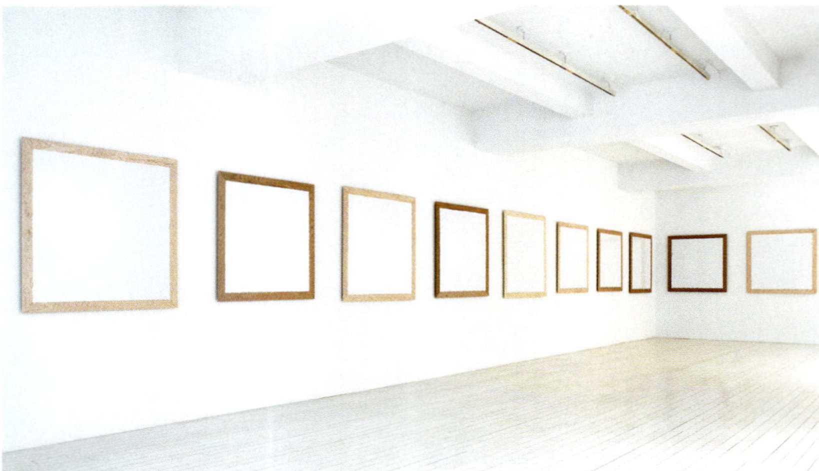

Robert Ryman, *Untitled* (1973). Double-baked porcelain enamel on five copper panels.

Robert Ryman, *No Title Required* (2006). Enamel on birch plywood with cherry, maple, or oak.

a feat of ideation (which is not the same as being an image or having a representational bias). Indeed, pragmatism draws attention to this lacuna in modernist criticism.[46]

Even under the best spectatorial conditions and enthusiastic, even material-oriented commitments, Ryman's paintings still evade summary. Many writers have noted the impediments to writing about Ryman's work, recuperating difficulties into their texts. Bruce Boice was one of the first writers to get at this conundrum in 1972, pairing Ryman with Brice Marden as limit cases for analysis: "One of the most interesting aspects of Marden's work is the virtual impossibility of spelling out what the interest is. The same could be said of Ryman's paintings, which, beyond concerns with process, seem to exist, like Marden's, so blatantly, so bluntly as to become almost instances of brute fact outside of perceptual or cultural associations."[47] (For Boice, this was a compliment. His polemic was against assignations of quality, which, he argued, exist within a preestablished value structure that is impossible to think about in relation to aesthetics, as art's "purpose" is not clear.)

Yve-Alain Bois similarly begins his 1981 "Ryman's Tact" as follows: "The question—despite its rhetorical flavor—must be asked at the very outset: why is it so hard to write about Robert Ryman's work?"[48] Bois continues: "Aren't his paintings themselves—preeminently antiillusionist, flatly literal—all the explanation the viewer or critic needs to penetrate their ineffable silence? Don't they reveal what they're made of, proudly, with a kind of routine generosity, thereby cutting short any attempt at associative readings? Simply, don't they seem to suggest their own commentary, to define their own discursive terrain?"[49] In a like vein in his 1986 "Making Distinctions," Robert Storr diagnoses Ryman's economy of means as "a trap both for those made chatty by silence and those who mistake single-mindedness for predictability." What is more, "the seemingly infinite nuance of which his work avails itself can only be arrived at by total concentration on sensory fact. Thus, it is with simple description that one must begin any serious critical assessment of Ryman's achievement, just as it is to the act of looking, of which description is the residue, that one must finally return."[50]

Here and elsewhere, Storr particularizes process. Despite his best attempts at description, however, he returns to the problems that are posed by the supposed muteness and lack of pretense in Ryman's work, pronouncing that "Ryman has persisted in the patient elaboration of one of the most sustained, considered and anti-rhetorical bodies of work in postwar American painting."[51] "From such a painter," Storr insists, "one no longer awaits breakthroughs, but what one has come to expect . . . is an authenticity thought to be all but lost by those who lament its disappearance with the greatest regularity and relish. Meanwhile, painting by painting, in a steady accumulation, art history, though perhaps not art news, is quietly being made."[52]

This assertion puts one in mind of Stella's disdain for retrospective-ready arcs and for accounts of rupture, synthetic appraisal, and triumphal progression—the very economy that eventually marred his own reputation. He had a breakthrough year, after which he improved, peaked, and then rather inconveniently kept producing work.[53] As Lucy Lippard quoted a "young and formerly admiring artist" in 1968: "Stella started out as a genius and ended up as an art student"[54]—a spectacle to which she devoted much of her review, condemning an art "star system" that requires unceasing production and makes public the failures that inevitably result.

It also recalls Ryman's own differently conceived jab at art's commercial epiphenomena, following a cover that he designed for *Art-Rite/Painting* in 1975.[55] The Institute for Art and Urban Resources purchased seven pages of ad space in the December 1976 issue of *Artforum* and invited Richard Nonas, Alan Saret, Patrick Ireland, Susan Rothenberg, Richard Tuttle, and Ryman to supply a page. Ryman put in a pat pitch for the magazine replete with his signature along the right edge: "It would be good if many people bought *Artforum*. *Artforum* has good pictures and a lot of good writing about many things. It is informative and good to have. It is nice to see it too. A great number of people already buy *Artforum*. It would be good if more people did. *Artforum* is a good magazine."[56] Asked about this recently by Vittorio Colaizzi, Ryman recalled that although he did not "remember now what it said," he knew it was edited before publication (the degree to which remains unclear). Ryman characterized *Artforum* as having

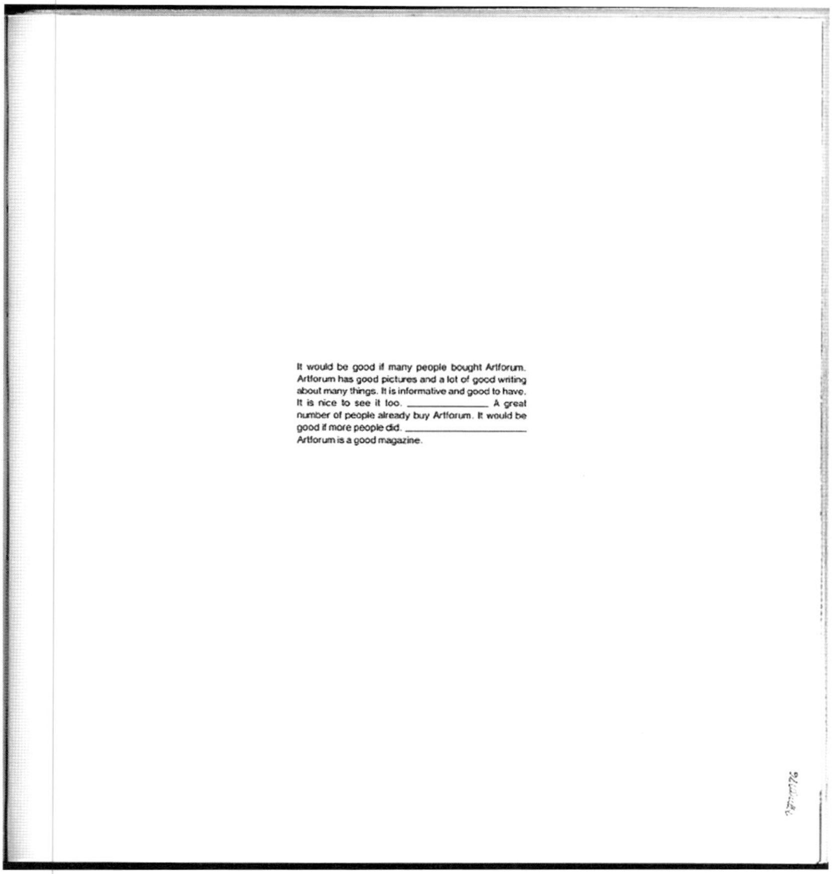

It would be good if many people bought Artforum. Artforum has good pictures and a lot of good writing about many things. It is informative and good to have. It is nice to see it too. ______________ A great number of people already buy Artforum. It would be good if more people did. ______________________ Artforum is a good magazine.

Robert Ryman, *Untitled, The Magazine Show, Artforum. Artforum* (December 1976). Commercial offset lithograph on paper.

"very serious type articles with big words and you would struggle through this thing and after you would finish reading it you would wonder what it was they were trying to say or what they were getting at."[57] Compared to Stella's parody of *Art News,* Ryman's *Artforum* "ad" is less aggressive than passive aggressive. It was not offensive enough to stop the magazine from asking Ryman to design the summer 1989 cover, and Ryman was hardly unsympathetic enough to the venue to decline the commission.

But Ryman's work is less about finding a way of painting "that you couldn't write about" than about drawing attention to the implicit relations between paintings—of painting to painting as opposed to painting to word. Art writing is another matter entirely and not necessarily a related one. To revise Storr's formulation, Ryman's painting is less "anti-rhetorical" than arhetorical. It is unconcerned with the discourse that seeks to pin it down yet critical of its grosser propaganda mechanisms or obscurantist prose paradigms. His subtle "shifts of emphasis" disenfranchise absolutism, revising each seemingly conclusive assumption in turn.

Ryman has avoided repetition. Each work revises the proposition and consequence of what has come before, while providing the impetus and method to continue with what follows. Sensitivity—a heightened sense of concentration about texture, scale, and so on—allows differences within and between works to be recognized and lends to each a specific gravity. To cite Storr once more: "Rather than pure painting, Ryman's work might be better described as 'plain' painting, the expression of a pragmatic classicism recalling William Carlos William's credo—'No ideas but in things.'"[58]

Although such an argument could stick in 1986, Ryman's work was certainly not apprehended in this way in the 1960s or 1970s. For some, Ryman's painting was residually expressionist, protominimalist, minimalist, or eventually postminimalist, while for others it was proto- or just plain conceptual. Lippard recounts that "Ryman was soon enveloped by 'anti-form' although his painting ideas had remained unchanged since the late 1950's, and until 1967 [at which time Ryman had a one-man exhibition at Paul Bianchini Gallery] his work had been ignored because it was too old-fashioned and 'expressionist.'"[59]

For his first solo outing at the Bianchini Gallery in 1967, Ryman showed *Standard,* which he made that year. None of the thirteen four-foot-square paintings of Swann's Down enamel paint on cold rolled-steel panels sold. They now comprise a multipart, twelve-panel work, with one painting held apart as a single panel. At the time of their debut, the paintings signified a dearth of labor (he used steel as a support) and a glut of duplication (the thirteen paintings were different only if viewers looked long or hard enough to see the modulations of loose horizontals strokes). In one of the few reviews of the show, Joseph Kosuth followed this logic and granted that it rendered interpretation unnecessary:

> The paintings are painted on thin sheets of steel. . . . When the brush was overloaded and the painting got complicated or painterly rather than just painted, he threw it out. What he ended up with was simple painted surfaces on which the paint was obvious and the square base for the paint—the metal sheets—were reduced to minor importance in the work. Ryman accepts the brush as a machine; he realizes that it is an element in his work. There is no need to study and project into these paintings because the brushed surface is all that is there. Perhaps there is no need to put one's thinking *into* painting because that necessitates interpretation.[60]

Antithetically, as Lippard imparts, for others they were somehow still too painterly or too open to emotionalism with their carefully apportioned paint and soft glimmer of steel. Two years later, a Fischbach press release also described his "prophetic exhibition at the Bianchini Gallery" as being "misunderstood by many as a throwback to action painting."[61]

When discussing this choice of steel as a support, Ryman ignored readings as aesthetic or otherwise and resorted to enumerating material qualifications: "I was just looking for a very thin material that would stand up on its own without any backing. Masonite wasn't so good and neither was aluminum. I thought, OK, steel is really very strong and very stable and very thin. That's how it happened. I looked into it, tested it, and worked it out."[62] As Kosuth

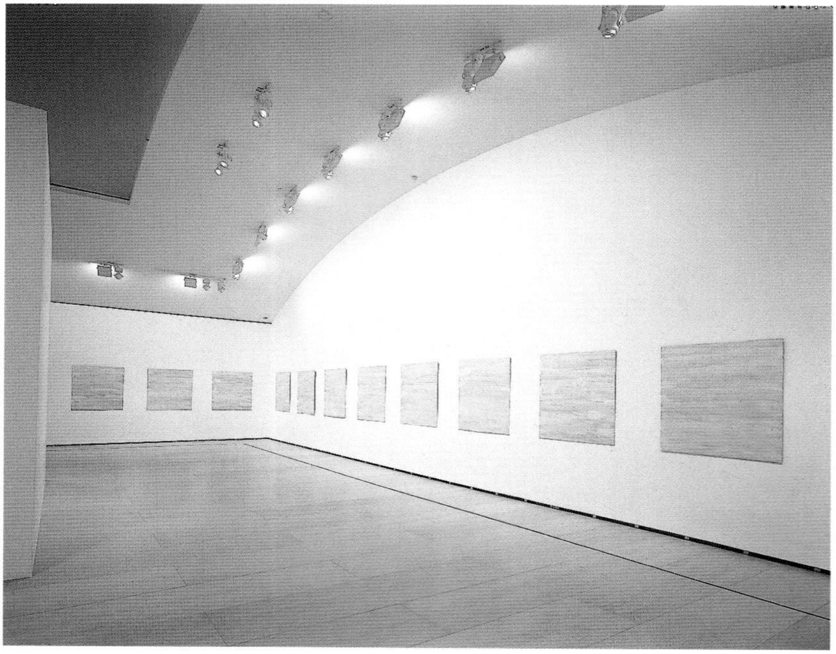

Robert Ryman, *Standard* (detail) (1967). Swann's Down enamel on cold-rolled steel.

knew but most ignored, Ryman completed fifty panels to arrive at the thirteen because the materials were unstable and the paint was slippery against its alloy ground. It proved exceedingly difficult to create works that were uniform enough to register the differences as almost indefinable but nonetheless there. Mel Bochner later wrote that "ordered proceduralism often led to an inversely proportional visual complexity,"[63] but less striking than Ryman's hand-painted surfaces were their modular formats and ostensibly programmatic production, smacking of nothing so much as the blankly affectless repetition of one thing after the next that marked much minimal sculpture.

Despite their commercial failure, Lippard still claimed that the polyptych had a pivotal status in art's course of "dematerialization":

> These thirteen all-white brushstrokes on steel supports were hung flat against the wall plane, denying object-quality to concentrate on surface, paint, and process, which, in 1968, became a "trend" called "antiform" and later "anti-illusionism," etc. Ryman had made a group of paintings without stretchers in 1964, and in 1967 began to tape or staple or paint (using paint as the adhesive) his white sheets of painted paper directly to the wall. Since then, he has continued to work with surfaces flat to the walls. . . . Ryman is primarily a painter, but these strategies enabled him to concentrate more fully on painting per se and freed him from a bulky, difficult-to-transport object; as such, this work is notable within the "dematerialization" process.[64]

Ryman's anticipatory status regarding dematerialization was further remarked in the above-cited Fischbach press release, which stated that "the 'dematerialization' process began in the early '60s when he mounted small canvases with rippling and unraveled edges directly against the wall and made a free-hanging tapestry-like painting."[65]

In the Anti-Illusion: Procedures/Materials exhibition catalogue in 1969, Marcia Tucker discusses Ryman's painterly qualities despite his overriding anti-illusionistic tendencies and dematerialized materials:

> Robert Ryman purifies painting to a further extreme by eliminating color as a formal element and concentrating on the act of putting paint on a surface. He uses white paint only, allowing the application of pigment to become the subject of the work. Each brushstroke affords a raw, immediate and spontaneous gesture whose intimations have nothing to do with narrative nor formal configuration. Moreover, he uses plain or corrugated paper, rejecting even the use of stretched canvas as a pictorial convention.[66]

However, when Greenberg and Fried were railing against the minimalists in "Recentness of Sculpture" and "Art and Objecthood," respectively, Ryman was painting a series on steel that was, for most, their first introduction to the artist's work. As dematerialization was ascendant, Ryman was painting on corrugated paper. And while he did return to canvas in short order—volunteering publicly that "linen or cotton on a stretcher . . . is probably still the best surface, when you come back to it"[67]—his experimentation with paper was quickly recuperated as emblematic of postminimalism, as is the case in the Anti-Illusion context. Seeing just one work—on steel, paper, or canvas—was not enough to confirm the scope of Ryman's project in the late 1960s. Differences between works and series mattered tremendously, but few could even see them at that time.

By 1965, Ryman had begun to develop systematic groupings, as in the *Winsors,* that said that the works should be seen relationally. Until this point, he had worked along similar lines, whether explorations of paint or properties of the support, but he had not conceived of any of these investigations as a discrete series. When there were many related works on unstretched canvas, for example, they remained just that. Even just after the *Winsors,* Ryman would make three related works in 1966 that derived their process and form from the *Winsors* but were not conceived as a series in and of themselves. *Mayco* and the nearly duplicative *Twin* and *Allied* were all made with a very wide, roughly twelve-inch brush, with paint coaxed along the surfaces in tidy bands. Unlike the *Winsors,* they do not divulge where Ryman reloaded his brush, as the heavy lines of paint reach from edge to edge (though the strokes remain unidirectional), instead of tapering off when the paint was expended.

Robert Ryman, *Mayco* (1966). Winsor White oil on stretched sized linen canvas.

The *Winsors* (1965–1966) were thus something new in the paintings' explicit branding as a series, but they were still produced one at a time. No two are alike. Even when the process remained utterly consistent, the effects did not; repetition served Ryman as a foil for difference. As Storr puts it: "Even as the nominal givens of his formal vocabulary seem among the most restricted of any contemporary abstractionist, Ryman has continued to avoid repetition, the Achilles heel of the reductivist enterprise. For, inasmuch as Ryman's art is materialistic and methodical, those very qualities are strategies designed to make repetition impossible."[68] Ryman later explained that when he approaches "paintings in that way, as a group, the feeling is very similar. But even though the approach is similar, the result tends to be a little different. And that was the interest. I wanted to see how the scale would change the painting and how different linen or maybe a slightly different paint consistency would affect it."[69]

Such was the game of the *Winsors,* where Ryman loaded a two-inch brush with paint and pulled it across the unprimed support from left to right until the paint was deposited and the brush bare. Then he would repeat the gesture, beginning just under the newly drawn streak of paint so that its bottom edge served as the demarcation for the next linear application. Once he reached the bottom of the canvas where the last bristled stroke of paint and the physical limit of support finally met with coinciding edges, he stopped. The resultant striations are highly irregular but overwhelmingly similar, all white and all equivalent widths as variably repeating compositional units. But they also betray the marks of their making, the registrations of uneven applications of pressure or the slips of a brush.

Ryman's alignment of stroke and edge and the means by which he uses the edge to circumscribe the pictorial activity that transpires within it reveal his method for actuating the *Winsors.* It comes dramatically close to the process that Stella employed in the *Black Paintings.* Coming forward is the question of influence, which may be felt more palpably here than with most of the other artists around whom Ryman was working. Stella's insistence on the facticity of his paintings (the "what you see is what you see" factor) and the unrepentant materiality of their surfaces that employed symmetry apart from perspective

Robert Ryman, *Winsor 34* (c. 1966). Winsor White oil on stretched sized linen canvas.

must have affected Ryman, who had been pursuing such ideas in his own work for half a decade by that time. All the same, with the *Winsors,* Ryman's laying down of trails of paint that established the boundaries for the application of the next horizontal band cannot help but resonate with Stella's own "deductive structures" (as Fried would name them), which play the literal shape of the material support off the depicted shape of its painted image in an insistent formal dialectic where shape becomes form that confirms its genesis as shape.[70]

Where Stella's works differ in composition from painting to painting or from shaped support to differently shaped support, Ryman's *Winsors* repeat a single compositional decision and implement (that same-size brush) over and again, noting, through such a repetition, the differences that would still emerge (in the choice of support and the relative scale of the lines to the size of each support), surviving a uniform set of procedural givens. In short, Ryman points to the series' structure more actively (because more questioningly) than would Stella. And to further emphasize the essentially relational if nonhierarchical logic of the *Winsors,* Ryman titled the paintings with arbitrary numbers to aid in their identification without implying a chronological sequence or a primary work from which the others evolved. There is no 1, for instance. Instead, there is *Winsor 6* (1965), *Winsor 5* (1965–1966), *Winsor 20* (1966), *Winsor 34* (1966), and later iterations of a similar horizontal stroke premise that bare no titular resemblance to the work of the mid-1960s, including *Paragon* (1974) and *Beacon* (1974). Related to this, in *Signet 20* (1966), a large *Winsor*-like painting on stretched sized cotton canvas with twenty-nine rows of overlapping horizontal stripes applied from left to right; the title refers to the brand and size of the brush Ryman used to make it. When Christie's auctioned *Signet 20,* staff members were at a loss for information regarding what they assumed were the preceding nineteen paintings and, as Ryman recalls, "were relieved to learn that no others existed."[71]

Differences—not distances from origins—formed the content of the paintings and ideated Ryman's longstanding premise that his painting was chiefly about making, not representing. Naomi Spector argues that, with the *Winsors,* Ryman ceased to use paint to make "something that could be seen at all apart from the paint itself. Now the work was about the nature of paint: the paint was the content of the paintings, as well as their form. They had no meaning outside the paint and the supporting material and the history of the process of the application."[72] As if to further literalize this, Ryman titled works according to paints, supports, and tools (like the aforementioned *Signet 20*). *Winsor* was derived from Winsor & Newton, the British paint manufacturers whose products—especially Winsor White—he used to complete these works, while *Dutch Boy Diamond* (1965) arises from Dutch Boy enamel. Similarly, *Medway* (c. 1968), the multipaper *Classico* series (1968–1969), and related works like *Lugano* (1968), index paper brands and exhibit watermarks, while *Van Dyke 9H #1* (1966), *Mars Lumograph 8H #1* (1966), *Eagle Turquoise 7H #3* (1966), *Koh-I-Noor 7H No. 1* (1966), *Castell 8H #2* (1966), and *Venus 7H No. 1* (1966) are all named for pencils.[73]

This, more than Stella's cagey *The Marriage of Reason and Squalor,* would frustrate interpretations beyond or in excess of the paint and the process by which it was applied. But Stella, too, had named works according to a paint brand in his *Benjamin Moore* series (1961).[74] Soon after, Stella declared that he hoped to "keep the paint as good as it is in the can."[75] Stella's use of pure paint registered his ambition for "the freshness of a pristine industrial object," as Caroline Jones writes, whereby paint is transferred "from container to surface, with as minimal interference as possible."[76] By contrast, titles for Ryman functioned expediently for identification. They have a "purely mnemonic function,"[77] as Bois asserts, and frequently forsake references to nonart objects, people, places, or even ideas in favor of the practical itemization evidenced by his material-oriented interviews.[78]

But there are exceptions. *To Gertrud Mellon* (1958) is a notable instance of a work renamed for symbolic reasons, while *Wedding Picture* (1961) is remarkable as a painting that was never untitled and always biographical (it was an unambiguous homage to Lucy Lippard and was completed in Maine, where they were married, shortly after the wedding). Titles also can have an ironic underbelly, as Naomi Spector asserts. Even materials and art supply brands—those most laconic of titles—evince a comparable duplicity.[79] In a discerning 1972

Robert Ryman, *Dutch Boy Diamond* (1965). Enamel on stretched linen canvas.

Robert Ryman, *Castell 8H #2* (1966). Graphite on Chemex coffee filter paper.

essay, "'Ryman' Brand Paintings," Spector plays with the multiple meanings that are embedded in Ryman's titles—for example, *Standard* (1967) as "ordinary, regular, usual . . . recognized as excellent and authoritative" and *General* (1970) as "common, widespread, not specific" or "in military terms, the highest rank." For Spector, "art manufacturers, like other businessmen, reach for elegance in their names; but the result is that whatever elegance was once there, now is lost. 'Venus' pencils is [*sic*] a beautiful example. And when Ryman titles a drawing *Venus,* after the pencil he used, he takes us one step further into the specific and ironic understanding of the word."[80]

Spector also writes that Ryman "doesn't make a project of finding these names":

> Rather, when he bothers to title his paintings at all, he just seems to hit on those with a special kind of ambiguity. They are almost all one-word titles, spare, dry, and condensed. For him the most important consideration is that the title should have nothing whatever to do with the painting itself. It has no interpretive, associative, symbolic, or any other kind of relation to the work. It is purely his way of identifying a painting from all the others. He says, "I get most of the names from the Yellow Pages (of the Manhattan classified telephone directory)—you know, brand names. They don't mean anything. I just want something that won't interfere with the painting." Naturally, he is not unaware of the humor in all this. His taste is for the ironic twist in American usage, and he handles it with great style. Thus, for example, there are the titles *Delta, Adelphi, Arista, Exeter, Essex, Impex.* These names cling to their traces of "class" as Blanche DuBois did to her remnants of gentility, but none of them really convince anybody.[81]

They don't convince anybody because Ryman chose the titles precisely for their anonymity.[82] Like Ryman's use of his name as a compositional element, repeated often to void its content, the ubiquity of product and company names thwarts their specificity, and having lost their original meaning, they circulate newly unmoored, ripe for Ryman's usage.

As mentioned earlier, titles became attached to specific paintings only when exhibited, and many early works remained untitled because they were never or only recently shown. By 1965, Ryman realized that he would probably be showing with enough regularity to precipitate identifying works. Lippard mentioned Ryman in passing in "Rejective Art" and "After a Fashion: The Group Show" of 1966 and "The Silent Art" of 1967, and she also named him as one artist among many who should have been included in the Whitney Annual—the first painting version in the Marcel Breuer building—in her 1968 review of the show.[83] References to Ryman remain scant until 1970, when Robert Pincus-Witten spoke of Ryman's "obvious polemical success"[84] (like an overnight success that was years in the making) in the pages of *Artforum*. By the time of Ryman's Guggenheim retrospective in 1972, Peter Schjeldahl claimed Ryman for his pantheon as "one of our great artists."[85]

Reviewing Ryman's 1970 Fischbach show, Pincus-Witten marked 1965 as a pivotal year for Ryman: "Five years ago, Robert Ryman began to pare his painting down to apparent essentials, reducing it to a reiterative kind of manipulative experience of white paint on a two-dimensional surface."[86] Pincus-Witten had the *Delta* series in mind, but instead of dealing with those paintings in the context of their current hanging at Fischbach, he read them retrospectively, noting how their look and meaning had changed over five years: "The *Delta* paintings—an alphabetical, non-referential designation—are three thoughtfully coated, nine foot squares painted in 1966. At that time one would have considered them as extravagantly desensitized although in 1970 they have a tender cast to them."[87] That is, the *Delta* series now functioned as a kind of stand-in for a bygone past where paintings were made on canvas supports rather than on sheets stapled to the wall or even drawn directly on it. They had appeared as minimalist in 1966, but by 1970 they appeared to be—and probably had been—more aesthetic than "desensitized."

For Pincus-Witten, the real import of works like the *Deltas* was what they had made possible for other artists. He was "put off by [Ryman's] ungenerous surfaces and by his serialized structurings, which press for a part-to-part comparison in a peculiarly taxing way."[88] Noting the prevalence of "non-stretcher-borne painting" in the work of artists like David Paul or Richard Tuttle, Pincus-Witten conceded that Ryman was nonetheless instrumental for "the swarm of young artists committed to pictorializing trends in sculpture."[89]

This shift to pictorializing sculpture had everything to do with a revaluation of minimalism, which could be historicized alongside Ryman's newly significant works. Pincus-Witten remarked on the way that minimalism once "made greater sense in sculpture than in painting,"[90] but this analysis was increasingly contravened and made categorically unstable by work such as Ryman's that hovered productively at painting's edge. For Pincus-Witten, Ryman's work occasioned a reconsideration of minimalism from the inside, where its more painterly aspects took precedence over its once dominant sculptural gestalts and architectonic forms. In this way, Ryman becomes the hinge from minimalism to postminimalism as exemplified in the work of someone like Tuttle, while minimalism itself is reappraised, even domesticated and made to count in terms of the new work of which it was generative. Ryman does not become a minimalist in this telling. Rather, he becomes another unwitting crux, anticipating the movement's splintered afterlife in a variety of process-driven forms.

In his abovementioned review of Ryman's 1972 Guggenheim retrospective, Schjeldahl also suggests that minimalism should be rethought through Ryman's work, designates Ryman as a minimalist, and then argues against this claim by suggesting that Ryman transcends such stylistic categorizations and group affiliations. In this, Schjeldahl reiterates his position of a year earlier, where, writing on Ryman's work at the Fischbach and Dwan Galleries, he posited Ryman as

> one of the most singular and underrated talents in American abstract painting since 1960. Ryman is not exactly unknown[,] . . . but such exposure has often served to obscure more than to illuminate the character of his very personal art, with the result that his reputation has suffered as much from easy acceptance as from easy dismissal. For though he is clearly "avant-garde"—what else do you call a maker of all-white paintings?—he seems finally to be

> at odds with some fundamental terms of the various movements from Minimal to Process and Conceptual, in whose ranks he has insensibly been lumped.[91]

In the Guggenheim retrospective catalogue, Diane Waldman again remarks that he "eludes categorization." "Since his is still a painterly response, the consequence of facing pictorial decisions," she reasons, "the results are of necessity fundamentally different from what we have seen in the sixties: a period characterized by the erosion of the position held by the 'specific object,' its dematerialization in the face of such external factors as the environment, and its subsequent banishment in favor of the 'idea as idea.'"[92] Waldman and Schjeldahl concur on the ambiguity of affiliation, except that the latter shifts the terms of the former back to a discussion of painting:

> Minimal art is usually considered a "sculpture movement," the painters connected with it being regarded as somewhat heterodox hangers-on. And, indeed, the intellectual program explicit in the major works of Morris, Judd, Andre, LeWitt, Flavin, et al. contains within it a kind of implicit death-of-painting esthetic attitude—an attitude that becomes an article of faith in the Post-Minimalism of such artists as [Bruce] Nauman, [Robert] Smithson, [Michael] Heizer, [Joseph] Kosuth, [Vito] Acconci, and [Keith] Sonnier, all of whom have advanced to a level where one may speak of a death-of-sculpture (or even death-of-art) presumption. It is exceedingly curious, then, that as all the willy-nilly *advancing* of the past decade begins to succumb to the inertia of familiarity, it should be the work of erstwhile Minimalist *painters* that emerges as perhaps the finest and most enduring legacy of the movement.[93]

This championing of minimalist painters attends Schjeldahl's view of minimal sculpture as anemic—little more than "used-up pedagogical visual aids, the relics of an esthetic education that, purely academic now, has lost its power to command our attendance."[94] If minimal sculptures were anodyne, minimal paintings were, by contrast, pleasingly rapt, commanding attention and *keeping* it. Ryman's paintings worked for Schjeldahl because they retained a sense of the hand and the volatility that it introduces, which had been repressed in much minimal sculpture. "The fun of esthetic discovery," Schjeldahl asserted, "curdled in the pedantry of most Minimalism, is delicately preserved in Ryman's astonishingly various art."[95]

Schjeldahl came to this understanding after seeing that Ryman's art was not singular but "astonishingly various." The Guggenheim show was crucial in this regard (as a 1993 Museum of Modern Art / Tate Gallery retrospective and permanent installations at Hallen für neue Kunst, in Schaffhausen, Switzerland, and Dia: Beacon would become) because it exhibited enough works for their distinctions to show. (Moreover, most catalogues at this time had few if any color reproductions. Ryman's vivid underpainting and the like would not reproduce well, and the works looked flat and absent of compositional incident on the catalogue page.) A concurrent early work show at the new John Weber Gallery (the "direct heir to the now-defunct uptown Dwan"),[96] which was organized because the Guggenheim did not include work made before 1965, also would have contributed to this revelation. Much early work still has not been exhibited, and when it is unearthed (as it was at the Whitechapel Art Gallery in 1977, MoMA in 1993, the Peter Blum Gallery in 2004, the Pennsylvania Academy in 2007, and the permanent installations at Schaffhausen and Dia), it is often appreciated on a continuum ranging from totally unexpected to all-out revelatory.

Back in 1972, few reviewed the shows as having this kind of connection. An exception was Ratcliff, who underscored that the Guggenheim reveals "how far Ryman has stayed from minimalism," a point made all the more striking by the early works downtown. Although they "include drawings in a style with roots in late-fifties New York gesture, there are no allusions at all. The interest is *entirely* in the question of how his brushstroke is able to cover the surface."[97] Denise Wolmer was unusually sensitive in description and argument when she wondered "if, in fact, he had painted in a radically different manner prior to their pure endgame reductions." In answer, the paintings at Weber show

> a wavering line of development, with Ryman's earlier works showing traces of an unconvinced infatuation with Abstract Expressionism. Hints of blue or green, even orange or red escape from the usually impastoed curls, ridges, and slips of gestural white. . . . It is now clear that he is one of the most categorically unflinching of painters, refusing, like Bishop, to be lazy, though the price of exertion, uptown retrospective notwithstanding, is the recognition of all-pervading doubt. I do not believe that Ryman is a Minimalist. He is a painter who, with every systematic white brushstroke, is seeking to reaffirm the value of his gestures amidst facile formalisms and pseudo-philosophic cant. I am reminded of Samuel Beckett's question, posed in relation to the painting of Bram Van Velde: "What do we do when we can't create art and we have to create art?"[98]

At the other end of the spectrum was Canaday, who denounced the Guggenheim show:

> A Frenchwoman was following close on my heels at the entrance, her admission fee clutched in her hand, but she took one surprised look at the place and said, "Mais, c'est vide!" and pocketed her fee and walked out. I must say, she hit the nail pretty much on the head, not exactly taking the words out of my mouth but doing better than I could have done in maximum compression of critical comment. . . . The idea of so trivial and obvious and even outmoded a body of work being given all this space in a major museum is ludicrous. *C'est vide,* buddy. . . . [99]

He finishes by saying that "if Robert Ryman never painted another thing, I would regard it as a commendable saving of canvas, paint, critics' ink and museum space."[100]

Of course, Canaday's arch conjunction of the trivial, obvious, and outmoded was not Ryman's sole public censure.[101] It is a typical avant-garde slight that repeats almost exactly David Bourdon's condemnation of a Tuttle retrospective at the Whitney Museum three years later. "Seldom has so little art been assembled in such ample space," Bourdon declared about Tuttle in the *Village Voice,* further deadpanning that the entire exhibition "would almost certainly fit into a single piece of carry-on flight luggage."[102] Hilton Kramer expressed outright scorn in the *New York Times:* "To Mies van der Rohe's famous dictum that less is more, the art of Richard Tuttle offers definitive refutation. . . . For in Mr. Tuttle's work, less is unmistakably less. It is, indeed, remorselessly and irredeemably less."[103] Thus, Canaday's remarks would not be worth repeating were it not for the fact that for some time they remained the only review that Ryman remembered "well enough to quote."[104]

Against Canaday's repudiation, Schjeldahl offered "aesthetic discovery" as evidence that Ryman was exempt from the strictures of both minimalism and postminimalism. An awareness of Ryman's aesthetic—and the approach to looking it put forward—became the necessary context for his work, especially as more of Ryman's works were exhibited in clusters or groups, whether congruent series or random hangings of work from many years. This reading overtook Ryman's supposed minimalism to such an extent that even the *Standards* became redolent of sensory pleasure. For Klaus Kertess: "Direct, deceivingly effortless, and, finally, pleasurable, there ensued a sensuous enlightenment that might have bespoken Ryman's sitting in Matisse's armchair."[105]

Eventually, painterly qualities trump all else in many reviews. Typical is a short blurb announcing a Pace Gallery show in 2002: "The snowman returns in a luxuriant temper with paintings whose frosty or creamy, brush-whipped whites interact discreetly with undercolors or the hue of raw canvas or linen. As is his wont, Ryman fusses eloquently with relations of paint masses to the shapes of blocky stretchers and, here and there, with how the stretchers are affixed to the wall. Familiarity with his pleasant worries makes one wonder how he could ever have been deemed minimalist. The style of this show is bashful baroque."[106] Here minimalism is upheld only to be cancelled by the hyperbolic, extravagant, and almost culinary language of the review that all but overwhelms the quiet, local materiality of the paintings that writers like Storr would emphasize.

Surprisingly, given his antipathy toward Tuttle, Kramer had written that Ryman's paintings at Fischbach in 1969 were "physically unimpressive but visually rather compelling, at least as a group. (Whether individual examples, removed from the purist atmosphere of the gallery, could sustain this visual power is rather doubtful.)"[107] In an *Artforum* review of his 1971 Fischbach show, Kenneth Baker details Ryman's use of serial structures to aesthetic ends, and he indicates that this realization was born of the interaction between works that the large show encouraged. (In writing about the same show, Ratcliff similarly remarked that "the self-sufficiency of each painting in this series [the *Generals*] is enhanced by the presence of so many near-duplicates.")[108] Baker discusses how Ryman's works "have no space in them" but grants that the show still managed "a marvelous feeling of depth to it owing to the fact that it changes as one spends time with it."[109] Baker writes:

> On entering one sees an array of paintings, all of them in white on gessoed canvas, one wall being unlighted, and they all look alike except for their sizes. But before long they begin to sort themselves out until each canvas appears as a distinct deviation from their original appearance of consistent whiteness. Pure white then comes to seem like an abstraction, something approachable only as a limit, like the line with which one depicts the edge of a form. A kind of pulse is set up among the square canvases of varying size and one notices that the variations in hue are so subtle even when they can be clearly seen that they cannot be "remembered" by the eye for comparison between any more than adjacent canvases.[110]

Ryman's paintings are serial but different, Baker infers, leading to his prescient interpretation of the work:

> Ryman's white paintings seem to make more sense of the idea of serial work than almost anyone else's do. The curious thing about

> these paintings is that they do not seem to depend upon the white of the gallery room to make them work; they work because they are all there. Whether their order is arbitrary or in some way necessary one simply cannot tell; all one can be sure of is their interdependence. Most striking perhaps is the way they energize the gallery space after a while by being entirely exterior to themselves. Watching them differentiate themselves from mere white is like seeing entropy reversed.[111]

Baker's commentary proposes the interdependence of Ryman's works, whether or not they are in an explicit series. It also gets at the spectatorial conditions that are dictated by the gallery space and yet oddly resistant to it, in that Ryman's works needed these white walls to mark out their individuated (and individuating) differences from them. The edges of these works rely on the wall plane to produce an effect of perceptual estrangement—what Baker names, with a nod to Robert Smithson, "entropy in reverse."

A few years later, Donald Kuspit took another tack by reading Ryman as a "cool" reductionist whose works "reveal themselves thermodynamically"—that is, as entropy. Kuspit even begins his essay with an epigraph culled from Ludwig von Bertalanffy's *General System Theory* (1968). For Kuspit, the differentiations in Ryman's paintings were irrelevant because they represented a "closed system" in which difference "tends to be displaced into its uniformity, like bits of coral generalized into a harmonious, self-same entity. Differentiation, here, represents a leveling of differences." Taken to its extreme for Kuspit, this means that Ryman's works are inevitably beholden to "a system of art which expects to have no power of intervention in the world and expects the world not to intervene in it."[112]

Marcia Hafif felt strongly enough about Kuspit's misunderstanding to reply the next month, recapitulating the position of Baker and those who by the late 1970s assumed that Ryman's work was less about closed systems or even serial uniformity and more about evocative differences within a reduced set of material and practical givens. Hafif insisted that Ryman's "paintings *are* different from each other, and the differences are *significant,*"[113] which is where the meaning of the work resides. An all-out attack on Kuspit answers many of his points in turn:

> Kuspit applies the adjective *cool* to Ryman's work, but cool in art means a standing back and a 'take it or leave it' attitude. Ryman's work is not cool, it is contemplative and human. *Reductionism* isn't right either because that suggests a process of reducing to an inevitable end, while Ryman's work does not do that, but rather uses a limited selection of elements in any given work for the purpose of clarity. And the range of elements he uses is large and expanding. One sees homogeneity, repression, narrow control and a closed system of art only if one is unable to see what is there and concomitantly expects bright colors and confusion, titillation for the bored, and blatant expressions of narcissism—if not political statements—to be the only worthy components of art. Ryman's painting has a great deal to say to the viewer willing to engage it.[114]

Even critics who failed to see the aesthetic of Ryman's work realized that it was advisable to reevaluate their positions based on the connections between paintings when those same paintings were exhibited in greater depth. In 1970, Pincus-Witten felt that Ryman's work was inassimilable apart from its fruitful role for other artists, but just two years later he recanted (admittedly in a rather circuitous manner). Ryman was a conceptualist who was interested only in "painting as theory" because he was "not interested in painting at all."[115] He writes: "It is largely because Ryman's pictures stop short of committing themselves as paintings that we have had to wait for his [Guggenheim] retrospective to appreciate the nature of his accomplishment. In his one-man shows, we were presented with individualized tentatives, the cumulative effect of which remained an elusive quantity. Seen chronologically, in the context of a retrospective, Ryman's special particularities reveal a consistent theoretical position."[116] This "theoretical position" put forward a Ryman who was "liberated from sensibility"[117] by virtue of a choice of brush or stroke that still constitutes an act of painting, even if it is divorced from the heroism or hyperbolic subjectivism with which such an act was once conceived.

Pincus-Witten later admitted that "these distinctions are not absolute" and that works like the *Surface Veils* (1970–1972) (discussed in chapter 5), twenty-eight or so related works that thinned their supports and allowed the paint to move ever closer to the wall, ironically nudged Ryman "away from theory back into sensibility."[118] Thus, Pincus-Witten could remark that "Ryman's work accepts certain traditional issues; for him art still remains an expression of the painting support, of paint itself, and of manipulation with that substance."[119] For Pincus-Witten, Ryman's "intellective processes"[120] overwhelm their plastic forms and aesthetic effects.

For me, contra Pincus-Witten, Ryman's choices, whether regarding the width of brush or the nature or size of his painting's support, precipitate intellective processes about the physical consequences of his material decisions even though results of those choices could not be predicted in advance of (or without) painting. The controlled devices beget spontaneous interactions and forms of creative experimentation, and this interaction vitiates claims for a purely conceptual basis for his work. Attempts to affiliate his work with conceptual art or to render binary the material or bodily and the conceptual or intellectual must fail.

Writing in 1971, Ratcliff had already sensed this interconnection between thought and materials:

> He wants to know how he can know what he is doing without giving himself over to anticipations so accurate they would take the knowledge of his act away from him, turning it into knowledge of an idea. To know what he is doing, he paints only very simple textures in rudimentary patterns; to keep this knowledge from extinguishing itself in accuracy, he allows these simplicities to be as complex as they can be without becoming complexities: Ryman paints always at the border between the absurd and the completely self-evident. He learns this only as he goes, intuitively—in order

> not to be too "well-informed" his paintings are illuminated by intuitive strength and steadiness, yet his brilliance is only *certain* in its knowledge of the way to avoid itself—to maintain an opacity which allows it to benefit somewhat from the illumination it provides, and so not give itself up to the transparent condition of merely having caused a surface to be painted white. Ryman made paintings of his signature in the late fifties and early sixties; he has arrived in the last few years at a point where the entire surface has the quirky directness, authenticity, and possible meaninglessness of his signature.[121]

For Ratcliff, Ryman's intuitive process lends his works their import, which is felt in diffuse surfaces that hover, simply and absurdly, between the twinned poles of meaning and meaninglessness. Cause and effect become not means and ends but, in Dewey's terms, "means and consequence," where "consciousness itself is the inception of such a transformation."[122]

In upholding a subjective dimension, this approach distinguishes Ryman's productions from the logic of conceptualism, which retained an emphasis on ideation above formalism and its phenomenological conditions of perception. In 1970, Bochner argued against just such a bifurcation. Conceptualism, Bochner wagered, was specious, and "for a variety of reasons"[123] he did not like the term. "Connotations of an easy dichotomy with perception are obvious and inappropriate. The unfortunate implication is of a somewhat magical/mystical leap from one mode of existence to another. The problem is the confusion of idealism and intention. . . . Outside the spoken word, no thought can exist without a sustaining support."[124] For Bochner, there are no ideas but in things, even if those things are no longer stable, categorical, or bounded, and even if "works of art are not illustrations of ideas."[125] Such is the paradox for Bochner not only of conceptualism but of writing about art more generally: "Ultimately, description as a critical method fails. Pretending to a non-subjective rendering of the object, it cuts off the peripheral pressures of experience."[126]

In a passage with undeniable relevance to Ryman's works that spread laterally across supporting walls, Bochner suggests that a better engagement could be offered by conceiving of sensible things as "'across' space, rather than 'in' space."[127] Illustrating this idea with a photograph of Ryman's *Prototypes* (1969), Bochner claims that the result of reading across space would be that "objects would cease to be the locus of sight. Then, no longer centers in themselves, they would demand to be perceived as the organization by everything around them. What might result from this conjecture is a sense of trajectory rather than of identity."[128] Contingency becomes key—in relation to the work's environment and the spectator's experience of it as it exists in a specific context and at a particular time.

To cite Dewey on experience:

> An experience has pattern and structure, because it is not just doing and undergoing in alternation, but consists of them in relationship. To put one's hand in the fire that consumes it is not necessarily to have an experience. The action and its consequence must be joined in perception. This relationship is what gives meaning; to grasp it is the objective of all intelligence. The scope and content of the relations measure the significant content of an experience. A child's experience may be intense, but, because of lack of background from past experience, relations between undergoing and doing are slightly grasped, and the experience does not have great depth or breadth. No one ever arrives at such maturity that he perceives all the connections that are involved. There was once written (by Mr. Hinton) a romance called "The Unlearner." It portrayed the whole endless duration of life after death as a living over of the incidents that happened in a short life on earth, in continued discovery of the relationships involved among them.[129]

Dewey further supposed that this operation of action and consequence, one of the guiding principles of his aesthetic theory, was also valid on the level of practice itself, which he understood as a microcosm (or practical elaboration) of his philosophy more generally. He writes that "a painter must consciously

Robert Ryman, *Untitled, Prototype* (1969). Acrylic polymer on fiberglass panel.

undergo the effect of his every brush stroke or he will not be aware of what he is doing and where his work is going. Moreover, he has to see each particular connection of doing and undergoing in relation to the whole that he desires to produce. To apprehend such relations is to think, and is one of the most exacting modes of thought."[130]

Dewey here offers a way out of the conceptualist bind by proposing that thought cannot be divorced from the materials through which they are actuated and against which they are tested. Ryman's work models just such an insight. Relationships between paintings and the connections born therein are primary, as are the edges of those supports that demarcate boundaries and allow for connections to be made from surface to surface and, in the swells of wall between them, from surface to environment. But just as crucial are connections between surface and viewer.

When asked to contribute to *Artforum* again in 1985, Ryman was less flip than in his Magazine Show artist's project. Amy Baker Sandback asked Ryman to comment on his painting, and he provided the following: "Painting does not exist independently as a thing, but exists in relationship. The meaning of painting depends not only on the interaction between a painting and the viewer, but on the painting's relationship with space. Painting interacts with space (the wall, ceiling, floor, light) and with the viewer. It is the interaction that initiates experience. You cannot understand painting by explaining something. You can only understand painting by experience."[131] By the early 1970s, this subjective experience of and concerted response to the incremental shifts and nuances in Ryman's works led to his increased critical prominence. As paintings were installed in groups that allowed their commonality and bases for disparity to be observed, Ryman's inscription into discourse continued, even as he resisted its overdetermination.

5

WALL

The May 1970 issue of *Artforum* contained Mel Bochner's assault on conceptual art, which was illustrated by Robert Ryman's *Prototypes.* But the salient photograph graced the issue's cover—Eva Hesse's *Contingent* (1969), a series of eight bannerlike rectangular fields of latex-covered cheesecloth that was suspended from the ceiling within fiberglass sheaths hung at right angles to the gallery walls. Hesse's death that month at the age of thirty-four rendered *Contingent* immediately historical. Yet, Hesse's nascent visibility turned retrospective summation was predicated upon the import of her work, more than the biographical circumstances (much less the accompanying interview) against which it registered. The work made a claim for an art that was on the edge of painting where "conventions, or institutions,"[1] of painting and sculpture were literally suspended and held in sharply oppositional relief. *Contingent* was a proposition—a series of paintings that were so flattened that they became edges that stood both as graphic lines and as tangible, physical borders. At once image and object, *Contingent*'s flags read as sculptures that insistently occupy space.

As Lucy Lippard has noted, Hesse's explicit questioning of the boundaries of practice shares much with Ryman's "unstretched and buckling" canvases of the early 1960s.[2] When posed against doctrinaire claims for the stability and integrity of the once sacrosanct medium, their work admits (although to different ends) a transformation of received formalist ideology. Nonetheless,

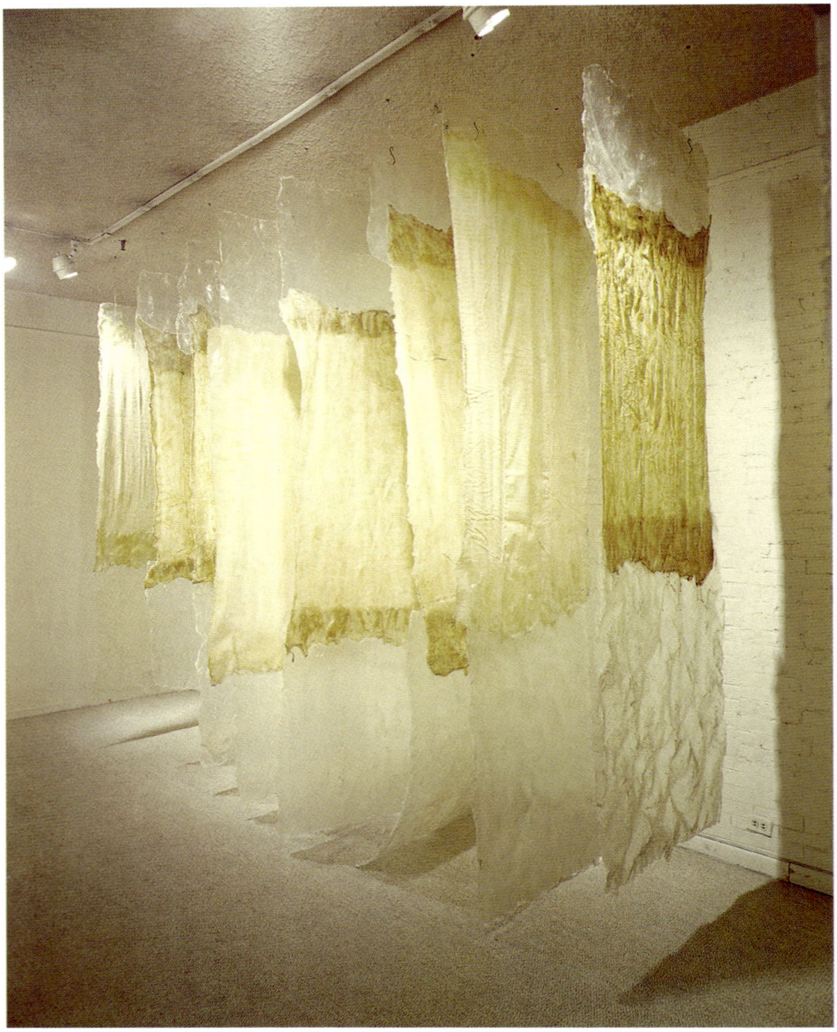

Eva Hesse, *Contingent* (1969). Fiberglass, polyester resin, and latex over cheesecloth.

Ryman remains within painting, even if painting in his hands becomes less ontologically than materially consequential, dependent on effects born of "painting" that justify its appropriation as such (as argued in chapter 3). Hesse limns its conventions to register the gap *between* painting and sculpture—not not-painting versus painting, not zero and one (as the distinction stands for Ryman), but painting versus a series of definable forms, which in Hesse's logic might be sculpture, space, or even the body that physically circumnavigates the installation.

Such was the significance of *Contingent*'s ideation as well as its corporeal structure. Its hanging emphasized the relations between its discrete entities, and it forced illusion to become external to its object. Its mooring in the schematics of the painted image was invoked only in terms of loss. This approach led Rosalind Krauss to the conclusion that with *Contingent,* "we feel ourselves to be in the affective terrain of painting. But *Contingent* is not a painting. And this is so because its flattened fields are not parallel but at right angles to the wall."[3] For Krauss, *Contingent*'s exemption from the category of painting derives from its relation to the wall. *Contingent* was sculpture or painting that approached the condition of sculpture obliquely as an unreachable if nameable limit.

To get at the complexities born of *Contingent*'s peculiar installation, Krauss suggests a hypothetical gallery where paintings by Rembrandt are, "through some caprice of the curator," installed at ninety-degree angles to the wall, allowing a frontal view of only the sides of frames: "In this hypothetical case the paintings, the Rembrandts, would have been rendered 'useless,' their normal function—that of making a certain order of things visible—annulled; and instead we would be given the extra-pictorial anomaly of the painting-object, or the painting-as-object. We would see, that is, the objecthood of the object (the painting-object) eclipsing its 'use.'"[4]

When the Rembrandts' object status displaces their pictorial illusionism, the paintings acknowledge their primary status as objects and therein make another "order of things visible." In this situation, the Rembrandts, with their offer of redoubled perspectives, exhibit the properties of anamorphosis as exemplified by a painting like Hans Holbein's *The Ambassadors* (1533). In *The Ambassadors,* the depicted dignitaries are surrounded by contrived displays of venality, and a looming, amorphous mass appears at their feet. When seen from a station at the painting's edge, the mass congeals into a foreshortened skull, a memento mori. This latent content provides a means of and cloaked allowance for spectatorial detection: "It insists that there are two different, mutually exclusive vantages: the one within the world from which death is not visible; and the one outside, or at an angle to it, from which death is seen because the 'world' is not."[5] Because these vantages diverge, a viewer cannot occupy a position at which to see both the images simultaneously. A physical parallax is needed that is unlike the one precipitated by the optical gestalt of figure against ground in, for instance, Ellsworth Kelly's oscillating figure and ground canvases.

Krauss argues that the Holbein example is critical to an understanding of *Contingent* because Hesse reinvents the anamorphotic condition: "From the front, the view is of the elements' edges with their sculptural condition eclipsing that of the pictorial; from a raking angle, one's perception is of the surfaces of the banners and the planarity of the rectangular fields, a perception that foregrounds the pictorial aspect of the experience. The problematic here is obviously very different from that of Holbein's *Ambassadors*."[6] But Krauss continues: "In *Contingent* . . . the issue is that of the mutual eclipse of the conventions, or institutions, of painting and sculpture as separate modalities of experience."[7] The literalism of minimalism distended illusionism into a lateral material spread across discrete objects and multiple parts, and Hesse pressed this division until form and matter were disjointed yet inextricable.

When Ryman turned to a similar problematic in the 1980s, he produced three related works—*Factor* (1983), *Pace* (1984), and *Pair Navigation* (1984). The pieces project outward from their wall planes at right angles, but Ryman still felt them to be squarely in the realm of painting so that any interpretation of them as sculptural was, in his words, at best "incidental."[8] This claim reiterates one that was voiced earlier in response to *Varese Wall* (1975), a huge structure that assumes the form of a wall. In an interview, Gary Garrels said that *Varese Wall* "is the most sculptural piece that you have done that I am aware of, dealing with the space in some ways as volume, not just as a plane."[9] Ryman replied:

> I wasn't really thinking about sculpture at all. It was all painting, although I can see how it could be thought of as three-dimensional, being a wall in the space. But that was incidental. That piece came about because I was working on a solution for Giuseppe Panza in Italy, who wanted me to do a room for him in his villa. I had been there before and knew how damp the walls and the weather there can be. I was trying to devise a way to line the walls with metal foil because I wanted to paint on wooden veneer panels. I was working on a way to join them together so that they would line the room on three walls. Behind them would be the metal foil to keep the moisture off of the wood, and the wood would be treated. I was going through all of this experimentation, bolting these panels together, and I realized that the room just wasn't going to work. But instead I thought I would make this piece and move it away from the wall. I wanted it to sit on the floor. I felt if it were attached to the wall, it wouldn't be the same situation. The aesthetic would be totally different. I wanted to attach it so you could see behind it. You would see it sitting on the floor, you could see the surface and so on. I wanted it to be totally naked. I wasn't sure how it was going to work, and in my studio I had it sitting on little foam blocks, just to keep it off the floor. The foam happened to be light blue. I became so used to these foam blocks that they became part of the painting. I just couldn't see it any other way. When I installed it in the gallery, I kept the foam blocks, because the floor was a little uneven and otherwise there would have been a gap underneath. So that was the way it turned out.[10]

Varese Wall's structure was thus practical as well as aesthetic. Its status as a frontal, planar painting—but also as an object that exists in a spatial and institutional situation—remained key, even though its frontality was only one mode of apprehending it. Similarly, when asked about the dividing line between painting and sculpture or relief, Ryman reiterated that he works from the point of view

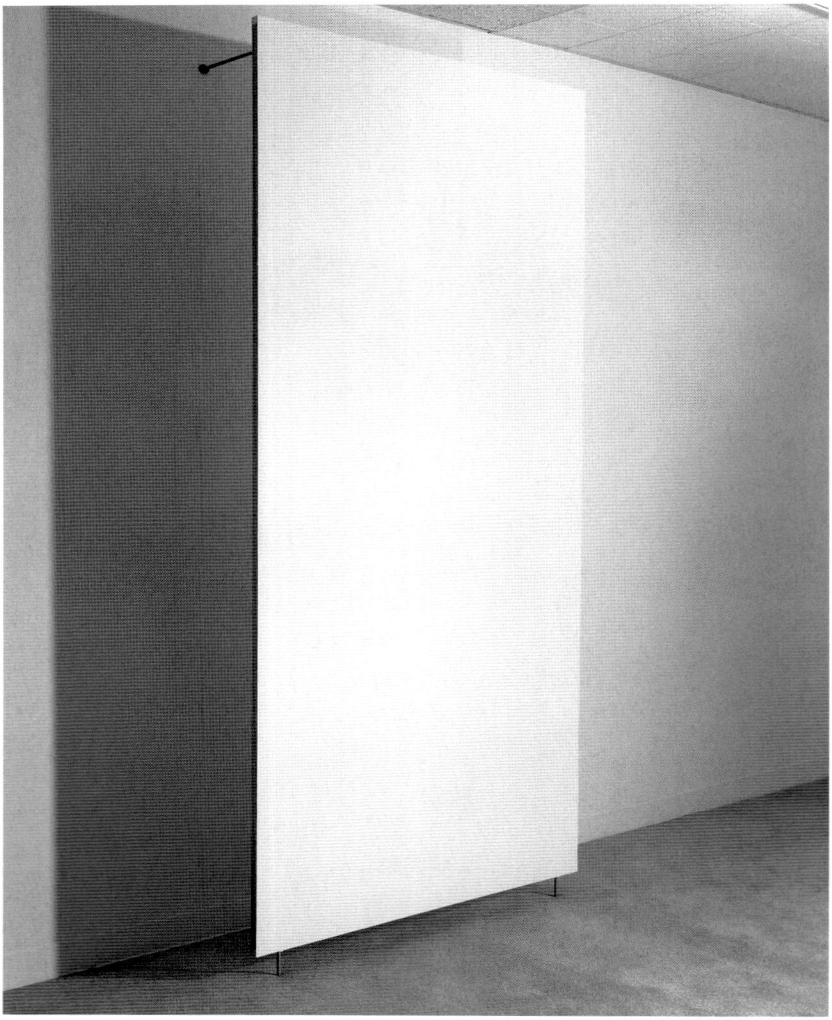

Robert Ryman, *Factor* (1983). Oil over Swiss Lascaux acrylic on recto, Swiss Lascaux acrylic with varnish on verso of fiberglass panel with honeycomb aluminum with epoxy edge, and metal rods with oval attachments.

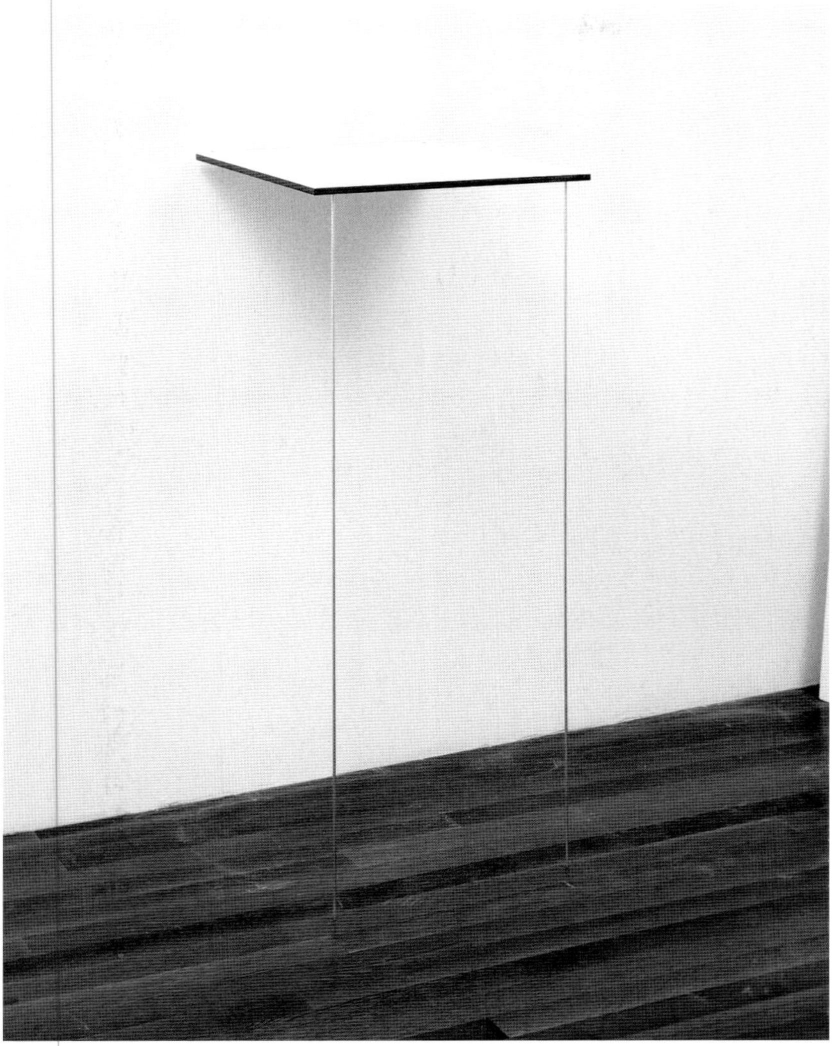

Robert Ryman, *Pace* (1984). Lascaux acrylic (synthetic polymer paint) on fiberglass panel with redwood edge with aluminum, stainless steel wall dowels, fasteners, and rods.

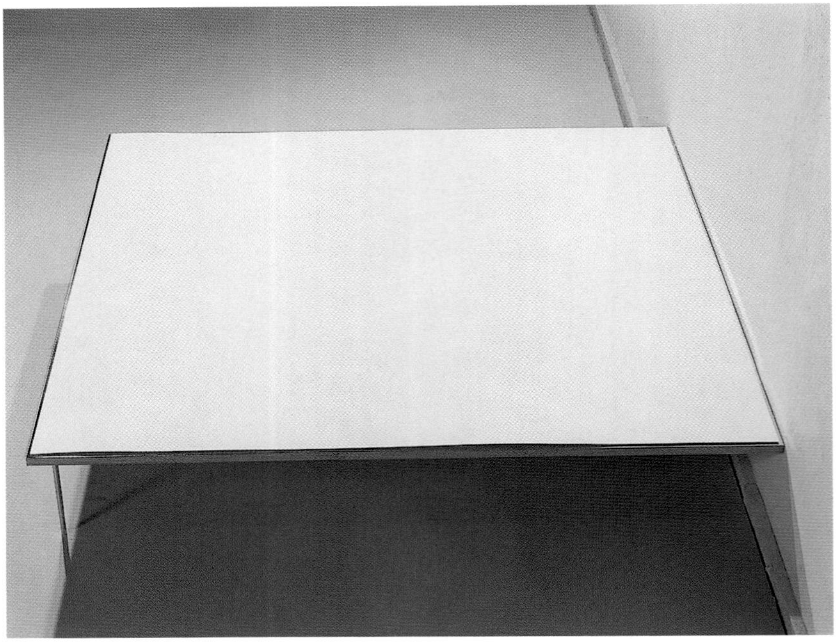

Robert Ryman, *Pair Navigation* (1984). Oil on fiberglass panel with redwood edge and metal frame, with four rod fasteners.

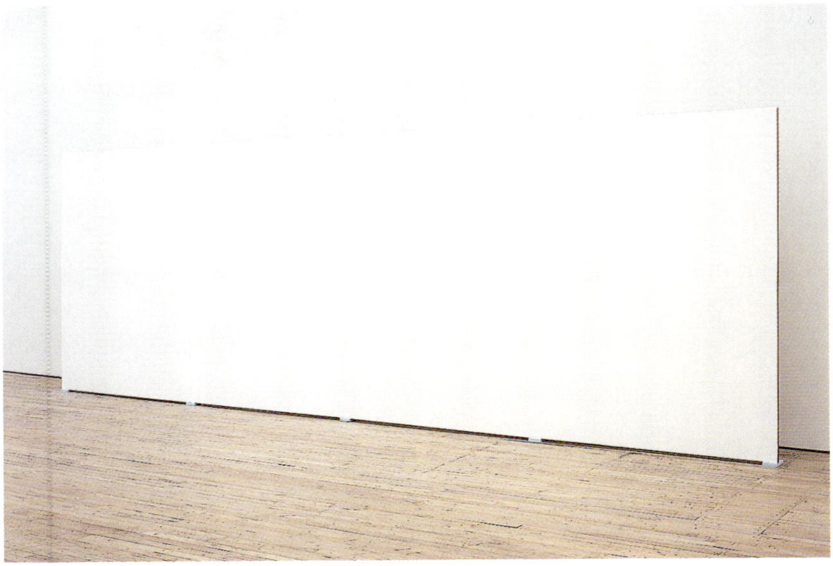

Robert Ryman, *Varese Wall* (1975). Vinyl acetate emulsion on six wood door panels, six metal rods, with five blue foam blocks.

of painting but that owing to gravity, paintings are stuck to the wall "so that they don't fall down." Offering another hypothetical scenario that suggests the turned Rembrandts, he imagined painting in outer space where the painting "would float around and you could see the front and the back and the edge of it and it would all make sense."[11]

When Ryman worked on *Factor, Pace,* and *Pair Navigation,* he painted two sides that are equally part of the "image" so that the image cannot be fully apprehended from a static position. *Factor,* for instance, has a matte, thinly brushed front and a shiny back of Swiss Lascaux acrylic varnish. It exploits the aspect of "seeing behind" the work that is present in *Varese Wall,* although on a double paint plane that extends some fifteen inches out from the wall, rendering the reverse visible. For *Pace,* too, Ryman utilized Lascaux acrylic, which he painted on fiberglass panels mounted on a redwood base with aluminum. This multilayer construction juts out from the wall horizontally as a counter would if it were supported by two narrow rods that extend down to meet the floor. At eye level, the unpainted wooden strip produces a line that is also the panel's edge, cleaving the painted surfaces above and below it to make more striking and irreconcilable their disparate visual effects. Where the glossy uppermost surface slickly reflects the cool, ambient light of the surrounding gallery, the underside of *Pace* is matte and absorptive.

Pair Navigation likewise induces perceptual play, but because it is less than a foot off the ground, it registers its competing vantages differently even as it presupposes the wall, floor, and light of the gallery as part of the work. It poses bright refraction against recession, which produces shadows that coagulate at *Pair Navigation*'s base. These pools are as much a part of the painting as the steel surface that hovers above. The steel in turn becomes a repository for the unattached fiberglass paint plane that rests lightly on it, in the process generating yet another dim silhouette on the steel. The painting is both the pigment-bearing surface and the appreciable shadows that its physical structure casts. Like *Pace, Pair Navigation* demands heightened engagement on the part of the viewer, who must crawl around the base of the work to inspect it at close range to see its subtle details. Akin to *Pace* in another respect, *Pair Navigation* has a narrow metallic edge between its "top" and "bottom" planes, dividing the fields above and below it.

The experience that these works instantiate reverses Krauss's terms for *Contingent,* as *Factor, Pace,* and *Pair Navigation* are in the "affective terrain" of sculpture, not painting. But they aspire to the category of painting, and they refer to the form of the easel painting. Ryman's production of paintings that torqued from their walls was the upshot of his questioning verticality as a condition of painting:

> I was just thinking how painting is always vertical, always against the wall. For good reason of course, because generally, they are pictures that need to be seen that way. I thought . . . since I'm not really making pictures, a work could possibly not be vertical. It could be just the opposite. I felt it was important that it be partly on the wall; the wall had to be in it. I thought I was a little crazy, but I thought "I'll try it; it'll be interesting, a challenge."[12]

Although the forms of *Pace* and *Pair Navigation* make horizontality a possibility for the painted field, the experiment was confined chiefly to these works. Notwithstanding the multiplaned *Accord* and *District* of 1985 and two works supported by elaborate mechanisms that propel edges off the wall, *Consort* and *Journal* of 1988, Ryman decided that he "didn't need to pursue the problem" further.[13] Ryman had examined the easel painting's logic in the 1950s. In compositions that lacked a fixed orientation, he broached issues of perception and modes of reading (see chapter 2).

But it was only with these later works that Ryman fully elaborated on their implications. If the painting was not representational (or even more accidentally illusionistic) it could be apprehended from any position, as could any object that plainly occupied space. Yet even if this analogy held, the painting remained a painting and not a sculpture or even an installation work because it made visible the spectatorial conditions that underlie the conventions of painting as pictorial (if not specifically representational) effects. Maybe most paintings

Robert Ryman, *District* (1985). Oil on aluminum panel with six hexagonal round-faced steel bolts.

are to be seen frontally, seeking a suspension of disbelief about the painting's objecthood in favor of its enclosed semblance (its image as a window onto a scene), but Ryman's decision to keep the edges in plain view invalidates optical recession into the picture plane. Ryman's paintings deflect attention from the surface alone, disprivileging it as just *one* side of the painting as object. Such an awareness, combined with a corollary desire to emphasize the materiality of his nonpictorial "image," prompted Ryman to designate his works as realist rather than representational or abstract because, as he put it, "the aesthetic is real"[14] and should be experienced as such.

A 1991 Dannheiser Foundation lecture in New York can be read as an epilogue to Ryman's critical predicament in the late 1960s and early 1970s. In it, he elaborated on what he meant by realism, a designation that he had arrived at some years before. As chapter 4 suggests, Ryman's elucidation of process had trumped all else traditionally. The Dannheiser lecture, "On Painting," thus represents one of the few instances where Ryman links materials and procedures to ideas of representation and where he looks at the why in addition to the how of his practice.

Ryman admitted his dissatisfaction with *abstraction* as a term and a practice because, like representational painting, abstraction necessarily cordons off the painted field from its greater environment. Abstract art is a form of containment; like representational art, it remains securely within its delimiting frame: "The frame is there for good reason," Ryman wagered in relation to representational art: "to focus the eye into the picture, because it is a picture, and to separate the illusion from the wall plane."[15] Even in the case of abstract painting, though, the same circumstances and interiorizing aesthetic obtain. In Ryman's account (which, it should be noted, is not wholly dissimilar from that of Clement Greenberg's in this instance), abstraction "kept the same devices that representation uses, such as the picture and symbolism. The story is still there, and often the frame is still isolating the illusion from the wall plane, and although in abstracting from things we know it opened up possibilities for painters, it is essentially very close to representational painting. The aesthetic there, again, is an inward aesthetic."[16]

By contrast, realism for Ryman implies an image without a picture, which is at once "outward" and concretely, physically "real."[17] Illusion is evacuated, even if painting in this vein retains elements "such as composition and color complexity, and surface and light, and line and so on."[18] This means, however, that when lines exist (or space exists or surface exists), the "lines are real, and the space is real, the surface is real and there is an interaction between the painting and the wall plane, unlike with abstraction and representation."[19] In representation or abstraction, lines are often graphic skeins or restrictive contours, but in Ryman's case they are the edges of painted fields or the brute boundaries of material objects, as with the emergent redwood stripe in *Pace* or the steel strip in *Pair Navigation:* "The edge was not a painted line, but the actual edge of the support would become another line."[20] And since these lines are really the edges where planes meet, they no more contain their painted fields than open onto what they adjoin. Painting that is realist in Ryman's sense is unbounded and exists in an unframed state. Porous and vulnerable in equal measure, Ryman's realist paintings regard light or gravity or the gallery as "literally a real element in the painting"[21] that acts on and through the painted surface and its support as an element of its composition.

It follows that light opens such a composition to its environment and activates a painting's internal syntax. Christel Sauer has written that "like no other painter before him, Ryman uses light itself as material and turns its subtle scale of refraction into form."[22] As Ryman puts it regarding light as well as the gallery context more broadly: "When you see the wall, the setting, the environment, it has a lot to do with the way they work. A lot of my paintings (I wouldn't say most, a lot) cannot really be shown to anyone in the usual way of dragging a painting out of the closet or the storeroom and saying, here's a painting. My paintings wouldn't work that way." He continues: "You can't drag a Flavin, for instance, out of the closet and say, here's a Flavin. All you would see is a couple of tubes. It has to be on the wall, in a situation. Then, it's complete. So the wall becomes very much a part of the work. But, I'm kind of tired of this wall business; I don't mean it that way. It's complete without the wall; but, it's not really."[23] In so making interaction and the experience that it generates the hallmark of his realism as well as its chief effect, Ryman underscores the context, both physical and institutional, in which his paintings are made visible—in which they become paintings at all.

Beginning with the steel-backed *Standards* in 1967, Ryman experimented with nontraditional supports to move the image as close to the wall as possible. From this decision others followed, their common characteristic being that the wall plane became instrumental to the forms that the paintings assumed. These newer works related to what Ryman had done years before in his exploration of the possibilities of the unstretched support and in his works on tracing paper from the late 1950s. An example such as 1959's *Untitled* reminds us of Ryman's longstanding commitment to varying supports—in this case, a translucent paper that acts both as the painting's ground and as a layered collage element sutured to it. In the work's small-square organization, different marks hover, sometimes tentatively (with light graphic marks carving out boxes and ginger arcs) and sometimes insistently (with black shading, parallel lines, and horizontal white paint bands). In all instances, marks stand out in pointed relief against the unassuming layers of paper (several of which are deposited in the lower right corner to twice record Ryman's signature) that are confined by a visual border and then, a couple inches away, by an actual frame.

Works like *Adelphi* (1967) were something new in their annexation of the wall plane as a compositional device that was not separated from the painted field by a frame. Or, more precisely, that it would not separate the painted field from its environment with a frame acting as a solid barrier between the space of the "inward aesthetic" and the space within which it existed. In *Adelphi,* Ryman employed a frame (or the vestiges thereof), only to empty it visually. A hazy expanse of oil on unstretched canvas painted with a twelve-inch brush in pendulumlike, swinging, multidirectional strokes is stapled directly to the wall, nestled within a waxed-paper border that crosses and overlaps at the corners and is crudely taped to the wall. (This tape now is often reinforced by a layer of glue to prevent it from detaching from the wall, but the glue, when used, is not visible and does not alter the visual terms of the painting.) The waxed paper is

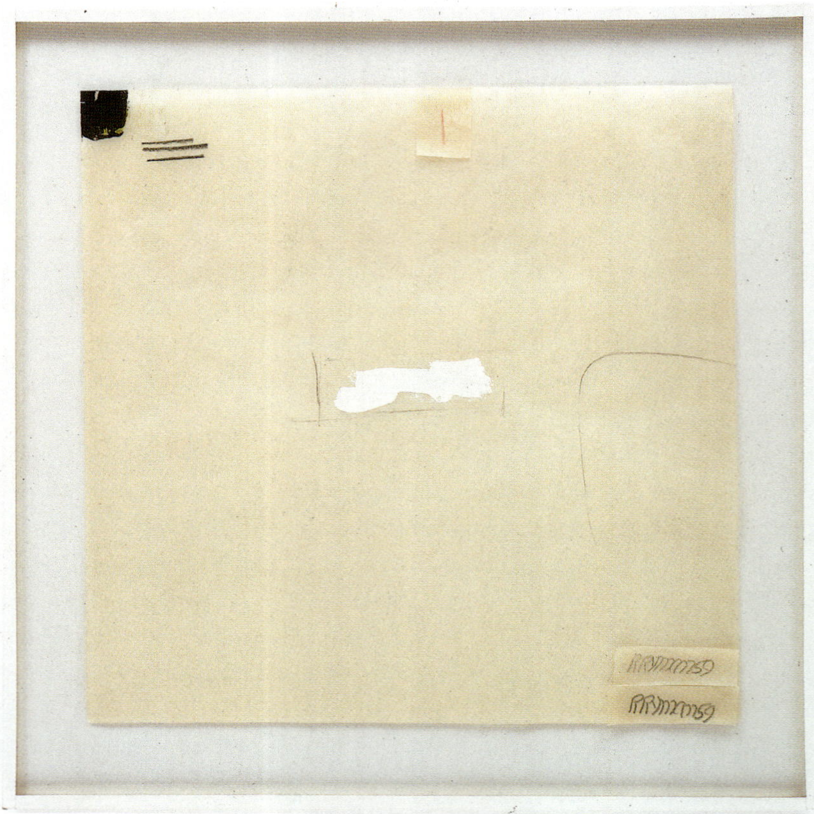

Robert Ryman, *Untitled* (1959). Graphite, colored pencil, and casein on collaged tracing paper.

Robert Ryman, *Adelphi* (1967). Oil on unstretched linen canvas, installed with staples, waxed paper, masking tape, canvas.

fragile and is site-specific insofar as it needs to be refashioned with each installation.[24] The waxed paper's translucent surface allows visitors to have a direct view of the wall that is amplified by the paper's slight reflective sheen, and it appropriates the wall into the image as part of the painting like the oil paint, linen canvas, or light that provides the painting with its proper illumination.

After *Adelphi,* Ryman used waxed paper and glassine frames in the series called the *Surface Veils.* He also worked with other panels that bore traces of tape and evinced subtractive marks where tape had been fastened and upbraided, highlighting passages from wall to alternate ground and back again. Ryman was incorporating the wall as a support and an "image." If there existed a medium that still separated the paint from the wall, the interference was made exceedingly thin or even transparent as it incorporated the wall back into the work. As a culmination of this formal and conceptual sequence wherein paint moved ever closer to the wall and extended well beyond the physical circumscription of the support, Ryman finally painted directly on the wall. Marking it as though it were another support, Ryman renders the wall imagistic.

Ryman painted directly on the wall a number of times: *Untitled, A. M. Sachs Gallery, New York, wall installation* (1967); *Untitled, Ace Gallery, Brentwood, California, wall installation* (1969); *Untitled, Jewish Museum, New York, wall installation* (1970); *Untitled, Lisson Gallery, London, wall installation* (1972); and *Untitled, John Weber Gallery, New York, wall installation* (1973). He also painted on sheets of watercolor paper at the 1976 Venice Biennale and at P.S. 1 that same year (as discussed below). Although neither the first nor last such intervention, Ryman's contribution to the Jewish Museum's Using Walls exhibition in 1970 is representative.

Untitled (1970) existed only for the duration of the Using Walls exhibition. This ephemeral project was likely encouraged by the premise of the show as well as by the logic of Ryman's practice at that time. Curator Susan Tumarkin Goodman's catalogue introduction states that the use of the wall by artists extends "as far back as cave painting of the Paleolithic period, through Egyptian tomb painting and Pompeiian wall painting, to the great mural frescoes of Giotto and Mantegna, and later apse and ceiling decorations" but that the wall "was most often viewed as an architectural support to be painted away, or a

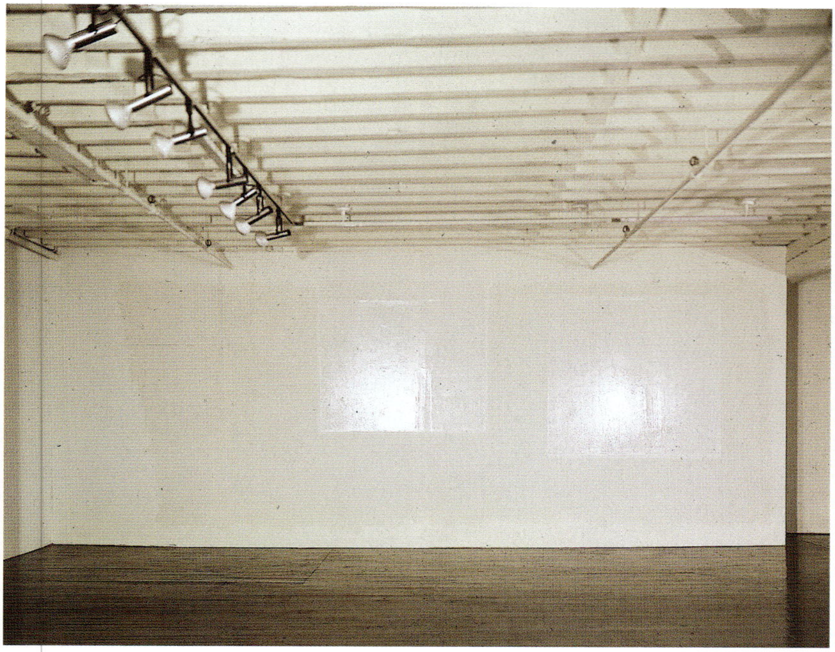

Robert Ryman, *Untitled, John Weber Gallery, New York, wall installation* (1973). Gloss enamel, Gripz, acrylic polymer, on wall.

surface to which decorative elements were added that served only to articulate the wall." By contrast, the wall in this exhibit's context "is no longer a surface simply to be covered with paint, or upon which to hang an object. Rather, it has become one of the elements in a work of art—indeed is an integral part of the work, itself."[25]

Ryman's published statement in the same catalogue addresses this transition that coopts the materiality of the wall but preserves the primacy of paint handling:

> The paintings consist of a square tape frame on the wall which determines the area of the paint. The intensity of the paintings and the wall can be controlled by the consistency of the paint. (They could all be of equal intensity, or of different intensity and that is decided at the time of installation).
>
> The paintings will be approximately 30 inches square but will not visually seem square as the paint will go off the 30 inch space onto the tape frame. The scale of the paintings and the number of paintings and the distance between each is determined by the overall space of the gallery wall. All measurements are done by eye.
>
> The wall of the gallery is, of course, the surface of the paintings and the wall is visually pulled into the paintings. While the concept is important, the work has to do primarily with visual response.[26]

That Ryman downplayed the "concept" hardly surprises. Nonetheless, it allowed him to achieve a visual response by using the same materials as before but now with an eye to their aesthetics and their function. The tape could be a compositional ingredient, not merely a functional way to fasten a work to a wall. (But it still was that. Hesse, for one, "got Ryman to show her how to frame her drawings cheaply with glass and tape.")[27] Tape, not unlike the red selvage thread of 1962's unstretched *Untitled,* proved to be a telltale procedural remnant, a kind of palimpsest, and a meditated aesthetic decision, whether present or removed, on paper or linen, as *Exeter* (1968) and *Untitled* (c. 1970) demonstrate.

Robert Ryman, *Exeter* (1968). Oil on unstretched linen canvas, installed with staples, masking tape, canvas.

Robert Ryman, *Untitled* (c. 1970). Acrylic on unstretched sized linen canvas.

When Ryman returned to working on paper after *Adelphi,* he manipulated tape and emphasized paper as a material through his registration of the brands on which the new pieces were actuated. "Classico," "Lugano," "Medway," "J. Green," and "A. Millbourn" (the handmade papers that he used) gave the works their titles, which are often reiterated in watermarks. One unique project from 1968, *The Watermark Series,* comprises five panels of light gray textured paper by Pietro Miliani Fabriano, each with a prominent central watermark of Raphael's *Madonna della Seggiola* (1513–1514) that is visible when the sheet is illuminated from behind. Around each watermark, Ryman drew a square that outlines or intersects the image. He likely developed this last composition in tandem with the much larger *Impex* (1968), an unstretched painted panel that is stapled to the wall. A blue chalk line extends from the linen diagonally up the wall from the upper right corner to the ceiling above the left edge in an angle governed by the ceiling height and at a fixed relation to it (fourteen inches to the left of the canvas is the farthest the line may go), which means that each time the work is installed, there is both a fixed rule and variability.

In other, more typical multipart works of 1968 (such as *Classico 5, Lugano,* and *Medway),* Ryman realized that paper, like the appreciably heavier if equally thin steel or the diffusely lucent waxed paper, could hug the wall so closely as to become almost inextricable from it. In these works, Ryman also differentiated the paintings from the walls to mark out differences between the image and its support or the painting and its architectural setting. Mounted nearly flush to the wall plane, *Classico 5, Lugano,* and *Medway* betray their differences from it in the slight cracks of space between individual sheets that allow glimpses of the walls to peek through the adjacent but just barely nonabutting sheets.

Ryman used acrylic paint to create the *Classico* series (six paintings), *Lugano,* and *Medway.* He painted the paper as it was taped directly to the wall, taking the pieces apart after completion and mounting the sheets on Featherboard (or foamcore or the like). The works then were glued back onto the wall in their previous phalanx. This process can be deduced from the splatters that have seeped onto the lower register of the painting, drips from above that made their way down the vertical support. The same thing can be seen clearly

Robert Ryman, *Medway* (c. 1968). Acrylic polymer on six sheets of overlapping handmade Medway wove mounted on foamcore panels.

Rcbert Ryman, *Impex* (1968). Oil paint on unstretched linen canvas and blue chalk line on wall.

in *Classico 4* (1968), where the contrast between the acrylic and the paper is even more pronounced than it was in *Classico, Lugano,* and *Medway,* meaning that the errant white pigment appears in starker relief against the comparatively creamier support. When these works needed to be moved, Ryman could simply "reach back with a spatula and just knock them off the wall."[28] Pulled from the paper as cleanly as possible, the tape still scarred the paper beneath it and left unevenly pulled patches in its wake. Having left a residue from the initial application, the tape's absence is thereafter a compositional device, as are the edges of the individual sheets that produce Ryman's "realist" lines. So-called realist lines propose a model of material truth as embeddedness. In their insistence on facticity, such lines and this notion of material truth more broadly amplify Ryman's pragmatic intuitions.

In *Classico 5,* these marks are highly visible and produce a pattern of barren squares within the larger grid on which spans an acrylic square in a brighter painted white. Each individual sheet contains part of the whole, and the twelve assembled fragments coalesce into a singular overarching image. Where the tape affixed the corners of the separate pieces of paper to the wall, notches that register the tape's crude removal pierce the painted areas in a syncopated pattern that adds to the work's visual complexity, appearing as sheltered forms within the overall lattice. Given their compositional prominence, they imply that these disparate panels are not unconnected, but, taken together are the painting as such.

This realization led Ryman to the *Surface Veils,* a series of about twenty-eight related works made between 1970 and 1972. Four large paintings are on traditional linen or cotton canvas, four thirty-nine-inch paintings are on a thin fiberglass called "Surface Veil" (hence the name of the series, derived from the brand of fiberglass used commercially to cover skylights), and still others incorporate waxed paper. Proceeding from the intuition that these different support structures were equivalently "realist" (in that they both incorporated a wall as part of a work that was no longer confined to the painted plane alone), Ryman decided that they could be integrated into a constellated grouping that was secured by a uniform title. The smaller *Surface Veils* are related but not sequential, whereas the twelve-foot canvases are numbered *Surface Veils I, II, III,* and *IV* as a series and are all the same size. The first two are on linen, and the second two are on cotton.[29]

Untitled, Surface Veil 22″ × 19″ (ca. 1970–1971) divulges its connection to *Adelphi* through its similar method of adhesion to the wall. It is altered with each installation, as the waxed-paper frame and the tape that imprints it on the wall need to be redone with each mounting. Unlike the waxed-paper frame in *Adelphi,* the same material when used in the *Surface Veils* assumes an additional utility by preventing the paint from seeping onto the wall. As Robert Storr writes: "Many of the small *Surface Veils* have taped waxed-paper underpinnings to prevent the paint from soaking through the mesh and sticking to the wall. To that extent they resemble *Adelphi* with its waxed-paper margins. But in the small *Surface Veils,* the waxed paper is less a framing device around the painting than a pictorial ground."[30] This difference is an important one, although Ryman still felt the waxed paper constituted an aesthetic—if not chiefly framing—device, and he insisted on its integration of the painting onto and into the wall plane.

When Ryman found out that a *Surface Veil* had come onto the market many years after it had been sold to a collector in Minnesota, he offered to buy it back. The collector had entombed the painting within a plexiglass box that Ryman promptly removed once it was back in his possession. He wanted the work to revert to its deliberate form "so it could work with the wall plane as originally intended."[31] By removing the plexiglass encasement, Ryman restored the integrity of the painting and its connection to the space around it, a maneuver that survived in the canvas *Surface Veil* works as well.

The four large *Surface Veils* are looming, physically imposing paintings that are hauntingly light in their effect. At twelve-foot square, they are some of Ryman's largest canvases, and they were so large that Ryman had to paint them flat and unstretched because his studio was not tall enough for them to be assembled. So he lined the works' perimeters with a fine blue chalk to demarcate their edges and provide guidelines for stretching the paintings once they had been completed. These blue lines survive as yet another material instantiation as aesthetic resolution and are related to a number of drawings like *Blue Line*

Robert Ryman, *Untitled, Surface Veil 12 1/16″ × 12 1/8″* (1970). Oil on fiberglass panel.

Robert Ryman, *Blue Line Drawing #5* (1969). Conté on thin matte Mylar panel.

Drawing #5 (1969), which was done at the same time. Ryman left these blue marks visible on the frontal plane of the *Surface Veils* rather than securing them on the sides or even the backs, and he also conspicuously left a margin of space between these blue marks and the edge of the raw canvas. Ryman recalls that "they were painted unstretched, and to mark my space, I used blue chalk. There is a blue line that runs down the edges that is partially painted over. . . it's not distinct. It's a kind of nebulous line, which I knew would be there—I didn't mind the blue on the edge. But it was also used to mark the edge of the canvas, for when it was stretched."[32]

Indeed, these nebulous lines are present and shown off to varying degrees within this series. For instance, in *Surface Veil I* (1970), a pigment membrane coats the surface up to the rim of the linen's front surface plane, where it bleeds into the faintest streak of blue that is, in turn, buried amid the oil and excavated beyond it. As a would-be limit of the painted activity, it both succeeds and fails, activating more than circumscribing what it might sequester were it not a "realist" element that divulges process and opens the paint to the edge of the composition and, in short order, to the wall. Attention is further drawn to the edges by the frenetic optical path contained within the painted area. The upper register and the left side of the composition are marked by vertical strokes that change direction and coagulate into a denser geometric patch at the lower right corner. This lower right section reverses the activity of the hatched strokes at its outskirts and pulls the eye back down and off the canvas edge.

Surface Veil II (c. 1970) is even more emphatic in its disjunction of these differently painted sections. Relying on the same composition—a configuration that all the larger *Surface Veils* share to a certain extent—Ryman here made the break in the work's surface more explicit. The dimensions of the break relate to his working practice and the reach of his arm across the massive support. Similarly, *Surface Veil II* has a notable interruption in facture midway up the left edge, where its suspended and broken-off vertical strokes denote temporal (and hence spatial) ruptures in the painting of the work. *Surface Veil III* (1971) presses this procedural-cum-compositional device yet again as it has a fractured

Robert Ryman, *Surface Veil II* (c. 1970). Oil and blue chalk on stretched linen canvas.

surface, a fissure two-thirds of the way up the cotton canvas that reveals the unpainted support as a material line dividing distinct periods of activity.

"Realist" lines also appear in the smaller panels—*Surface Veil* (1970), a square of oil on fiberglass on Featherboard, and *Surface Veil 4* (1970), a square of oil on fiberglass on Featherboard. In *Surface Veil,* the surface is heavily worked with raking impastolike smears of paint that trail down in large swaths, serpentine curves, and short choppy segments. Paint juts out, condenses into orbs, and just below the painting's midline is pulled across the surface in a thick, blocky rail, again showing diachronic sequences of action. The line's concreteness and mass are juxtaposed with a comparatively empty passage to its left, a relatively blank point in the composition that exerts a magnetic push, repelling the top and bottom edges on either side of it. What is above and below this aperture bristles with movement but never meets, hovering just to the exposed ground without overstepping it.

In *Surface Veil 4,* Ryman revisited this idea of the spatial cavity less as a fissure than as a passed-over seam. Again the result of different stages of work, this joint is different from those in the larger *Surface Veils,* where such marks additionally registered the impossible reach of Ryman's brush across the huge support. Since the ground in *Surface Veil 4* is more uniform than that in *Surface Veil,* the space where the paint is not filled in becomes simply empty. It does not redirect the strokes or alter their nature, but it does call attention to the fact that the painting stops there, tapering off to the left edge or breaking in a hairline crack from the outside in. It pressures the edge and inversely makes it central. Even more obviously perhaps, the corners do this, too. They are notched with irregular square indentations that carve out space from the painted zone and are reminders of the ubiquitous tape pits in *Classico 5, Lugano,* and *Medway* or the tape frame anchoring *Exeter.*

Although these incisions suggest a passage from painting to wall, they now stand in for it. Instead of referencing their material origins, as in the case of the pulled if spectrally present tape, these marks are painted, not scraped. They function as enacted composition instead of composition as residual material consequence. In Ryman's developing grammar, they nevertheless came to refer to the real (or realist) opening of work onto space.

In 1976, Ryman began to use various fasteners to secure works to the wall. By making visible his paintings' method of hanging and by moving that armature to the front of the support, Ryman proposed a new form of transparency that made radically plain the fact that paintings rely on walls and are understood as paintings through this interchange. Moving from masking tape to oxide fasteners or steel bolts made this interdependence more direct. It also made it more stable than, for example, the use of tape, since these physically inextricable fasteners would survive innumerable installations.

An additional, cannier benefit of the protruding fasteners was that they disenfranchise particular kinds of installation practices, warding off restriction within plexiglass boxes or beneath glass. These works come preframed as it were, and they make other frames impracticably cumbersome and nearly impossible to envisage. Because they lie on or project from the pictorial surface to which they are fixed, the fasteners are likewise compositional elements that often provide a shock of color to an otherwise "white" painting. In a sort of hardware fetishism, fasteners range from black-oxide steel plates to cadmium bolts, and these bits and pieces—whether nudged into and onto the painting or withdrawn to its physical edges—manage the gap between painting and environment and redraw this spatial transition as a compositional effect.

Embassy I (1976) is one of Ryman's first instances of visible fasteners, notwithstanding *Untitled* (c. 1961) (discussed in chapter 2). Onto *Embassy I*'s oil and Elvacite on plexiglass ground, Ryman secured four black-oxide fasteners and four-sided bolts—two of each on the top and two of each on the bottom—that held the work to the wall. Ryman was pleased that the support didn't shatter when he drilled holes in the plastic ground for the application of the hardware, and this small practical success led to numerous works with fasteners. Works like *Embassy I* were successively alternated with (or often produced alongside) paintings with hidden components, some of which project the work off the wall quite obviously, as would later be true of *Pace* or *Pair Navigation*. Others are more restrained in their manipulation of this mechanism so that the hidden braces that buoy the work off the wall remain unseen, like in *Monitor* (1978), a painting that accentuates its connection to the wall by floating off of it. About *Monitor,* Ryman noted:

> In this work, I used metal fasteners to make the painting project from the wall. All my canvases at that time extended off the wall a few inches. It seemed to make them actually closer to the wall, curiously . . . because you saw it attached, and you saw it coming off the wall, but it was also very much part of the wall. It was important that it had an immediate relationship with the wall plane, because this was not a picture of anything. So I wanted it to really look like it and the wall were together. They had to be together for it to be complete. And so you would see it attached. And when it came away from the wall—it looked more as if it were a thing of its own, with the wall.[33]

While this connection to the wall was, as Ryman describes, emphasized in *Monitor,* other works like *Alliance* and *Arrow* relied on the visible fasteners to produce a like result of a "thing of its own, with the wall."

Concord (1976), *Summit* (1978), *Anchor* (1980), *Academy* (1982) and *Context* (1989) employ oil on linen that is fixed firmly to the wall plane with steel fasteners, while *Phoenix* (1979) and *Archive* (1980) render pigment on steel grounds set with steel fasteners. Still others—like *Crown* (1982), *Access* (1983), and *Range* (1983)—work on fiberglass supports that bleed off onto the wall in various ways as Ryman's fasteners became increasingly complex over time. This litany is merely a representative sample, as Ryman produced scores of like works from the 1970s to the present, suggesting this format's continued relevance. In all these works, Ryman made the painting and the wall inextricable. Commensurate with this attention to environmental materiality was an acknowledgment of the fundamental question that such a ploy raises—namely, where does a work begin and end, whether spatially, perceptually, or conceptually?

Robert Ryman, *Monitor* (1978). Oil on stretched cotton canvas with metal fasteners and four bolts, canvas.

Robert Ryman, *Alliance* (1976). Acrylic polymer on blue Acrylivin panel, with four sanded plexiglass fasteners, cadmium-plated steel pentagonal bolts.

Robert Ryman, *Arrow* (1976). Oil on sanded plexiglass panel, four sanded plexiglass fasteners and hexagonal cadmium plated steel bolts.

Robert Ryman, *Phoenix* (detail) (1979). Panel 1: 13⅞₁₆ × 13⅞₁₆ in. Varathane on eight steel panels, each with four fasteners and bolts.

With these works came Ryman's sense of his paintings as "realist" objects that should be taken in from all sides. This approach became so essential to the experience of Ryman's paintings that a 1990 catalogue of new paintings photographed all works on a slanting angle under strong light to set off their surfaces, emphasize their edges, and show their depth of projection from the wall, regardless of whether fasteners were used.[34] The fasteners became their own code, a way to read not only these works but Ryman's other paintings with supplemental texts that were external to their objects. As Ryman's fasteners suggest their own protocols for proper installation and refuse containment in extraneous secondary frames, the paintings with fasteners and later even those without them propose a method of engagement apart from written accompaniments.

Writing in 1977, Krauss described as apposite to 1970s art a converse phenomenon of mute artworks that required textual accompaniments. She found in a morphologically dissimilar range of mediums and practices a structural similarity based on the index, which, as Charles Peirce first formulated it, is a sign that "refers to the Object that it denotes merely by virtue of characters of its own, and which it possesses, just the same, whether any such Object actually exists or not."[35] Krauss contended that much new art was beholden to the indexical organization of photography (this art was indexical rather than iconic because it only secondarily resembles its object or resembles it because of its direct physical connection to it), which was increasingly becoming the "operative model for abstraction."[36] Through this appropriation, the works at issue admitted an insufficiency. Presence was not enough to secure meaning, thus obliging a caption—a flood of words or narratives—to correct for what Roland Barthes calls a "message without a code."[37] In relation to abstract painting, Krauss pointedly maintained that it bowed to "the implied necessity to add a surfeit of written information to the depleted power of the painted sign."[38]

To make this claim, Krauss took as her example many incongruent works on view at one site at one time—the inaugural, principally installation-based show that was curated by Alanna Heiss at P.S. 1 in 1976 and was simply titled Rooms. Even as this 1976 exhibition provided the focus of her seminal thesis, Krauss's 1977 structural reckoning became historical. She sought to locate this art in relation to prior instances of the index in abstract expressionism.[39] In a

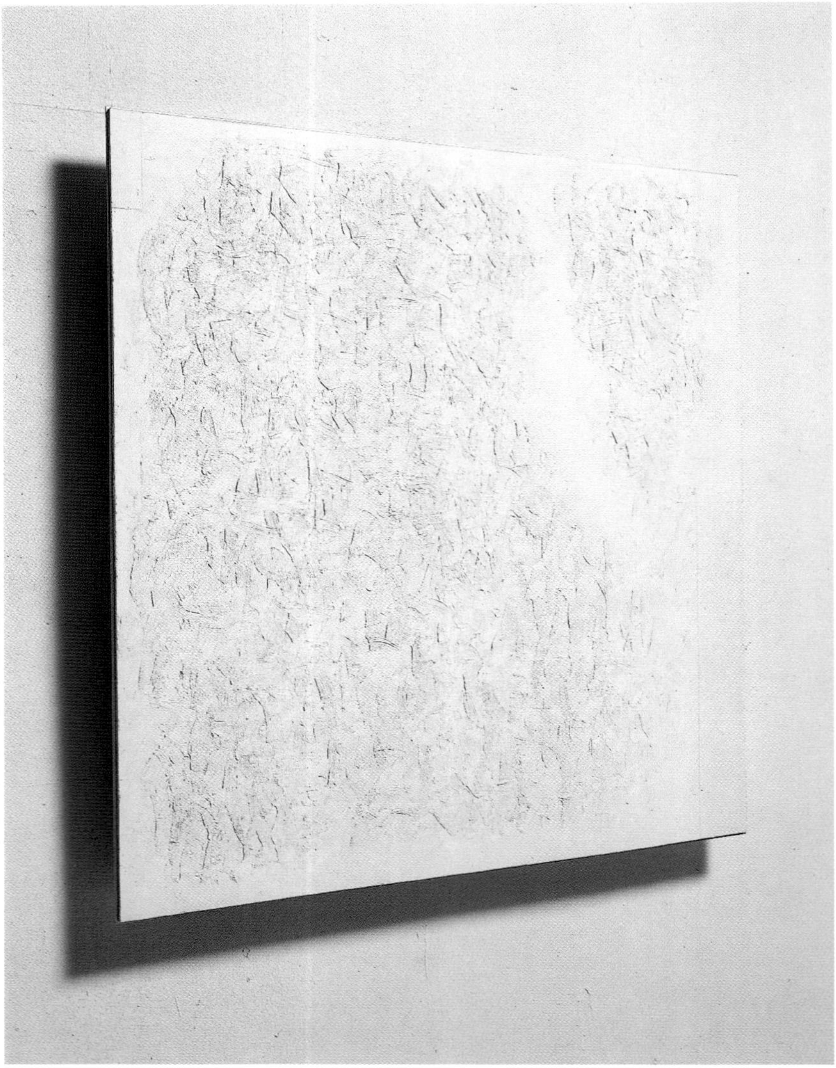

Robert Ryman, *Roll* (1989). Oil and graphite on gatorboard panel with aluminum frame mount.

footnote, Krauss returned to a kind of interpretive genealogy that was otherwise absent from this synchronically oriented piece:

> The pressure to use indexical signs as a means of establishing presence begins in Abstract-Expressionism with deposits of paint expressed as imprints and traces. During the 1960s, this concern was continued although changed in its import in, for example, the work of Jasper Johns and Robert Ryman. This development forms a historical background for the phenomenon I am describing as belonging to 1970s art. However, it must be understood that there is a decisive break between earlier attitudes towards the index and those at present, a break that has to do with the role played by the photographic, rather than the pictorial, as a model.[40]

The passage's final distinction between the pictorial and the photographic is the hinge on which much of Krauss's thinking here relies, and it provides a language of difference—of chronology as well as incipient causality—that distinguishes the art of the 1970s, as exemplified by the Rooms exhibit, from what came even a decade before.

In the case of Ryman, though, such a note is misleading. In short, his work relies on neither the pictorial (which implies a mooring in abstraction, according to the terms of his 1991 lecture) nor the photographic (which implies a foundation in conceptualism and by extension a technical deskilling that is anathema to his process).[41] Krauss rightly perceived that Ryman's work did not fit into her account except as an "earlier" qualitatively and ideologically separate precedent. Hence, the work that Ryman had on view at P.S. 1 remained outside of Krauss's purview to such an extent that it is unclear from Krauss's essay that Ryman was even in the Rooms show at all. He contributed a painting in two sheets—twin squares of matte white acrylic on watercolor paper, one positioned slightly higher than the other on a brown and green wall.[42] (Worth noting, too, is that Ryman was invited to inaugurate P.S. 1's formal exhibition wing shortly thereafter with a "remarkable display" of seventeen recent works, Robert Ryman: Paintings 1976.)[43]

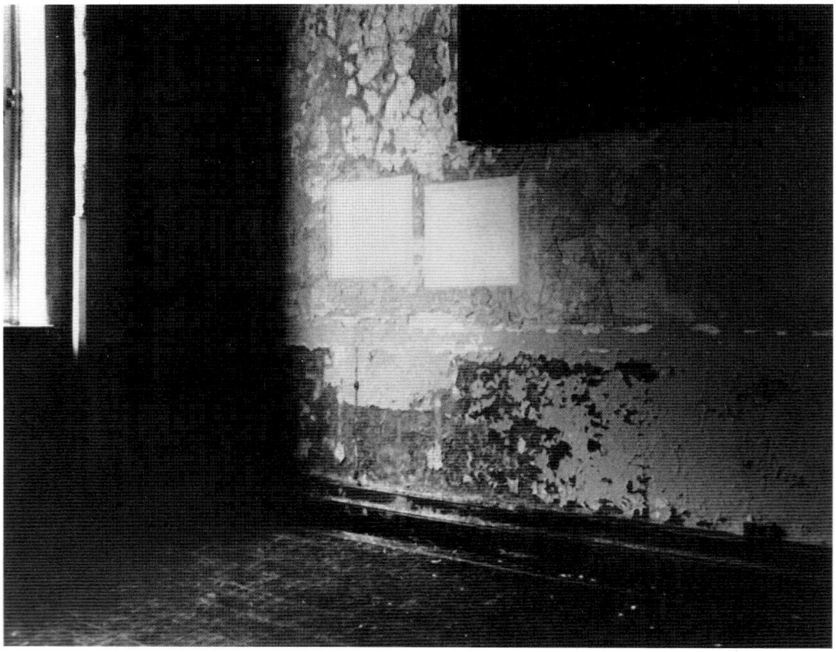

Robert Ryman, *Untitled, P.S. 1, Long Island City, New York, wall installation* (1976). Acrylic polymer on two sheets of watercolor paper.

At issue in all of this is Ryman's contrary and antigenerational belief (as Krauss would have it) in the nondepleted power of the painted sign. His sheets pasted to the wall at P.S. 1 still counted for him as a painting without requiring further description or elaboration. They were as real as the walls on which they hung. In counterpoint to other work that, as Krauss contends, reduced the "conventional sign to a trace" that requires a "supplemental discourse,"[44] Ryman's paintings here and elsewhere transform and enfold the conventions of painting in a way that constitutes the effects that generate "painting" out of this material. Where other works in Rooms reflected the world itself as the "connective tissue binding the objects contained by the photograph . . . rather than that of a cultural system"[45] (such as painting that imposes its own internal rules on the matter at its disposal), Ryman's painting upholds a logic that answers itself in paint.

Contrary to Krauss's example of Lucio Pozzi, whose painted panel works *P.S. 1 Paint* (1976) are "strictly accountable to the wall within which they are visually embedded and whose features they replicate,"[46] Ryman's paintings are related to the wall insofar as they rely on it and call attention to this fact. They are not cropped, reduced, and hence quasi-photographically indexical impressions of it. Whereas Pozzi's panels redoubled, continued, and extrapolated their wall planes so that if the wall diagonally changed colors, the panel followed suit, Ryman's panels hovered against the derelict wall of layered, chipped paint as wholly distinct units. Rather than effacing or estranging the wall beneath the work hanging on it, Ryman's individuating works announced its presence. This affirmation is coextensive with Ryman's realism, such that he is less interested in displacement or associational contiguity than in primary visibility—that is, the object rather than its trace. Since the object is all there (if not there all at once, as would be the case in Clement Greenberg or Michael Fried's bounded modernist painting), there is no need to look outside it for something to decode it or to supplement it as Krauss suggests was the case for Pozzi and the others at P.S. 1.

For Ryman, it comes down to experience that has been—or that can be—garnered contextually. The painted sign, the support on which it is put down, the edge that rims it and connects it to the wall, and the wall that finally completes the circuit all form the empirical relay that justifies the painting's existence and generates its effects. To look carefully at the work is to read the work, and this experience, Ryman suggests, is enough. When asked about the best mode of engagement with his painting, Ryman mildly recommends that, above all, "people should just look."[47] This is why he abhors wall texts, feeling that they do not encourage understanding but restrict it or, in their most dire manifestations, supersede it altogether.

Ryman's massive 1993 Museum of Modern Art / Tate Gallery retrospective (which also traveled to Madrid, San Francisco, and Minneapolis) was displayed without the interdiction of wall text, a decision that was pioneered in the early 1980s in the permanent installation at InK (Halle für internationale neue Kunst, Zurich) and the Hallen für neue Kunst at Schaffhausen, Switzerland, and recapitulated in Ryman's 2003 Dia: Beacon installation. At the Tate, though, the lack of wall-bound didactic materials was so striking that the *London Times* mentioned it: "No captions are permitted to disturb the impeccable white walls in Robert Ryman's Tate retrospective. All the picture titles are confined to a simple list near the door of each room. The implication to visitors is clear: concentrate on the paintings. Such a purist priority hardly comes as a surprise."[48]

Although the lack of wall text might not have come as a surprise to the reviewer, the Tate played it safe in its handout, which consisted of a list of exhibited works, a biography, and an inventory of materials. Simon Wilson, the Tate's curator of education, channeled Leo Steinberg's essay "Contemporary Art and the Plight of Its Public"[49] when he captured "Ryman's Vision" for his assumedly lay audience: "The history of Western art since the Renaissance is precisely the history of those artists who have expanded our way of seeing, but their work has, for that reason, sometimes baffled or alienated contemporary audiences, especially when taken 'to the furthest limits.'"[50] After a snappy blurb, the *Sun* quoted Wilson explaining, "Modern art is like a football match. If you don't understand the rules, you won't enjoy it."[51]

In the place of wall texts at the Museum of Modern Art, there was a brochure like the Tate's that incorporated a floor plan with a checklist, quotations

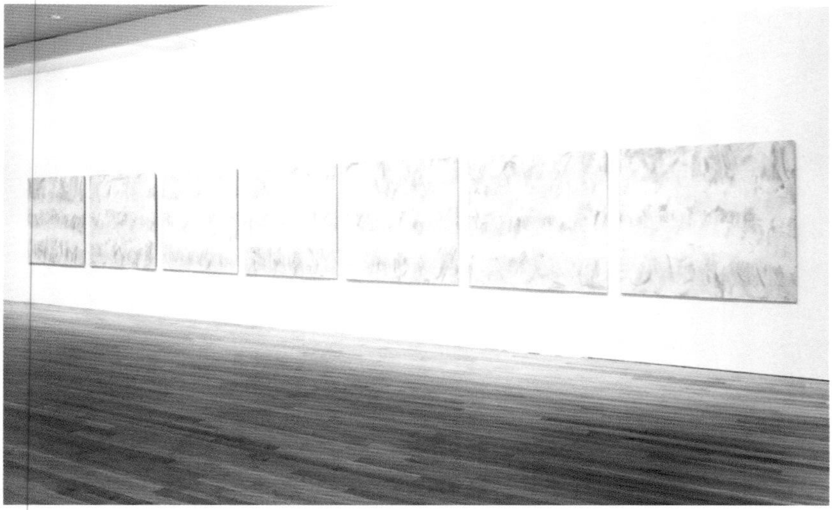

Robert Ryman, Installation view of the exhibition, Robert Ryman (1993–1994), The Museum of Modern Art, New York. Robert Ryman, *VII* (1969). Enamelac on seven corrugated paper panels mounted on aluminum.

from the artist that were culled from interviews, and a text by Robert Storr, the show's curator. In his text, Storr emphasized Ryman's realism, beginning by writing that "when we look at paintings, we are generally looking *for* something *in* painting, something that paint describes, or suggests, or evokes. It may be an image, a symbol, or an idea. Frequently it involves a synthesis of all three. Even in its most abstract form, therefore, painting has usually been *about* something outside or beyond itself. . . . For the past forty years, Robert Ryman has approached painting from the opposite direction."[52] Storr emphasized Ryman's realism and the act of looking that was encouraged by Ryman's objective to "paint the paint" in all its material immediacy. He encouraged people to pay close attention. He also emphasized Ryman's connection to MoMA, persuading viewers to visit the permanent collection galleries to see the works that Ryman had observed as a guard.

Storr thus acknowledged the retrospective's status as an institutional appropriation. Ryman's work is acclaimed, and so is the institution itself for producing an artist who showed that painting, and by extension the Museum's position as that painting's proper receptacle, was secure. Storr writes: "Thus, while a retrospective normally looks back to summarize an artist's career, this one looks back in order to look forward and to show how, even at its most reductive, painting itself continues."[53] In a comment that Storr must have relished, Arthur Danto gushed that the Ryman retrospective "is a treat even for those who think the art world has moved beyond painting."[54]

Reviewing the retrospective, Roberta Smith noted its unusual format and the simple act of looking that it augured: "Contrary to the usual display methods at major museums, there's not a single label or text panel in sight, a condition that even the most seasoned art viewer may find a bit disorienting. It's akin to being tossed into the deep end without one's water wings. The only typeface visible will be found in the hands of those visitors who pick up a checklist and exhibition map at the beginning of the show."[55] The institutional sanctioning of Ryman's brand of realism seemed to render commentary analogously outside the frame. By the end of her piece, Smith concluded that discursive restraint worked, with the paintings primary but neither involuted nor as opposed to (or even outside of) language as Ryman would suggest:

> What is finally so uplifting about this exhibition is how much other, often earlier painting, and even how much nature, seeps unexpectedly into these almost hermetically sealed galleries. Mr. Ryman's art reminds us that it is paint, scale and color that we look at first and last in all painting, but that at its best, painting also leads us inexorably outward toward the world.[56]

During his 1993 retrospective, Ryman talked with David Carrier about his practice and the ways in which he felt that it had developed over the years. His impetus to conduct the interview, as Carrier succinctly put it, was the fact that "most published accounts of his work show a strange disregard for his own sense of his development."[57] In the interview that transpired, Ryman discussed what had been omitted up to this point:

> In books and magazines, people see reproductions, and they see photographs of paintings. And they read what people have said about different paintings. Their perception is geared by that. They might have preconceptions about what they are to see or what they might expect, without ever having seen a painting.
>
> I think most paintings are discussed or described by the story or the symbolic meaning that they convey outside the painting itself. That's the most popular means of experiencing a painting, by the "what" of the painting, as I like to call it; the image, the story, the symbolism. And the history of that story is talked about; what the story was, and what it might refer to, and how it came about, why the artist painted this particular image. But very little is said about the "how" of the painting, I mean what I call the real part of the painting, which is the "how" of the painting. . . .
>
> I don't want to criticize, but I think a lot of writers have an idea or something they want to write about, and work it in with an article on an artist's work. It can work that way sometimes. I know of a writer who wrote something on my painting without ever seeing a painting. He had seen photographs. He had something

> he wanted to say, and he was getting information from the photographs, and from what he had heard.
>
> Painting is a visual experience. People can write about historical or philosophical points they want to get across using certain examples of painting, maybe work that they think might be similar. They could make a point in so doing, but it usually has very little to do with the painting itself. I do something with the paint, but I'm not painting a picture of anything. I'm not manipulating the paint into an illusion of something other than what the paint does. I make a painting.
>
> Painting will go on. Painting is by far not finished, it will never be finished, because it's too rich. The medium is so challenging. What could be more challenging than to have endless possibilities. I think that there is much more to be done. We will see things probably in the future we wouldn't have thought. Maybe it won't be like the painting we know now.[58]

This flow of words is one of the most sustained passages in any of his published interviews. Much needed to be clarified, Ryman seemed to wager, and old grievances warranted remuneration.

Lest this be read as primarily defensive, Ryman's setting forth of his ideas has an earnestness to it. In its plain-spoken realism, it is also the closest Ryman has come to outlining a position in the context of such an exchange. The interviews that circulate in the fairly small discursive universe of writings on Ryman have become a disproportionately privileged mode of responding to Ryman's practice.[59] In most cases, Ryman's restraint and emphasis on the procedural and material qualities of works lead to an uneasiness in his interviewers, who seem to want to unearth metaphor or shore up meaning. Although many interviewers take Ryman as the authority through which to articulate their own interests and agendas (which, as Ryman notes above, is not unlike what happens in many authored texts), Ryman deflects efforts to fix ideas or to transmute them into truth claims or kinds of evidence. If the interviewers sometimes indulge in psychological probing, Ryman projects a protective strategy that counters misreadings, generic misappropriations, or flamboyant interpretations. Otherwise, Ryman admits, he usually "just go[es] along with whatever happens to come out; it doesn't really affect me at all I don't think . . . I'm just talking about what I know."[60]

In addition, Ryman moves from discussing particular paintings to painting at large. Ryman's conclusion in the aforementioned passage, which for all the other talk about inadequate reproductions and critical fallibility, is really his monologue's fulcrum. For it is there that Ryman clarifies his conception of painting and its history as it relates to his work but also as it stands apart from it. Ryman's disciplined optimism is not a concession, but a countervailing assertion of broad application, as painting becomes a proper name that is imbued with agency apart from the artist's manipulation of it. In this move, Ryman shifts from his usual sense of speaking and making in the present tense to an atypical bet on expectations. Futurity in this usage has everything to do with the possibilities of painting that are born of conditionality and contingency.

In 1986, Ryman had already concluded that painting was far from an anachronistic form. He told Nancy Grimes: "I think painting is moving too slowly, but, of course, it's the nature of painting to evolve slowly. You become impatient for more. I feel that the possibilities of painting are so great and that we've just scratched the surface, and I think that it's a matter of learning to see in different ways and developing our capacity to see things we're not seeing now."[61] For Ryman, the possibilities that are still afforded by painting plausibly, even demonstrably, point forward but offer no guarantees.

This is Ryman's pragmatism, his line in the sand. Ryman questions what a "painting" is every time that he makes a painting, and he sees no reason why this experimentation cannot continue. Ryman's painting is precisely an experiment in keeping the experiment going, just as for William James, who formulated such matters in relation to his own pragmatic method, things appear "less as a solution, then, than as a program for more work, and more particularly as an indication of the ways in which existing realities may be *changed. Theories thus become instruments, not answers to enigmas, in which we can rest.*"[62] Ryman, in the pragmatist tradition of Charles Peirce, William James, and John Dewey, asks what practical or meaningful effects this experiment and related experiences have for himself and for his viewers. The question, as Ryman's paintings come to formulate it, is something like "what is the consequence of believing in painting?" and, because of this belief, making them.

In this, Ryman's riposte to apocalyptic critics suggests a comparison with James's fundamental tenets of philosophy—less to render systematic or foundational a philosophy than to propose a way of *doing* philosophy. James was famously a depressive, and he treated his chronic ill health as a philosophical problem. In 1870, he had a provisional "breakthrough" after reading Charles Renouvier, declaring in his diary that he could "see no reason why his definition of Free Will—'the sustaining of a thought *because I choose to* when I might have other thoughts'—need be the definition of an illusion. At any rate, I will assume for the present—until next year—that it is no illusion. My first act of free will shall be to believe in free will. . . . Not in maxims, not in *Anschauungen* [contemplations], but in accumulated *acts* of thought lies salvation."[63] James's epiphany correlated belief and action and persuaded him of the utility and even necessity of acting in advance of popular validation or philosophical confirmation—since it never came. Some twenty-six years later, this insight formed the basis of his pragmatism in "The Will to Believe."

James's moment of optimism was short lived, but Ryman's pragmatism is formed along (and in effect, forges) a similar understanding that all too often registered in critical misunderstanding. Ryman acted on painting by painting, and he continues to do so. He has never waited for retrospective consolidation or validation (although they have come despite his avowed disinterest in them). He has pushed paint around, made paintings, and left the commentary for others. Daniel Buren, one of Ryman's friends and a perceptive commentator, offers a pertinent analysis:

> This also teaches us that a profound, analytical and sensitive examination of painting as an object can be so innovative, rich, complex and unexpected that, initially, no one will see it as painting in the

> true meaning of the term. One could even risk saying that true painting, in other words, a true work of art from any movement whatsoever, in the most noble sense of the word—innovative, intriguing and beautiful to boot—cannot initially be seen as such. This was such a powerful argument that the fiercest critics would claim that Ryman's work could in no way be considered painting; and that it is even a pure negation of it, an anti-painting! What they all forget, of course, is that this type of painting cannot be appreciated at first sight as a painting, even if its creator swears that it is nothing but that! This work overturns commonly held beliefs about painting to such an extent that it cannot be immediately assimilated as such. At worst, it is considered to be an insignificant object; at best, as an intriguing, therefore undefined and unclassifiable object. Accepting it as painting would mean a re-examination of the painting that preceded it, but would also expand the inner vision that we have had about art up to this time. For this same reason, one could logically affirm today that, although Ryman's work is certainly linked to a historical movement in Western painting, it is also dissociated from it to such an extent that we can speak of the history of painting before Ryman, and after.[64]

The questions now become what painting is after Ryman and what Ryman does after his own retrospection.

Conclusion

An image that illustrates Robert Storr's essay in the 1993 Robert Ryman retrospective catalogue divulges much about the artist's practice. The image shows a push-pinned, photograph-covered wall in Ryman's studio, much like the one reproduced here. The wall chronicles in meticulous if limited detail (what Amy Baker Sandback calls "ghost stand-ins for near-impossible-to-reproduce original paintings")[1] works from the beginning of Ryman's career. This mural of black-and-white photographs makes an expanding grid, lacking in visual incident by virtue of its scale and gray tones and, crucially, indifferent to sequence in its ad hoc assemblage. As Ryman proposed in 1969 and would repeatedly assert, the basic problem was always what to do with paint: "There is never a question of what to paint, but only how to paint."[2] Order, which is to say, linear history is here undone by the shifts and permutations of Ryman's decades-long interest in a square format, an arsenal of white pigments, and a multiplicity of support structures. Works on steel, canvas, linen, and paper are navigable in a loose, associative way without rank or succession.

Befitting Ryman's practical tendencies, this working archive was meaningful to him, not to his commentators. Although it resonates for people who are interested in documenting Ryman's process, his repertoire of materials and forms, his approach to retrospection, and so on, it now offers a different object lesson that is based less on an investment in the sanctity or viability of the visual

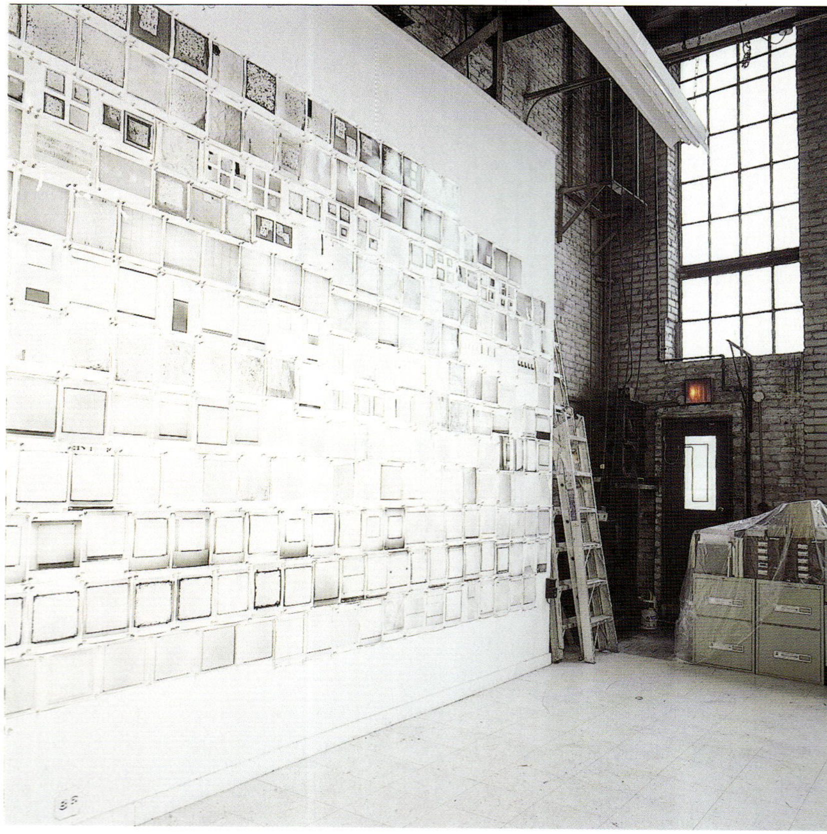

Installation view of Ryman's studio.

library than its ultimate incompatibility with practice. Not long after this installation shot was taken, Ryman removed the photos from the wall in his studio because he felt that they had grown out of control and were doing him more harm than good. There is a danger of overshadowing the contemporary with phantoms of works past. For Ryman to keep painting, he had to keep painting from a clean slate. He could continue to do so not because of his proximity to tangible evidence of past experiments, but because of the experience gained in their production, as lessons assimilated over time and impossible to un-learn. As John Dewey appraises: "While the content of knowledge is what *has* happened, what is taken as finished and hence settled and sure, the *reference* of knowledge is future or prospective. For knowledge furnishes the means of understanding or giving meaning to what is still going on and what is to be done."[3]

Ryman's recent works are examples of how he makes new painting without losing sight of what had constituted its import before. Alteration within a set of options and material givens has proven the mainstay of Ryman's practice, and as the no longer extant image wall makes clear, this mutable and expansive field is less delimited by what has been than suggested by what else might be. For a show at the PaceWildenstein Gallery in New York in 2004–2005, Ryman pursued something that was implicit but not attempted in his prior work: He finally decided to make "white paintings" on the model of his *Untitled (Orange Painting)* from decades earlier (see chapter 2). This new series must have proven a source of consternation to those who, like one anonymous *New Yorker* reviewer, had recently christened Ryman "the snowman"[4] and assumed that he had been making white paintings all along.

Painting white paintings was something Ryman had long disavowed, as when he answered a question about this in 1971:

> No, it may seem that way superficially, but there are a lot of nuances and there's color involved. Always the surface is used. The gray of the steel comes through; the brown of the corrugated paper comes through; the linen comes through, the cotton (which is not the same as the paint—it seems white): all of those things are

Robert Ryman, *Untitled* (1960). Oil on stretched sized cotton canvas.

> considered. It's really not monochrome painting at all. The white just happened because it's a paint and it doesn't interfere. I could use green, red, yellow, but why? It's a challenge for me to use paint and make something happen with it, without having to be involved in reds, greens, and everything which would confuse things. But I work with color all the time. I don't think of myself as making white paintings. I make paintings; I'm a painter.[5]

To avoid misunderstanding in the PaceWildenstein context, Ryman wrote his own catalogue essay, which appeared without an interview or additional critical commentary. In making plain his intentions, Ryman sidestepped his usual meditations on procedure and turned to meaning insofar as it attends method.

In these works, Ryman is painting white, as opposed to using white as a neutral paint that is capable of producing a wide range of effects. He decided to do so because he had never tried it before. As Ryman writes: "When I complete each group of paintings, I try to change my approach, as it gives me a new challenge so that I don't become too comfortable with my painting. It is important that painting always be new for me."[6] Ryman elaborated on how this series occasioned doubts for him. After all, was this experiment really different from those preceding it? Could white *be* the painting but not its image? Could white paint smeared against a dark ground enact composition without standing apart from its support? These questions led to others that were less intimately formal and opened onto a different sort of self-reflection:

> So, to begin, I had the different whites, the dark ground, different sizes, and lean paint, but no plan as to how the paintings would be. At the beginning I have to somewhat blindly find my way and it is only after several months that I can finally see how the paintings are developing. Then it becomes more clear how they are working, how they feel. How the paintings look can be deceiving, but the way they feel is more important. Usually they are not what I

Robert Ryman, *Series #12 (White)* (2004). Oil, gesso on stretched cotton canvas.

Robert Ryman, *Series #24 (White)* (2004). Oil, gesso on stretched cotton canvas.

> expected, although I don't know exactly what I expect. At the same time I am surprised at how the paintings develop into something I hadn't foreseen and at times there are doubts. You would think at my age, doubt in painting would be a thing of the past, but it happens on occasion. I think it is because my technical approach is always somewhat different and I am not so clear about it. Anyway, I have learned to accept doubt as part of the process.[7]

As recently as June 2004, Holland Cotter wrote that "Mr. Ryman has remained untroubled by doubts."[8] I have to imagine that, for Cotter, Ryman's above remarks must have startled. More than the surprise of rendering white as subject, Ryman's uncertainty and his willingness to give it voice was the show's real revelation, especially because of something that Ryman had written many years earlier in 1983:

> Even though some people may have liked my painting, they didn't know what to do with it because it was not really the correct thing—it didn't fit. Sometimes I myself couldn't see where it was going to lead; I had doubts and at times was not so sure of myself. Then one day in 1965 I felt that I had just finished being a student. I felt very confident. I felt that I knew exactly what to do. I felt mature. There was no more hesitation, no more doubt. It didn't have to do with any particular paintings I was doing or any outside recognition. It just had to do with myself and my painting.[9]

Had these 1983 comments appeared after those from 2004, the latter would have secured a resolute temporality of before-and-after, as triumphal in its unidirectional, consummately modernist trajectory as conclusive in its verdict. But as with the jumbled photo wall, this scrambling of assumed chronology—the assertion of confidence that is undercut by its eventual dissipation—tells another story that is poignantly encapsulated in the title of the large oil painting *Best or Worst* (1996–1997).

Like William James declaring his cure from depression in his diary one day in 1870 only to lapse back into it soon thereafter (and repeat this process for the remainder of his years), Ryman's shifting relation to the ease with which he facilitates production is something of a leitmotif. Unmarred by histrionics, his doubt is nevertheless countered by assurance, and so it begins again. Ryman's doubt is worth taking seriously chiefly because it is procedural. It is also embedded in the approach of pragmatist thought wherein doubt produces insights that are based not on metaphysical confirmation but on humane fallibility. The choice to believe assumes importance only against a backdrop of supposed improbability, and this doubt makes the act of painting consequential for Ryman. Indeed, to return to the works at Pace, why should he take up painting white paintings when most assumed that he was already doing so?

For all the critiques of pragmatism as yoked to blithe liberation, can-do exuberance, positivism, or crass, efficacious utilitarianism, pragmatism for James was foremost a way to allow for—but not to argue for—belief. As he succinctly put it, "God is real since he produces real effects."[10] The irony was that James was perpetually despondent; he never believed. Louis Menand writes that "James was a moralist who gave a great deal of his time and intellectual energy to the business of trying to understand religion. But although he believed in the legitimacy of the religious response to the universe, he was never able to attain its consolation for himself."[11] Philosophy here is a kind of "moralism,"[12] as Menand names it, but one that even James did not always have the compunction to face. He could not always, in his words, be on "such constant duty."[13]

Anecdotally, apocryphally, or otherwise, Gertrude Stein's remarks about studying with James resonate here. Stein claimed that while at Radcliffe she wrote to James: "I am so sorry but I really do not feel a bit like an examination paper in philosophy to-day." To this, James is said to have responded, "I understand perfectly how you feel. I often feel like that myself."[14] He also gave her the highest grade in the class. The implication was that Stein understood James. James knew that philosophy was insufficient, but in the end it was what he had, even if he could not live in a state of perpetual acuity, much less unfettered optimism. One can create a philosophy of hope without finding reason for it. Put differently, one can believe that believing in something would have certain consequences without believing in that thing oneself. To admit as much was James's honesty and the source of his philosophy's validity. It was also the acknowledged core of its perverse generosity. Here is Menand on James once more: "James was too wise to believe that true melancholy can ever be overcome by a theory, and he was too honest to pretend to a spiritual satisfaction he was never able to feel. . . . What lends authenticity to his philosophy is not its triumph over the unhappiness in his own life, but its failure."[15]

To be willing to believe and to act on that belief in the face of skepticism are no small feats. For James, the willingness to act "as if" and see what happens thereafter offered the best hope of mediating contingency and adapting to its exigencies, and this is why his pragmatism remained at the level of method. It remained an idea, a social tool, a justification to make choices (without suggesting what those choices should be or why they occur in the first place), and a way of being. For James (as for Dewey, as discussed in chapter 1), pragmatism never congealed into a totemic ideology, except when misunderstood and wrongly appropriated. "Meanwhile," James advises, "we have to live to-day by what truth we can get to-day, and be ready to-morrow to call it falsehood."[16] But this openness at the level of thought *as* regulative practice does not ensure or valorize acclimatization, nor does it signal uncritical affirmation. It inversely registers mutability as a function of uncertainty about morality and about belief, which, in this formulation, are less "solving names,"[17] magic words, or punctual solutions to metaphysical riddles than they are events or processes to which truth provisionally "happens."[18]

Ryman was painting as declarations were being made about painting's demise as a historically potent form. Despite such eulogies, painting's promise for Ryman should not be taken as a capitulating, head-in-the-sand position. Rather, Ryman's experiment is an act of faith despite doubt and maybe because of it. Ryman has not operated outside history, historicist teleologies, or critical narratives, but as Daniel Buren suggests in chapter 5, he has dissociated from them to such an extent that we must rethink the applicability of such mechanistic frameworks on the basis of his achievement. What beliefs do such systems of thought or modes of apprehension abet and confirm? What does believing in the value of such narratives do for the writing of history or criticism, and how might practices operate beyond or beneath them?

Ryman's wish for exemption from such strictures, concomitant with his sustained working at an angle oblique to them, raises questions about the dangers of categorization—of style, group affiliation, and the like. Ryman's doubt is answered in particular examples that are based on specific trials, but generalizations can nonetheless be extrapolated from those trials. Suggestive in this model is Ryman's attempt to work apart from the front-loaded assignation of value or meaning.

Ryman's work begs for close attention and rewards the concentration expended on it. Key to Ryman's pragmatism, the subject that his paintings solicit is marked by doubts that are commensurate with the restive practice on which such subjectivity is forged. Ryman's paintings are radically open, both physically (in their relation to the wall and the ambient space of the gallery in which they are sited) and theoretically (in their arhetorical stance) and have been prone to prolonged interpretive misrecognition. At best, Ryman's paintings offer a site of resistance against responses that are predicated on the deferral of meaning beyond the material. Yet this same condition of openness is often expropriated as a suggestive emptiness that is awaiting a critical supplement.

With a full awareness of the fickleness of taste and the volatility of generational approaches to the framing of artworks into culturally intelligible artifacts, Ryman has produced paintings. And an understanding of contingency and fallibility prompts Ryman to keep painting into a present where it might or might not be apprehended. In the meantime, a dialogue about and around his painting can commence and be sustained. By extension, this project moves painting along, but the larger stakes and the specific results (as specific paintings) are no more certain than are those of Ryman's own practice.

Pragmatism remains at the level of method and therefore "stands for no particular results."[19] Ryman might believe painting to be in its infancy, but this proposition remains at the level of belief and as such is attended by doubt. It is a speculation that will be tested and possibly discredited, but it is not a forgone conclusion. To act as though it were would confirm such a thesis, whereas to believe otherwise is to produce radically antithetical effects. By regarding painting as an available possibility—a condition of possibility—Ryman is betting that there are positive consequences in assuming this position. Ryman paints pragmatism and leaves the tallying for some other time.

Notes

A Note on the Illustrations

1. Christel Sauer, "Introduction," in Urs Raussmüller, ed., *Ryman Paintings and Ryman Exhibitions, Raussmüller Collection* (Frauenfeld: Raussmüller Collection, 2006), 8. See also Thierry de Duve, "Ryman irreproductible," *Essais Datés I 1974–1986* (Paris: La Différence, 1987), 119–158.

2. Douglas Crimp, "On the Museum's Ruins," in Hal Foster, ed., *The Anti-Aesthetic* (Seattle: Bay Press, 1983), 50.

3. Robert Ryman cited in Phyllis Tuchman, "Robert Ryman," *MoMA Magazine* (Fall 1993): 10.

Introduction

1. "The Avant-Garde: Subtle, Cerebral, Elusive," *Time* 92, no. 21 (November 22, 1968): 70.

2. Ibid.

3. Ibid.

4. Ibid.

5. Ibid.

6. Ibid., 77.

7. "New Art Show Really Is a Bit of All White!," *The Sun* (London), February 18, 1993. See also Gregory Battcock, "An Experiment with Art in Education," *Art Education* 24, no. 1 (January 1971): 10–12.

8. Yasmina Reza, *Art,* trans. Christopher Hampton (New York: Faber and Faber, 1996), 61.

9. Vivien Raynor, "Robert Ryman," *New York Times,* January 31, 1986.

10. Leo Steinberg, "Contemporary Art and the Plight of Its Public," *Other Criteria: Confrontations with Twentieth-Century Art* (1962; New York: Oxford University Press, 1972), 12.

11. "Drawing a Blank!," *Leyland Guardian* (Chorley, England), March 4, 1993.

12. Paul Cummings, "Interview of Robert Ryman, Part 1," interview conducted October 13, 1972, unpublished transcript, Archives of American Art, Smithsonian Institution, 5.

13. For an extended discussion of Ryman's relation to Tristano, see Vittorio Colaizzi, "'How It Works': Stroke, Music, and Minimalism in Robert Ryman's Early Paintings," *American Art* 21, no. 1 (Spring 2007): 29–49, and Vittorio Colaizzi, "Robert Ryman: Painting as Actuality," Ph.D. dissertation, Virginia Commonwealth University, 2005. Colaizzi compares Ryman's painting to the dictates of his musical tutor, a comparison that privileges process (the act of execution conceived as analogous to musical play), an exhibition of temporality, the discrete stroke, and an irrevocability of each stroke once put down. See also Ethan Ryman, "Jazz Tunes and White Paint," *Yard Magazine* (2005): 14–21.

14. Cummings, "Interview of Robert Ryman, Part 1," 7. See also Lucy Lippard, "Living Space," in David Frankel, ed., *Sniper's Nest: Art That Has Lived with Lucy R. Lippard* (Annandale-on-Hudson, NY: Bard College, 1996), 1.

15. Cummings, "Interview of Robert Ryman, Part 1," 7, 9.

16. Robert Ryman, in Robert Ryman and Peter Blum, *Robert Ryman: Works on Paper 1957–1964* (New York: Peter Blum Edition, 2004), 64.

17. Victor D'Amico, *Experiments in Creative Art Teaching: A Progress Report on the Department of Education, 1937–1960* (Garden City, NY: Doubleday, 1960), 14–15.

18. Lucy Lippard, "Biting the Hand: Artists and Museums in New York since 1969," in Julie Ault, ed., *Alternative Art New York, 1965–1985* (Minneapolis: University of Minnesota Press, 2002), 82.

19. "Interview with Lucy Lippard," Oral History Project with Sharon Zane, Unpublished transcript, Museum of Modern Art Archives, New York, 1999, 18.

20. Ibid., 39. Ryman and Merrill Wagner have been married since 1969.

21. Lucy Lippard, "New York Letter: Rejective Art" (1965), *Changing: Essays in Art Criticism* (1965; New York: Dutton & Co., 1971), 143.

22. Cited in Colaizzi, "Robert Ryman: Painting as Actuality," 73.

23. Jan Dibbets, *Robert Ryman* (Brussels: Xavier Hufkens, 2005), n.p.

24. Robert Ryman, cited in Nancy Grimes, "White Magic," *Art News* 85, no. 6 (Summer 1986): 89.

25. Phyllis Tuchman, "Robert Ryman," *MoMA Magazine* (Fall 1993): 9.

26. Many have made comparisons between Ryman and Malevich on morphological grounds as well. See Donald Kuspit, "Introduction," *Out of the South* (Atlanta: Heath Gallery, 1982), 7. See also Barbara Rose, *Monochromes: From Malevich to the Present* (Berkeley: University of California Press, 2006).

27. Robert Ryman, in Barbaralee Diamonstein, *Inside New York's Art World* (New York: Rizzoli, 1979), 340.

28. Robert Storr, "Robert Ryman: Making Distinctions," *Art in America* 74, no. 6 (June 1986): 92.

29. This position is not unique. It can be thought of in relation to ekphrasis and through the writings of figures as disparate as Vasari, Denis Diderot, and Walter Benjamin. Nonetheless, it is crucial here for Ryman's work, which seems especially impervious to "translation."

30. Robert Storr, "Simple Gifts," *Robert Ryman* (London: Tate Gallery; New York: Museum of Modern Art, 1993), 37.

31. See Lawrence Alloway, *Systemic Painting* (New York: Solomon R. Guggenheim Foundation, 1966), 63.

32. Robert Ryman, "The '60s in Abstract: Thirteen Statements and an Essay," *Art in America* 71, no. 9 (October 1983): 124.

33. See "Joseph Kosuth and Seth Sieglaub Reply to Benjamin Buchloh on Conceptual Art," *October* 57 (Summer 1991): 153. See also Cummings, "Interview of Robert Ryman, Part 1," 21.

34. Konrad Fischer and Heiner Friedrich visited Ryman's studio in 1967, and each bought a work, Ryman's first major sales. Following this, they each gave him a show in 1968 and then 1969.

35. "Robert Ryman Exhibition at Guggenheim Museum March 3–April 30," press release, Guggenheim Museum, New York, 1972. The press release states that Ryman's exhibition was "the third in a series of shows devoted to artists identified with the Minimalist movement of the 1960s," following Carl Andre and Robert Mangold. Diane Waldman's original conception of the show was that it would be shared between Ryman and Mangold, but for space and other reasons she separated them into two solo shows. See Paul Cummings, "Interview of Robert Ryman, Part 2," interview conducted November 7, 1972, unpublished transcript, Archives of American Art, Smithsonian Institution, 25.

36. Ryman contributed to this installation, feeling that "it isn't time for that kind of thing [a comprehensive, canon-making retrospective], so I wanted it to be a very concise group." Ibid., 26. But neither did he want to make any new work, a point criticized by Lawrence Alloway, who felt the show was "monotonous in the absence of any direct painting done on the wall, which is the artist's especial contribution." He likewise critiqued Waldman for allowing "his withholding of the one gift that might have made his show extraordinary (Ryman paints Frank Lloyd Wright)." Alloway tied this to a larger argument about curators who acquiesced to the desires of artists, dealers, and collectors. Lawrence Alloway, "The Great Curatorial Dim-Out," *Artforum* 13, no. 9 (May 1975): 32–34.

37. Diane Waldman, *Robert Ryman* (New York: Guggenheim Museum, 1972), n.p.

38. Peter Schjeldahl, "Robert Ryman at the Guggenheim," *Art in America* 60, no. 3 (May–June 1972): 33.

39. "Robert Ryman: Making Distinctions," 96.

40. "Robert Ryman: April 26–May 15, 1969," press release, Fischbach Gallery, New York, 1969.

41. Patrick Frey, "The American Robert Ryman at InK, White: An Empire of Colors," *Robert Ryman* (Zurich: InK, Halle für internationale neue Kunst, 1980), 5.

42. Naomi Spector, *Robert Ryman* (Amsterdam: Stedelijk Museum, 1974), 1.

43. Yve-Alain Bois, "Ryman's Tact," *Painting as Model* (Cambridge: MIT Press, 1993), 225.

44. Yve-Alain Bois, "Painting: The Task of Mourning," *Painting as Model,* 242.

45. Ibid., 232. Bois posits Ryman as working through painting's end, such that his paintings arrive at "the condition of the photograph or of the readymade, yet remain at the threshold of simple negation."

46. Maurice Berger, *Political Geometries* (New York: Hunter College Art Gallery, 1986), n.p.

47. Ryman is the only artist for whom there is no image in the catalogue. While Ryman shuns the possibility of perfect reproduction of his work, this is still an egregious omission that turns a deliberately material practice into a conceptual abstraction unmoored from its objects.

48. Douglas Crimp, "The End of Painting," in Frances Colpitt, ed., *Abstract Art in the Late Twentieth Century* (Cambridge: Cambridge University Press, 2002), 97.

49. Robert Storr, *Robert Ryman* exhibition brochure, Museum of Modern Art, New York, 1993, 8.

50. Storr, "Simple Gifts," 37.

51. Urs Raussmüller has remained immune to these squabbles by foregrounding his own support of Ryman. In 1978 he presented the artist's work at InK, the Halle für internationale neue Kunst in Zurich; in 1983 he added his work to the permanent exhibition of paintings at the Hallen für neue Kunst in Schaffhausen; and in 2006 he installed his collection at Inverleith House, Edinburgh. See Urs Raussmüller, *Ryman Paintings and Ryman Exhibitions, Raussmüller Collection* (Frauenfeld: Raussmüller Collection, 2006).

52. John Dewey, *The School and Society* (1899; Mineola, NY: Dover, 2001), 52.

53. John Dewey, *Experience and Education* (1938; New York: Simon and Schuster, 1997), 87.

54. Ibid., 86.

55. Ibid., 87.

56. William James, *Pragmatism: A New Name for Some Old Ways of Thinking* (1907; New York: Longmans, Green, 1912), 54.

57. Ibid., 51.

58. Ibid., 45.

59. Charles S. Peirce, "How to Make Our Ideas Clear," in Edward C. Moore, ed., *The Essential Writings: Charles S. Peirce* (1878; Amherst, NY: Prometheus Books, 1998), 156–157.

60. Jean Frémon, "This Is Not a White Square," *Robert Ryman: peintures récentes,* trans. Ann Cremin (Paris: Galerie Maeght Lelong, 1984), 22.

Chapter 1

1. Paul Cummings, "Interview of Robert Ryman, Part 1," interview conducted October 13, 1972, unpublished transcript, Archives of American Art, Smithsonian Institution, 10.

2. Robert Storr, "Simple Gifts," *Robert Ryman* (London: Tate Gallery; New York: Museum of Modern Art, 1993), 12. See also Cummings, "Interview of Robert Ryman, Part 1," 11.

3. Cited in Storr, ibid., among many sources.

4. Howard Singerman, *Art Subjects: Making Artists in the American University* (Berkeley: University of California Press, 1999), 119.

5. Ibid., 4.

6. Thomas Crow, *The Rise of the Sixties: American and European Art in the Era of Dissent* (New York: Abrams, 1996), 116–117.

7. Ibid., 117.

8. . Robert Ryman, in Robert Ryman and Peter Blum, *Robert Ryman: Works on Paper 1957–1964* (New York: Peter Blum Edition, 2004), 63.

9. Ibid., 64.

10. Cummings, "Interview of Robert Ryman, Part 1," 9.

11. See Victor D'Amico, *Creative Teaching in Art* (1942; Scranton, PA: International Textbook, 1953).

12. They are also remarkably similar to a primer—a book and activity kit replete with acrylic paints (titanium white, zinc white, flake white, and yellow ochre), oil pastels (white, grey,

and brown), brushes, a palette, light and dark paper, and a box frame—that Ryman published decades later. The activity book suggests projects that incorporate one's signature and date, as well as an "experimental painting" that involves testing brushes and long and short strokes without a "set plan." Other tips include underpainting, using a system, erasing with white, and using different whites in the same composition. See Janet Boris, *Robert Ryman* (New York: ArtEd Series, Inc., 2001).

13. Charles J. Martin and Victor D'Amico, *How to Make Modern Jewelry* (New York: Simon and Schuster, 1949), 5.

14. Ibid.

15. Victor D'Amico, Frances Wilson, and Moreen Maser, *Art for the Family* (New York: Simon and Schuster, 1954), 5.

16. Ibid., 17.

17. Ibid., 19.

18. Ibid., 29.

19. Ibid., 101.

20. Ibid., 105.

21. Ibid., 17.

22. Robert Ryman, in Nancy Grimes, "White Magic," *Art News* 85, no. 6 (Summer 1986): 92.

23. Teaching materials included "New Forms of Our Time," "Adventure in Modern Art," and "What Is Modern Painting?" See Victor D'Amico, "Creative Art," *Bulletin of the Museum of Modern Art* 19, no. 1 (Fall 1951): 15. These texts closely followed museum programs, publications, and ideologies and were meant to complement exhibitions, increase attendance, and garner interest in modernism.

24. For a discussion of the carnivals, see D'Amico, "Creative Art," 11–13; Carol Morgan, "From Modernist Utopia to Cold War Reality: A Critical Moment in Museum Education," in John Elderfield, ed., *Studies in Modern Art, The Museum of Modern Art at Mid-Century: Continuity and Change,* vol. 5 (New York: Museum of Modern Art, 1995), 150–173; and Mary

Anne Staniszewski, *The Power of Display: A History of Exhibition Installations at the Museum of Modern Art* (Cambridge: MIT Press, 1998), 79–80.

25. For a history of museum education in America and its complexities at this moment, see Terry Zeller, "The Historical and Philosophical Foundations of Art Museum Education in America," in Nancy Berry and Susan Mayer, eds., *Museum Education: History, Theory, and Practice* (Reston, VA: National Art Education Association, 1989), 10–89.

26. Under the subject heading "More Science, Less Art," D'Amico vented similar frustrations in his 1960 progress report on the Education Department, reiterating: "The most recent problem confronting art education results from the emphasis on meeting our need for national safety. All over the country, schools are adding and stepping up courses in mathematics and science without considering the effect on the student's total education or on his ability to master these subjects. . . . Of course it is vital for education to produce scientists for the nation's defense program; but this need not be done by coercing children who lack aptitude for science nor by giving a one-sided education to those who have it. The unfortunate aspect of this problem is that the extra time given to science is in many instances taken from the arts. In some schools, art has been dropped from the curriculum entirely, while in others only those who do not rate high academically or who have a low I.Q. are encouraged to elect it. Some schools are compelling students with high I.Q.s to take an all-academic program with no art, against the students' own wishes and without their parents' approval." He continues: "In one of his early addresses citing the need for more scientists, President Eisenhower emphasized that we must not develop science at the expense of the humanities, that the best science education was one balanced with the humanities. Eminent scientists and scholars have underscored the President's view by cautioning educators not to destroy our cultural foundations through a hysterical rush toward an overweighted science program. If we lose our cultural freedom and sacrifice the richness of a broad program of learning, we shall unwittingly play into the hands of the enemy and fulfill his wishes by our own lack of wisdom and foresight." Victor D'Amico, *Experiments in Creative Art Teaching: A Progress Report on the Department of Education, 1937–1960* (Garden City, NY: Doubleday, 1960), 20.

27. D'Amico, "Creative Art," 10.

28. Ibid., 20. D'Amico pioneered the use of television programs to instruct in art education across America. Although suspicious of mass mobilization, technology, and incipient social conformity (as even evidenced in a paint-by-number craze of which he was resolutely criti-

cal), he too tried to reach a wider audience through the medium of television in 1952 and 1953. His series *Through the Enchanted Gate* was cosponsored by the Museum and the National Broadcasting Company (NBC) and was another outlet for conveying his creative art teaching. See D'Amico, *Experiments in Creative Art Teaching,* 57–58.

29. Sybil Gordon Kantor, *Alfred H. Barr, Jr. and the Intellectual Origins of the Museum of Modern Art* (Cambridge: MIT Press, 2002), 74.

30. Alfred H. Barr, Jr., "Chronicle of the Collection of Painting and Sculpture," *Painting and Sculpture in the Museum of Modern Art, 1929–1967* (New York: Museum of Modern Art, 1977), 620.

31. Ibid., 629.

32. In the midst of all of this, in 1939 the museum moved to a new building at 11 West Fifty-Third Street that had ample gallery space to hang more works (triple that of the previous site). In 1942, Gertrude Vanderbilt Whitney died, and talks about consolidating the Whitney Museum of American Art into the Metropolitan Museum of Art were instigated if ultimately repudiated in 1948. Crucially, in 1943, Barr was forced to resign as director of the Department of Painting and Sculpture, a post curtly given to his friend James Thrall Soby. (René D'Harnoncourt was subsequently named museum director in 1948.) By the time the talks resumed after the war, MoMA was in a much stronger position than it had been a decade earlier, and the "feeder" model no longer applied. For a thorough discussion of these circumstances and the intricacies and implications of the intramuseum proceedings, see Kirk Varnedoe, "The Evolving Torpedo: Changing Ideas of the Collection of Painting and Sculpture of The Museum of Modern Art," in John Elderfield, ed., *Studies in Modern Art, The Museum of Modern Art at Mid-Century: Continuity and Change,* vol. 5 (New York: Museum of Modern Art, 1995), 12–73.

33. James W. Husted, cited in Varnedoe, "The Evolving Torpedo," 40.

34. Cited in "An Important Change in Policy," *Bulletin of the Museum of Modern Art* 20, no. 3–4 (Summer 1953): 3.

35. Cited in Varnedoe, "The Evolving Torpedo," 47.

36. Russell Lynes, *Good Old Modern: An Intimate Portrait of the Museum of Modern Art* (New York: Atheneum, 1973), 212.

37. Cited in Staniszewski, *The Power of Display,* 139.

38. D'Amico, "Creative Art," 5.

39. Jane Addams, "A Function of the Social Settlement," in Louis Menand, ed., *Pragmatism: A Reader* (1899; New York: Vintage Books, 1997), 274–275.

40. William James, cited in ibid.

41. Morgan, "From Modernist Utopia to Cold War Reality," 155.

42. John Dewey, *Art as Experience* (1934; New York: Perigree, 1980), 84.

43. John Dewey, *Experience and Education* (1938; New York: Simon and Schuster, 1997), 17.

44. D'Amico, "Creative Art," 7.

45. Dewey, *Experience and Education,* 6.

46. Louis Menand, *The Metaphysical Club* (New York: Farrar, Straus and Giroux, 2001), 438.

47. Dewey, *Experience and Education,* 5.

48. Ibid., 6.

49. However, even now the Victor D'Amico Institute of Art (commonly referred to as The Art Barge) exists as a summer art school and study center—replete with Art Carnivals and many other hallmarks of D'Amico's programs—on Long Island, New York.

50. Staniszewski, *The Power of Display,* 70. For the canonical critique of MoMA's curatorial apparatus, see Carol Duncan and Alan Wallach, "The Museum of Modern Art as Late Capitalist Ritual," *Marxist Perspectives* 1, no. 4 (Winter 1978): 28–51.

51. Cited in Staniszewski, *The Power of Display,* 62.

52. See Alfred H. Barr, Jr., *Matisse: His Art and His Public* (New York: Museum of Modern Art, 1951), 12, 4.

53. Marilyn Aronberg Lavin, *The Eye of the Tiger: The Founding and Development of the Department of Art and Archaeology, 1883–1923* (Princeton, NJ: Princeton University, 1983), 5.

54. Cited in ibid., 10.

55. Cited in ibid., 12 (emphasis mine).

56. Erwin Panofsky, "Art History in the United States," *Meaning in the Visual Arts* (1955; Chicago: University of Chicago Press, 1982), 326.

57. Ibid.

58. Paul Sachs, cited in Kantor, *Alfred H. Barr,* 65.

59. Ibid., 62.

60. Ibid., 74.

61. Ibid., 91.

62. Ibid., 102.

63. For a discussion of this exhibition and its critical reception, see Staniszewski, *The Power of Display,* 143–152.

64. Cited in Kantor, *Alfred H. Barr,* 161.

65. Benjamin Buchloh ascribes a kind of negative or perverse importance to Barr's travels in the Soviet Union. The meaning of this trip is, for him, encapsulated by and damned because of Barr's later refusal to convey to an American audience the stakes of a vanguard modernism that was promised to a new socialist culture but instead was delivered to a totalitarian regime. In short, Buchloh cannot forgive Barr for highlighting the formal inventions of suprematism and constructivism discrete from praxis without popularizing productivism. Benjamin Buchloh, "From Faktura to Factography," *October* 30 (Fall 1984): 84. On the apposition of art to politics in this context, Buchloh follows a much earlier critique made by Meyer Schapiro in 1937. Schapiro also faults Barr's *Cubism and Abstract Art* catalogue for being "unhistorical" and derides the assumption that abstraction is purely aesthetic. Meyer Schapiro, "Nature of Abstract Art," *Modern Art: Nineteenth and Twentieth Centuries* (1937; New York: George Braziller, 1978), 185–211.

66. Alfred H. Barr, Jr., "Russian Diary 1927–28," *October* 7 (Winter 1978): 15.

67. Ibid., 36.

68. Ibid., 37.

69. Panofsky, "Art History in the United States," 328–329. See also Michael Ann Holly, *Panofsky and the Foundations of Art History* (Ithaca: Cornell University Press, 1984), 97–113.

Chapter 2

1. This painting was mentioned in a few places and reproduced in black and white twice before being printed in color in the Tate/MoMA catalogue in 1993. See Christel Sauer, *Robert Ryman* (Zurich: InK Halle für internationale neue Kunst, 1980), 25; Yve-Alain Bois and Christel Sauer, *Robert Ryman* (Paris: Musée national d'art moderne, Centre Georges Pompidou, 1981), 23; and Robert Storr, *Robert Ryman* (London: Tate Gallery; New York: Museum of Modern Art, 1993), 49.

2. In 1972, Ryman brought the painting to New York, where he met with the conservator Orrin Riley to address some of these issues. The painting now is mounted on wood panel for structural reinforcement.

3. Although every work could be seen as inhabiting this position of being a productive failure, here I suggest that the work was a failure to Ryman as well. Any work might stand or fall as a failure for himself as his first viewer but also for anyone else, hence the anxiety about making works public but also the generosity of the act. Ryman additionally makes visible this common structure of doubt, having rendered it constitutive of the act of production. This position can be compared to that explored in Maurice Merleau-Ponty's writing on Cézanne. See Maurice Merleau-Ponty, "Cézanne's Doubt," in Galen A. Johnson, ed., *The Merleau-Ponty Aesthetics Reader: Philosophy and Painting,* trans. Michael B. Smith (Evanston, IL: Northwestern University Press, 1994), 59–75.

4. Ryman, cited in interviews with Catherine Kinley on April 11, 1992, and Lynn Zelevansky on July 1 and 7, 1992. See Catherine Kinley, Lynn Zelevansky, and Robert Ryman, "Catalogue Notes," in Storr, *Robert Ryman,* 48.

5. Robert Storr, "Simple Gifts," *Robert Ryman* (London: Tate Gallery; New York: Museum of Modern Art, 1993), 16.

6. For Danto, Ryman's "entire evolution has consisted in making painting that takes the all-over white square as a kind of Platonic ideal." Arthur C. Danto, "RRyman," *The Madonna of the Future: Essays in a Pluralistic Art World* (New York: Farrar, Straus and Giroux, 2000), 21.

7. Cited in numerous sources around the time of MoMA's reopening, including Hal Foster, "It's Modern But Is It Contemporary?," *London Review of Books,* December 16, 2004, <http://www.lrb.co.uk/v26/n24/fost01_.html>, accessed September 2007.

8. Interview with Bruce Kurtz, in "Documenta 5: A Critical Preview," *Arts Magazine* 46, no. 8 (Summer 1972): 42.

9. In this, Ryman unwittingly conjures the debate for the primacy of line or color—or *dessin* or *coloris*—as played out in theories of representation in relation to structure and ornament from antiquity to Roger de Piles in the seventeenth century and beyond (often in the guise of contest between the Poussinistes and Rubenistes). For the longstanding gendered implications of color as cosmetic, see Jacqueline Lichtenstein, "Making Up Representation: The Risks of Femininity," *Representations* 20 (Fall 1987): 77–87, and Jacqueline Lichtenstein, *The Eloquence of Color: Rhetoric and Painting in the French Classical Age,* trans. Emily McVarish (Berkeley: University of California Press, 1993).

10. Yve-Alain Bois, "Ryman's Lab," *Abstraction, Gesture, Ecriture: Paintings from the Daros Collection* (Zurich: Scalo, 1999), 115.

11. Robert Ryman, cited in Nancy Grimes, "White Magic," *Art News* 85, no. 6 (Summer 1986): 89.

12. Paul Cummings, "Interview of Robert Ryman, Part 1," interview conducted October 13, 1972, unpublished transcript, Archives of American Art, Smithsonian Institution, 11.

13. Vittorio Colaizzi, "Robert Ryman: Painting as Actuality," Ph.D. dissertation, Virginia Commonwealth University, 2005, 74.

14. Ibid., 41.

15. Likewise, despite their initial impression, Ryman's unstretched canvases from the early 1960s are not trials for other "finished" works, either.

16. Thierry de Duve, *Look, One Hundred Years of Contemporary Art,* trans. Simon Pleasance and Fronza Woods (Ghent: Ludion, 2001), 147.

17. Ibid. See also Thierry de Duve, "Taking Care of Painting," *Robert Ryman Paintings from the Sixties* (Brussels: Xavier Hufkens Gallery, 2000).

18. However, one could also argue that Ryman's repeated use of his signature is a play on abstract expressionism's obsession with signature styles.

19. John Elderfield, "Preface," in John Elderfield, ed., *Studies in Modern Art, The Museum of Modern Art at Mid-Century: At Home and Abroad,* vol. 4 (New York: Museum of Modern Art, 1994), 8.

20. Taped conversation with the author, August 5, 2003.

21. Harold Rosenberg, "The American Action Painters," *The Tradition of the New* (New York: Horizon Press, 1959), 26.

22. Ibid., 33.

23. De Duve, *Look, One Hundred Years of Contemporary Art,* 148.

24. Ibid., 148–149. De Duve here moves beyond repeating the tautology that Ryman's paintings are solely about painting to soliciting a viewer who will or will not be "touched" by Ryman's painting.

25. See Jeffrey Weiss, "Robert Ryman, Interview by Jeffrey Weiss (8 May, 1997)," *Mark Rothko* (Washington, DC: National Gallery of Art, 1998), 367–370.

26. "Interview with Lucy Lippard," Oral History Project with Sharon Zane, unpublished transcript, Museum of Modern Art Archives, New York, 1999, 66.

27. Charles Wylie, *Robert Ryman* (New Haven: Yale University Press for the Dallas Museum of Art, 2006), 13.

28. Maurice Poirier and Jane Necol, "The '60s in Abstract: Thirteen Statements and an Essay," *Art in America* 71, no. 9 (October 1983): 123.

29. Dore Ashton, *About Rothko* (1983; New York: Da Capo, 1996), 112–113.

30. David Carrier and Robert Ryman, "Robert Ryman on the Origins of His Art," *Burlington Magazine* 139, no. 1134 (September 1997), 632–633.

31. Donald Kuspit, "Robert Ryman at Peter Blum," *Artforum* 43, no. 3 (November 2004): 222.

32. For example, see Robert Pincus-Witten, "Ryman, Marden, Manzoni: Theory, Sensibility, Mediation," *Artforum* 10, no. 10 (June 1972): 53.

33. Rauschenberg would say the following of his works: "My black paintings and my white paintings are either too full or too empty to be thought—thereby they remain visual experiences. These pictures are not Art." Cited in Branden W. Joseph, "White on White," *Random Order: Robert Rauschenberg and the Neo-Avant-Garde* (Cambridge: MIT Press, 2003), 33, 57.

34. Cited in Danto, "RRyman," 21.

35. Bois, "Ryman's Lab," 115.

36. Kinley, Zelevansky, and Ryman, "Catalogue Notes," 52.

37. While trying to get to the bottom of *The Paradoxical Absolute,* Danto (in the great imaginative critical tradition of Denis Diderot) claims that the artist was reading Schopenhauer against Ryman's protests to the contrary. Danto, "RRyman," 26.

38. For a discussion of Picasso's relation to semiotics, see Rosalind Krauss, *The Picasso Papers* (Cambridge: MIT Press, 1999), especially "The Circulation of the Sign," 25–85, and Yve-Alan Bois, "The Semiology of Cubism," *Picasso and Braque: A Symposium* (New York: Abrams, 1992), 169–208. For a reading of Johns centered on metonymy, see Fred Orton, *Figuring Jasper Johns* (Cambridge: Harvard University Press, 1994).

39. Kinley, Zelevansky, and Ryman, "Catalogue Notes," 70.

40. Naomi Spector, "Robert Ryman at the Whitechapel," *Robert Ryman* (London: Whitechapel Art Gallery, 1977), 12.

41. Ryman in conversation with Storr, in Storr, "Simple Gifts," 44 and n. 39.

42. Even earlier, Ryman stated that his painting had to be "a very direct feeling and a very sure approach. There can't be any doodling. I mean it has got to come out right away; and if it doesn't, you can always tell when it's been fussed with." Cummings, "Interview of Robert Ryman, Part 1," 29. Only in 2004 did he decide to "work" the paint. See Robert Ryman, *Robert Ryman* (New York: PaceWildenstein, 2004), 6, and Vittorio Colaizzi, "'How It Works': Stroke, Music, and Minimalism in Robert Ryman's Early Paintings," *American Art* 21, no. 1 (Spring 2007): 29–49, as well as my conclusion in this volume.

43. Robert Ryman, in Barbaralee Diamonstein, *Inside New York's Art World* (New York: Rizzoli, 1979), 337–338.

44. Robert Ryman, in Grace Glueck, "The Twentieth-Century Artists Most Admired by Other Artists," *Art News* 76, no. 9 (November 1977): 99.

45. Carter Ratcliff, "New York Letter," *Art International* 16, no. 6 (Summer 1972): 76.

Chapter 3

1. Robert Ryman, in Ward Jackson, *Art Now: New York* 3, no. 3 (September 1971): 3.

2. Catherine Kinley, Lynn Zelevansky, and Robert Ryman, "Catalogue Notes," in Robert Storr, *Robert Ryman* (London: Tate Gallery; New York: Museum of Modern Art, 1993), 164.

3. Yve-Alain Bois, "Ryman's Lab," *Abstraction, Gesture, Ecriture: Paintings from the Daros Collection* (Zurich: Scalo, 1999), 120–121.

4. Clement Greenberg, "Modernist Painting," in John O'Brian, ed., *Clement Greenberg: The Collected Essays and Criticism,* vol. 4 (1960; Chicago: University of Chicago Press, 1993), 90.

5. Ibid., 85.

6. Ibid., 86.

7. According to Greenberg: "And I cannot insist enough that Modernism has never meant, and does not mean now, anything like a break with the past. It may mean a devolution, an unraveling, of tradition, but it also means its further evolution. Modernist art continues the past without gap or break, and wherever it may end up it will never cease being intelligible in terms of the past." Ibid., 92.

8. Ibid., 86.

9. Ibid., 90.

10. This reduction of the picture plane to the flatness of its support was soon recoded in the service of "specific objects" by Donald Judd or as objects as such by other artists and critics in the context of minimalism. On these grounds, Hal Foster named minimalism as a crux in that it "consummated one formalist model of modernism, completed and broke with it at once." Hal Foster, "The Crux of Minimalism," *The Return of the Real* (Cambridge: MIT Press, 1996), 35.

11. This shift led Rosalind Krauss to argue for opticality as an index of its self-differentiating capacity. She writes that "no sooner had Greenberg seemed to isolate the essence of painting in flatness than he swung the axis of the field ninety degrees to the actual picture surface to place all the import of painting on the vector that connects viewer and object. In this he seemed to shift from the first norm—flatness—to the second—the delimitation of flatness—and to give this latter a reading that was not that of the bounding edge of the physical object but rather the projective resonance of the optical field itself—what in 'Modernist Painting' he had called the 'optical third dimension' created by 'the very first mark on the canvas [which] destroys its literal and utter flatness.' This was the resonance he imputed to the effulgence of pure color as he spoke of it, not only as disembodied and therefore purely optical, but also 'as a thing that opens and expands the picture plane.' 'Opticality' was thus an entirely abstract, schematized version of the link that traditional perspective had formerly established between viewer and object, but one that now transcends the real parameters of measurable, physical space to express the purely projective powers of a preobjective level of sight: 'vision itself.'" Rosalind Krauss, *A Voyage on the North Sea: Art in the Age of the Post-Medium Condition* (New York: Thames & Hudson, 1999), 29. See also Rosalind Krauss, "Reinventing the Medium," *Critical Inquiry* 25, no. 2 (Winter 1999): 289–305, and Rosalind Krauss, "The Crisis of the Easel Picture," in Kirk Varnedoe and Pepe Karmel, eds., *Jackson Pollock: New Approaches* (New York: Museum of Modern Art, 1999), 155–179.

12. Clement Greenberg, "After Abstract Expressionism," *Clement Greenberg,* 4: 131–132.

13. Thierry de Duve, "The Monochrome and the Blank Canvas," *Kant after Duchamp* (Cambridge: MIT Press, 1996), 216. De Duve further elaborates that Greenberg shifted his position to uphold his aesthetic doctrine despite its consequences for medium-specificity. He did this under duress and in the face of the blank canvas and its evacuation of the last essential element of painting—that it needs to be painted to be considered a painting. Greenberg abstained from naming the stretched and tacked up canvas a picture (if not a successful picture), instead decrying it "bad art" in "How Art Writing Earns Its Bad Name" in 1962. For de Duve, this proves that Greenberg abandoned a sense of the medium as derived from its specific history for a reading that redrew the distinction in generic terms. Ibid., 221–222.

14. Christopher S. Wood, "Ryman's Poetics," *Art in America* 82, no. 1 (January 1994): 67–68.

15. Naomi Spector, *Robert Ryman* (Amsterdam: Stedelijk Museum, 1974), 8–9.

16. Yve-Alain Bois, "Cézanne: Words and Deeds," *October* 84 (Spring 1998): 42.

17. Ibid. This citation comes from Walter Benjamin, "Painting, or Signs and Marks," in Marcus Bullock and Michael Jennings, eds., *Walter Benjamin: Selected Writings, Volume 1: 1913–1926* (Cambridge: Harvard University Press, 1996), 83.

18. About drawing, Ryman says: "It's kind of a basic theory of thinking about drawing that it has to do with line. I don't work with line in that way with my painting at all. When I draw, I'm usually thinking about line, and what kind of line it can be." Robert Ryman, cited in Robert Storr, "Simple Gifts," *Robert Ryman* (London: Tate Gallery; New York: Museum of Modern Art, 1993), 180.

19. For an account of the ways that the grid's materialism has been yoked to symbolic and spiritual ambitions, see Rosalind Krauss, "Grids," and "The Originality of the Avant-Garde," in *The Originality of the Avant-Garde and Other Modernist Myths* (Cambridge: MIT Press, 1986).

20. Barbara Reise, "Robert Ryman: Unfinished II (Procedures)," *Studio International* 187, no. 964 (March 1974): 123.

21. Ibid.

22. Storr, "Simple Gifts," 17.

23. Leon Battista Alberti, *On Painting,* trans. Cecil Grayson (London: Penguin Classics, 1991), 54.

24. Ibid., 58.

25. Naomi Spector, "Robert Ryman at the Whitechapel," *Robert Ryman* (London: Whitechapel Art Gallery, 1977), 15.

26. Mondrian should not be equated with Kelly, and Kelly should not be read as a latter-day neoplasticist. Kelly strove for a mode of acomposition that would differentiate him from this formal lineage, and he did so with the curve, the absent if primary referent (even showing the grid as a collection of bathroom tiles in a 1951 work), and his use for a time of readymade colors. For an expanded discussion of Kelly's acompositional strategies and his wrongly ascribed association with Mondrian, see Yve-Alain Bois, "Ellsworth Kelly in France: Anti-Composition in Its Many Guises," *Ellsworth Kelly: The Years in France, 1948–1954* (Washington, DC: National Gallery of Art, 1992), 11–19.

27. Cited in ibid., 14.

28. Kelly was not trying to be Duchamp. Ibid., 18. Kelly's fear of the critical "source hunting" that he worried would attend this work has been born out in much of the critical literature on the artist, from E. C. Goossen's monograph to more recent work, such that Bois's piece stands as an explicit corrective to such projects. See, for example, E. C. Goossen, *Ellsworth Kelly* (New York: Museum of Modern Art, 1973).

29. Email to author, November 16, 2007.

30. Bois, "Ellsworth Kelly in France," 22.

31. Ibid., 10.

32. For a discussion of Kelly's tablets, see Yve-Alain Bois, "Pichenette," *Ellsworth Kelly Tablet 1948–1973* (New York: Drawing Center, 2002), 198–201.

33. Although Kelly began by using red, yellow, and blue, he shifted his palette to red, green, and blue for these figure and ground works. Sarah Rich has noted that red, green, and blue are the colors of light projection rather than the primaries of pigment and that they thus relate to color television. Rich makes a case that these colors are similar to the Technicolor red, green, and blue xylophone logo of NBC (which was a cultural symbol because NBC was the first media corporation to broadcast in color nationwide). For Rich, such a reading suggests a non-Greenbergian trajectory of abstraction, as Kelly embraces the popular or at least admits to the spectacular conditions under which the artist was working. See Sarah K. Rich, "Ellsworth Kelly's Spectacular Painting *Red Blue Green*," *Ellsworth Kelly: Red Green Blue: Paintings and Studies, 1958–1965* (San Diego: Museum of Contemporary Art, 2002), 36.

34. This is the first of Kelly's works that use these colors on a massive, architectural scale, which makes its return to his first work with these colors on a smaller scale all the more pointed in its reference to a history of past citation from within Kelly's own oeuvre.

35. Alberti was explicit about the harmony of colors and the ways that they should be made to interact to achieve the best composition: "I should like, as far as possible, all the genera and species of colors to appear in painting with a certain grace and amenity. Such grace will be present when colors are placed next to others with particular care; for, if you are painting Diana leading her band, it is appropriate for this nymph to be given green clothes, the one next to her white, and the next red, and another yellow, and the rest should be dressed

successively in a variety of colors, in such a way that light colors are always next to dark ones of another genera. This combining of colors will enhance the attractiveness of the painting by its variety, and its beauty by comparisons. There is a kind of sympathy among colors, whereby their grace and beauty is increased when they are placed side by side. If red stands between blue and green, it somehow enhances their beauty as well as its own." Alberti, *On Painting,* 85. Kelly has turned this on its head, intentionally exacerbating the dissonance between red and green and the complementary pairing of blue and green.

36. Wood, "Ryman's Poetics," 68–69. See also Meyer Schapiro, "Nature of Abstract Art," *Modern Art: Nineteenth and Twentieth Centuries* (1937; New York: George Braziller, 1978), 196.

37. Rosalind Krauss, "A View of Modernism," *Artforum* 11, no. 1 (September 1972): 50.

38 Ibid., 48.

39. Ibid., 50.

40. Ibid.

41. Along these lines, de Duve posits not one unified Greenberg but three disparate Greenbergs. As he writes: "The first is the doctrinaire Greenberg, who very early on formed a conviction as to the role of the avant-garde. He is the one I admire the most and from whom I have learned the most. The second is the art critic who wrote from day to day, who discovered Pollock, panned Rouault, changed his opinion on Mondrian—he's the one I enjoy the most, the one whom I would really like to see emulated. The third—the one who most interests me—is the theorist who, under the pressure of 'advanced art,' took up debates with Croce and even Kant on the terrain of theoretical aesthetics." See Thierry de Duve, *Clement Greenberg Between the Lines,* trans. Brian Holmes (Paris: Éditions Dis Voir, 1996), 8.

42. Ibid., 147.

43. Ibid., 148–149.

44. Robert Ryman interview with Robert Storr (1986), in Rosemarie Schwarzwälder, *Abstract Painting of America and Europe: Brice Marden, Gerhard Richter, Helmut Federle, Robert Mangold, Robert Ryman* (Klagenfurt: Ritter Verlag, 1988), 213.

Chapter 4

1. Dorothy C. Miller, ed., *Fifteen Americans* (New York: Museum of Modern Art, 1952), 5.

2. Dorothy C. Miller, "Forword and Acknowledgement," in Dorothy C. Miller, ed., *Sixteen Americans* (New York: Museum of Modern Art, 1959), 6.

3. Dorothy Miller, as cited in Lynn Zelevansky, "Dorothy Miller's 'Americans,' 1942–63," in John Elderfield, ed., *Studies in Modern Art, The Museum of Modern Art at Mid-Century: At Home and Abroad,* vol. 4 (New York: Museum of Modern Art, 1994), 70.

4. See Katharine Kuh, "A Contemporary Canvass of the American Canvas," *Saturday Review* (January 23, 1960): 29, 40; Thomas B. Hess, "U.S. Art, Notes from 1960," *Art News* 58, no. 9 (January 1960): 24–29; and Stuart Preston, "Art: 'Sixteen Americans,'" *New York Times,* December 16, 1959.

5. "There is not a dealer in town," Canaday writes, "nor a collector, nor yet a painter hoping to hang in the Museum of Modern Art who doesn't study each of Mr. Barr's syllables in an effort to deduce what he should offer for sale, what he should buy, or what he should paint. If Mr. Barr sees 'a new concern with figure, and a movement toward a new severe style,' there is going to be a vast weeding out in the gallery lists this fall, a vast indifference on the part of buyers to what they fought to get hold of last year and a rush toward the art stores where those little books called 'How to Draw' are for sale." John Canaday, "In the Gloaming: Twilight Seems to Be Settling Rapidly for Abstract Expressionism," *New York Times,* September 11, 1960.

6. John Canaday, "It Talks Good: Story-Telling Is Taboo, But Painting Today Is an Adjunct to Words," *New York Times,* March 6, 1960.

7. Ibid.

8. Ibid.

9. John Canaday, "Perhaps Drastic: A Moratorium on Art Might Be Nice for a While But Could Be Dangerous," *New York Times,* September 4, 1960.

10. Robert M. Coates, "The 'Beat' Beat in Art," *The New Yorker* (January 2, 1960): 61.

11. Following T. J. Clark and Thomas Crow, who have written about the recuperation of Jackson Pollock's abstraction as design, James Meyer locates this phenomenon in relation to

the 1966 Jewish Museum show, Primary Structures: Younger American and British Sculpture. At the show's opening, a woman who wore a white boxlike dress (which Meyer dubs the "Primary Structure" dress) signaled a merging of art and fashion in which the modernist drive to abstraction led to a "minimal look" in design in both sculpture and clothing. See James Meyer, *Minimalism: Art and Polemics in the Sixties* (New Haven: Yale University Press, 2001), 24–30. See also T. J. Clark, "Jackson Pollock's Abstraction," in Serge Guilbaut, ed., *Reconstructing Modernism: Art in New York, Paris, and Montreal 1945–1964* (Cambridge: MIT Press, 1990), 219; and Thomas Crow "Fashioning the New York School," *Modern Art in the Common Culture* (New Haven: Yale University Press, 1996), 39–48.

12. See Zelevansky, "Dorothy Miller's 'Americans,'" 81.

13. Robert Ryman cited in Robert Storr, "Simple Gifts," *Robert Ryman* (London: Tate Gallery; New York: Museum of Modern Art, 1993), 25.

14. Cited in Vittorio Colaizzi, "Robert Ryman: Painting as Actuality," Ph.D. dissertation, Virginia Commonwealth University, 2005, 283.

15. For a discussion of Stella's suit and its implications, see Caroline Jones, "Frank Stella, Executive Artist," *Machine in the Studio: Constructing the Postwar American Artist* (Chicago: University of Chicago Press, 1996), 116.

16. Carl Andre, "Frank Stella," Miller, ed., *Sixteen Americans,* 76.

17. Bruce Glaser, "Questions to Stella and Judd," in Gregory Battock, ed., *Minimal Art: A Critical Anthology* (Berkeley: University of California Press, 1995), 158.

18. Tom Donnelly, "But Is That Avalanche on Everest Really Necessary?," *Washington News,* February 9, 1960.

19. Ibid.

20. Yve-Alain Bois, "Surprise and Equanimity," *Robert Ryman: New Paintings* (New York: Pace Gallery, 1990), n.p.

21. Grace Glueck, "Like a Beginning," *Art in America* 57, no. 3 (May–June 1969): 118.

22. Ryman, in Phyllis Tuchman, "An Interview with Robert Ryman," *Artforum* 9, no. 9 (May 1971): 53.

23. Dan Cameron, "Robert Ryman: Ode to a Clean Slate," *Flash Art* 159 (Summer 1991): 91– 93.

24. Bridget L. Goodbody, "Robert Ryman," *Time Out New York* (December 30, 2004–January 5, 2005): 56.

25. Christel Sauer, "Robert Ryman's Realism," *Robert Ryman,* trans. Gertje Utley (Paris: PaceWildenstein, 1999), 6.

26. Emily Genauer, "Sixteen-Artist Show Is on Today at Museum of Modern Art," *Herald Tribune,* December 16, 1959.

27. Ibid.

28. Frank Stella quoted in "An Artist Writes to Correct and Explain," *Herald Tribune,* December 27, 1959.

29. "The Higher Criticism," *Time* 75, no. 2 (January 11, 1960): 59.

30. Stella, in Jones, "Frank Stella," 120.

31. As Fried summarizes: "When minimalists looked at the transition from Pollock to Kenneth Noland to Frank Stella, they saw art becoming a unitary thing, no longer a matter of part-by-part construction. This is what fascinated me; it was as if the minimalists were the ones who really believed the Greenbergian reduction—that there was a timeless essence to art that was progressively revealed. And in their reading, the timeless essence turned out to be not just the delimited flat surface of painting but the literal properties of the support." Further, they realized "that the support itself is a limited, compromised form of literalness. So why not go all the way and isolate, hypostatize, and project literalness as such—go beyond painting and sculpture altogether and simply make things like primary objects? If literalness was behind the entire development of modernism, if it was the motor that made it run, why not just go after it directly? That was the logic of the minimalists." Michael Fried, "Theories of Art after Minimalism and Pop: Discussion," in Hal Foster, ed., *Discussions in Contemporary Culture,* vol. 1 (Seattle: Bay Press, 1987), 73.

32. Ibid., 79.

33. Michael Fried, quoted in Amy Newman, *Challenging Art: Artforum 1962–1974* (New York: Soho Press, 2000), 435.

34. Hal Foster, "The Crux of Minimalism," *The Return of the Real* (Cambridge: MIT Press, 1996), 53.

35. Ibid.

36. Rosalind Krauss, "Eva Hesse: Contingent," *Bachelors* (Cambridge: MIT Press, 1999), 99.

37. Ibid.

38. Ibid., 99–100.

39. Thierry de Duve, *Look, 100 Years of Contemporary Art,* trans. Simon Pleasance and Fronza Woods (Ghent and Amsterdam: Ludion, 2001), 144.

40. Willis Domingo, "Ryman at Fischbach," *Arts Magazine* 44, no. 5 (March 1970): 66.

41. Carter Ratcliff, "Robert Ryman at Fischbach," *Art News* 69, no. 2 (April 1970): 72.

42. De Duve, *Look, One Hundred Years of Contemporary Art,* 146.

43. This painting was damaged beyond repair a short time after it was initially exhibited. For the most sustained discussion of it, see "Robert Ryman with Phong Bui," *The Brooklyn Rail* (June 2007), <http://brooklynrail.org/2007/6/art/ryman>, accessed July 2007.

44. Clement Greenberg, "Where Is the Avant-Garde?," *Clement Greenberg: The Collected Essays and Criticism,* vol. 4, ed. John O'Brian (1967; Chicago: The University of Chicago Press, 1993), 259–265.

45. Clement Greenberg, "Recentness of Sculpture," in ibid., 254.

46. For a similar critique, see also Leo Steinberg, "Other Criteria," in *Other Criteria* (New York: Oxford University Press, 1972), 55–91.

47. Bruce Boice, "The Quality Problem," *Artforum* 11, no. 2 (October 1972): 70.

48. Yve-Alain Bois, "Ryman's Tact," *Painting as Model* (Cambridge: MIT Press, 1993), 215.

49. Ibid.

50. Robert Storr, "Robert Ryman: Making Distinctions," *Art in America* 74, no. 6 (June 1986): 92.

51. Ibid., 97.

52. Ibid.

53. See Harry Cooper and Megan Luke, *Frank Stella 1958* (New Haven: Yale University Press, 2006). See also Foster, *The Return of the Real,* 78. For an economic analysis of Stella as well as Ryman, see David W. Galenson and Bruce A. Weinberg, "Age and the Quality of Work: The Case of Modern American Painters," *Journal of Political Economy* 108, no. 4 (August 2000): 761–777.

54. Lucy Lippard, "Constellation by Harsh Daylight: The Whitney Annual," *Hudson Review* 21, no. 1 (Spring 1968): 178.

55. See the cover of *Art-Rite/Painting* 9 (New York, Spring 1975).

56. Robert Ryman, "The Magazine Show," *Artforum* 15, no. 4 (December 1976): 21.

57. Colaizzi, "Robert Ryman: Painting as Actuality," 291.

58. Storr, "Making Distinctions," 97. See also Kirk Varnedoe, *Pictures of Nothing: Abstract Art since Pollock* (Princeton: Princeton University Press, 2006).

59. Lucy Lippard, *Eva Hesse* (New York: Da Capo Press, 1992), 137.

60. Joseph Kosuth, "In the Galleries: Robert Ryman," *Arts Magazine* 41, no. 8 (Summer 1967): 63–64. See also Diane Waldman, "Reviews and Previews: Robert Ryman," *Art News* 66, no. 4 (Summer 1967): 65.

61. Press release, Fischbach Gallery, New York, 1969.

62. Tuchman, "An Interview with Robert Ryman," 49.

63. Mel Bochner, "Excerpts from Speculation [1967–1970]," *Artforum* 8, no. 9 (May 1970): 71.

64. Lucy Lippard, *Six Years: The Dematerialization of the Art Object from 1966 to 1972* (1973; Berkeley: University of California Press, 1997), 25–26, expanded from Lucy Lippard and John Chandler, "The Dematerialization of Art," *Art International* 12, no. 2 (February 1968): 31–36.

65. Press release, Fischbach Gallery, New York, 1969.

66. Marcia Tucker and James Monte, *Anti-Illusion: Procedures/Materials* (New York: Whitney Museum of American Art, 1969), 28.

67. Robert Ryman in Barbaralee Diamonstein, *Inside New York's Art World* (New York: Rizzoli, 1979), 337.

68. Storr, "Making Distinctions," 96.

69. Catherine Kinley, Lynn Zelevansky, and Robert Ryman, "Catalogue Notes," in Robert Storr, *Robert Ryman* (London: Tate Gallery; New York: Museum of Modern Art, 1993), 118.

70. Fried argues of Stella that "in each painting the stripes appear to have been generated by the framing edge and, starting there, to have taken possession of the rest of the canvas, as though the whole painting self-evidently followed from not merely the shape of the support, but its actual physical limits." Michael Fried, "Shape as Form: Frank Stella's Irregular Polygons," *Art and Objecthood: Essays and Reviews* (Chicago: University of Chicago Press, 1998), 79–80.

71. Kinley, Zelevansky, and Ryman, "Catalogue Notes," 118.

72. Naomi Spector, *Robert Ryman* (Amsterdam: Stedelijk Museum, 1974), 9.

73. Thierry de Duve has discussed the implication of the tube of paint as a readymade. See Thierry de Duve, "The Readymade and the Tube of Paint," *Kant after Duchamp* (Cambridge: MIT Press, 1996), 163.

74. He had also alternately titled *Turkish Mambo* (1959–1960) as *Requiem (Tristano),* thus referring to the musician with whom Ryman studied. See Colaizzi, "Robert Ryman: Painting as Actuality," 44.

75. Glaser, "Questions to Stella and Judd," 157.

76. Jones, "Frank Stella," 124–125.

77. Yve-Alain Bois, "Ryman's Lab," *Abstraction, Gesture, Ecriture: Paintings from the Daros Collection* (Zurich: Scalo, 1999), 105.

78. Although Stella named his series the *Black Paintings,* Ryman did not call a work a white painting until 2003, when he began to designate works with white in parentheses after the work's number. See the conclusion to this book for a discussion of these works.

79. This playfulness is surprising given Spector's other writings, which are rather terse. About this, Bois writes: "In Naomi Spector's lengthy essay on Ryman, she undertakes a systematic chronological description of Ryman's work from the point of view of process. Painstakingly, she establishes each painting as a procedural document, reconstructing Ryman's process of production in the smallest detail." Bois, "Ryman's Tact," 215. See Spector, *Robert Ryman;* and Naomi Spector, "Robert Ryman: une chronologie," *Macula* (Paris) 3–4 (September 1978): 115–131.

80. Naomi Spector, "'Ryman' Brand Paintings," *Bilder. Objekte. Filme. Konzepte* (Munich: Stadtische Galerie im Lenbachhaus, 1973), 156.

81. Ibid.

82. This could be compared to Jasper Johns choosing numbers, letters, or even ale cans for their ubiquity.

83. See Lucy Lippard, "Rejective Art," *Art International* 10, no. 8 (October 1966): 33–36; Lucy Lippard, "After a Fashion: The Group Show," *Hudson Review* 19, no. 4 (Winter 1966–1967): 620–626; Lucy Lippard, "The Silent Art," *Art in America* 55, no. 1 (January–February 1967): 58–63; Lucy Lippard, "Constellation by Harsh Daylight: The Whitney Annual," *Hudson Review* 21, no. 1 (Spring 1968): 174–182; and Lucy Lippard, "Top to Bottom, Left to Right," *Grids* (Philadelphia: Institute of Contemporary Art, 1972).

84. Robert Pincus-Witten, "Robert Ryman, Fischbach Gallery," *Artforum* 8, no. 8 (April 1970): 75.

85. Peter Schjeldahl, "Robert Ryman at the Guggenheim," *Art in America* 60, no. 3 (May–June 1972): 35.

86. Pincus-Witten, "Robert Ryman, Fischbach Gallery," 75.

87. Ibid.

88. Ibid. Pincus-Witten revised this view after seeing more of Ryman's work in his Guggenheim retrospective.

89. Ibid.

90. Ibid., 76.

91. Peter Schjeldahl, "The Ice Palace That Robert Ryman Built," *New York Times,* February 7, 1971.

92. Diane Waldman, *Robert Ryman* (New York: Guggenheim Museum, 1972), n.p.

93. Schjeldahl, "Robert Ryman at the Guggenheim," 33.

94. Ibid.

95. Ibid.

96. Peter Schjeldahl, "The Malaise That Afflicts SoHo's Avant-Garde Galleries," *New York Times,* June 11, 1972. See also James McElhinney, "Interview with John Weber," interview conducted March 21 and April 4, 2006, unpublished transcript, Archives of American Art, Smithsonian Institution, Washington, DC.

97. Carter Ratcliff, "New York Letter," *Art International* 16, no. 6 (Summer 1972): 75–76.

98. Denise Wolmer, "In the Galleries: Robert Ryman, Weber," *Arts Magazine* 46, no. 7 (May 1972): 64–65.

99. John Canaday, "Ryman's White-on-White Oeuvre," *New York Times,* March 4, 1972.

100. Ibid.

101. One particularly keen one from these years: "The logic and the happy craziness in Ryman's work, the endless refinement, the laborious isolation of one element of painting after another—stretcher, support, fastening, medium, edge—need constant pointing out if more than a fraction of the public is going to see anything in such work beyond whiteness in various sizes. Though public reaction should have no bearing on what the artist chooses to do, still at a place like the Whitechapel, deep in the East End, with juggernaut lorries thundering past, unemployment rising and inner-urban squalor on all sides, there is the uncomfortable reaction that art like Ryman's is worlds apart from common experience. Maybe that makes it an inspiration; maybe too it makes it signify next to nothing to almost everyone." William Feaver, "Robert Ryman, Whitechapel Art Gallery," *Art News* 76, no. 10 (December 1977): 126.

102. David Bourdon, "Playing Hide and Seek at the Whitney," *Village Voice,* September 29, 1975, 97.

103. Hilton Kramer, "Tuttle's Art on Display at Whitney," *New York Times,* September 12, 1975.

104. Nancy Grimes, "White Magic," *Art News* 85, no. 6 (Summer 1986): 91.

105. Klaus Kertess, "Robert Ryman, *Standard,* 1967," *Artforum* 35, no. 1 (September 1996): 95.

106. "Robert Ryman," *The New Yorker* (November 4, 2002): 29.

107. Hilton Kramer, "Etienne Hajdu's Sculptures on View," *New York Times,* May 31, 1969.

108. Carter Ratcliff, "Robert Ryman's Double Positive," *Art News* 70, no. 1 (March 1971): 54.

109. Kenneth Baker, "Robert Ryman, Fischbach Gallery and Dwan Gallery," *Artforum* 9, no. 8 (April 1971): 78–79.

110. Ibid., 79.

111. Ibid.

112. Donald Kuspit, "Robert Ryman: Reductionism → Entropy," *Art in America* 67, no. 4 (July–August 1979): 89.

113. Marcia Hafif, "Robert Ryman: Another View," *Art in America* 67, no. 5 (September 1979): 88.

114. Ibid., 89.

115. Robert Pincus-Witten, "Ryman, Marden, Manzoni: Theory, Sensibility, Mediation," *Artforum* 10, no. 10 (June 1972): 50.

116. Ibid.

117. Ibid., 52.

118. Ibid.

119. Ibid., 50.

120. Ibid.

121. Carter Ratcliff, "New York Letter," *Art International* 15, no. 2 (February 1971): 69–70.

122. John Dewey, *Art as Experience* (1934; New York: Perigee, 1980), 25.

123. Mel Bochner, "Excerpts from Speculation [1967–1970]," *Artforum* 8, no. 9 (May 1970): 70.

124. Ibid.

125. Ibid., 71.

126. Ibid., 72.

127. Ibid.

128. Ibid.

129. Dewey, *Art as Experience,* 44.

130. Ibid., 45.

131. Robert Ryman, cited in Amy Baker Sandback, "Art on Location," *Artforum* 24, no. 3 (November 1985): 4.

Chapter 5

1. Rosalind Krauss, "Eva Hesse: Contingent," *Bachelors* (Cambridge: MIT Press, 1999), 99.

2. Lucy Lippard, *Eva Hesse* (New York: Da Capo Press, 1992), 135.

3. Krauss, "Eva Hesse: Contingent," 98.

4. Ibid.

5. Ibid., 99.

6. Ibid.

7. Ibid.

8. Catherine Kinley, Lynn Zelevansky, and Robert Ryman, "Catalogue Notes," in Robert Storr, *Robert Ryman* (London: Tate Gallery; New York: Museum of Modern Art, 1993), 178.

9. Gary Garrels and Robert Ryman, "Interview with Robert Ryman at the Artist's Studio," *Robert Ryman* (New York: Dia Art Foundation, 1988), 13.

10. Ibid., 13–14.

11. Ryman interview with Robert Storr (1986), in Rosemarie Schwarzwälder, *Abstract Painting of America and Europe: Brice Marden, Gerhard Richter, Helmut Federle, Robert Mangold, Robert Ryman* (Klagenfurt: Ritterverlag, 1988), 217.

12. Kinley, Zelevansky, and Ryman, "Catalogue Notes," 178.

13. Ibid.

14. Robert Ryman, "On Painting," in Christel Sauer and Urs Raussmüller, eds., *Robert Ryman* (Schaffhausen, Switzerland: Hallen für neue Kunst, 1991), 59.

15. Ibid., 57.

16. Ibid., 57–59.

17. Ibid., 59.

18. Ibid., 61.

19. Ibid., 59.

20. Ibid., 65.

21. Ibid., 63.

22. Christel Sauer, "Robert Ryman's Realism," *Robert Ryman,* trans. Gertje Utley (Paris: PaceWildenstein, 1999), 5.

23. Robert Ryman in Phyllis Tuchman, "An Interview with Robert Ryman," *Artforum* 9, no. 9 (May 1971): 47.

24. Ryman feels that he does not need to be present for each reinstallation. He also says that the placement of tape was largely instinctive. Even so, subsequent hangings mimic the exact spacing and angles of the tape as he first applied it. He has noted in relation to a *Surface Veil* (a work that also needs new waxed paper and masking tape for each hanging) that people often pore over documentation of his original tape configurations to replicate them exactly, which

he finds "curious" because "it was a very immediate, intuitive thing." Kinley, Zelevansky, and Ryman, "Catalogue Notes," 140.

25. Susan Tumarkin Goodman, *Using Walls (Indoors)* (New York: Jewish Museum, 1970), n.p.

26. Robert Ryman statement in ibid., n.p.

27. Lippard, *Eva Hesse,* 67.

28. Kinley, Zelevansky, and Ryman, "Catalogue Notes," 128.

29. Exactly twenty years later, Ryman returned to a similar project. He made sixteen paintings between the summer of 1991 and the spring of 1992. They are all titled *Versions* and are comprised of large, medium-sized, and small panels that, like the *Surface Veils,* vary in their mediums and supports but unify in their courting of flatness by alternate means. Several *Versions* have waxed-paper frames; many *Versions* also have prominent grid structures, dates, and Ryman's signature. As is customary for Ryman's works, they proceed from the results of earlier experiments and press them into new directions. See Christel Sauer, *Robert Ryman Versions* (Schaffhausen, Switzerland: Hallen für neue Kunst, 1992).

30. Robert Storr, "Simple Gifts," *Robert Ryman* (London: Tate Gallery; New York: Museum of Modern Art, 1993), 30.

31. Kinley, Zelevanksky, and Ryman, "Catalogue Notes," 140.

32. Ibid., 144.

33. Ibid., 164.

34. See *Robert Ryman: New Paintings* (New York: Pace Gallery, 1990).

35. Charles S. Peirce, "Logic as Semiotic: The Theory of Signs," *Philosophical Writings of Peirce* (1903; New York: Dover, 1955), 102.

36. Rosalind Krauss, "Notes on the Index, Part 2," *The Originality of the Avant-Garde and Other Modernist Myths* (Cambridge: MIT Press, 1997), 210.

37. Ibid., 211.

38. Ibid., 219.

39. The first part of Krauss's essay establishes the index's parameters and its historical debt to the work of Duchamp, who also saw and exploited a connection between the index and the photograph. See Rosalind Krauss, "Notes on the Index, Part 1," *The Originality of the Avant-Garde and Other Modernist Myths* (Cambridge: MIT Press, 1986), 196–209. But in the second installment, Krauss writes that she is "not so much concerned here with the genesis of this condition within the arts, its historical process, as I am with its internal structure as one now confronts it in a variety of work." Krauss, "Notes on the Index, Part 2," 210.

40. Ibid., 212 n. 2.

41. David Joselit provides a recent example of reading Ryman's practice as one that manifests a deskilling of the painterly gesture. See David Joselit, *American Art since 1945* (New York: Thames and Hudson, 2003), 48.

42. This painting is similar to the one that Ryman completed for the Venice Biennale of 1976.

43. John Russell, "Robert Ryman, P.S. 1," *New York Times,* February 4, 1977.

44. Krauss, "Notes on the Index, Part 2," 211.

45. Ibid., 212.

46. Ibid., 215.

47. Taped conversation with the author, August 5, 2003.

48. Richard Cork, "Made of the White Stuff," *The Times,* March 5, 1993.

49. Leo Steinberg, "Contemporary Art and the Plight of Its Public," *Other Criteria: Confrontations with Twentieth-Century Art* (1962; New York: Oxford University Press, 1972).

50. Simon Wilson, "Ryman's Vision," *Robert Ryman* (London: Tate Gallery, 1993), n.p.

51. "New Art Show Really Is a Bit of All White!," *The Sun* (London), February 18, 1993, 3.

52. Robert Storr, *Robert Ryman* exhibition brochure, Museum of Modern Art, New York, 1993, 1.

53. Ibid, 8.

54. Arthur C. Danto, "RRyman," *The Madonna of the Future: Essays in a Pluralistic Art World* (New York: Farrar, Straus and Giroux, 2000), 28.

55. Roberta Smith, "Robert Ryman Derives Poetry from White on White," *New York Times,* September 24, 1993.

56. Ibid.

57. David Carrier and Robert Ryman, "Robert Ryman on the Origins of His Art," *Burlington Magazine* 139, no. 1134 (September 1997): 631.

58. Ibid., 632–633.

59. For a discussion of Ryman's relation to the interview, see my "Robert Ryman, Retrospective," *Art Journal* 64, no. 3 (Fall 2005): 62–69.

60. Taped conversation with the author, August 5, 2003.

61. Robert Ryman in Nancy Grimes, "White Magic," *Art News* 85, no. 6 (Summer 1986): 92.

62. William James, *Pragmatism: A New Name for Some Old Ways of Thinking* (1907; New York: Longmans, Green, and Co., 1912), 53.

63. William James, "The Letters of William James," in Louis Menand, ed., *Pragmatism: A Reader* (New York: Vintage Books, 1997), xviii.

64. Daniel Buren, "The Ineffable," *Robert Ryman* (Paris: Beaux Arts Magazine, 1999), 38. This was reprinted in Philip Armstrong, Laura Lisbon, and Stephen Melville, eds., *As Painting: Division and Displacement* (Cambridge: MIT Press, 2001), 243–249. This is of particular interest given the nature of the exhibition (at the Wexner Center for the Arts, The Ohio State University) and the book, which turn on the question of what counts as painting after minimalism. See, in particular, Melville, "Counting/As/Painting," in ibid., 1–26.

Conclusion

1. Amy Baker Sandback, "Art on Location," *Artforum* 24, no. 3 (November 1985): 4.

2. Robert Ryman, in Elayne H. Varian, *Art in Process IV* (New York: Finch College Museum of Art, 1969), n.p.

3. John Dewey, *Democracy and Education* (1916; New York: Free Press, 1997), 341.

4. "Robert Ryman," *The New Yorker* (November 4, 2002): 29.

5. Robert Ryman in Phyllis Tuchman, "An Interview with Robert Ryman," *Artforum* 9, no. 9 (May 1971): 46.

6. Robert Ryman, *Robert Ryman* (New York: PaceWildenstein, 2004), 6.

7. Ibid., 6–7.

8. Holland Cotter, "Exactly What about White Don't You Understand?," *New York Times*, June 4, 2004.

9. Robert Ryman, "The '60s in Abstract: Thirteen Statements and an Essay," *Art in America* 71, no. 9 (October 1983): 123.

10. William James, in Frederick H. Burkhardt, ed., *The Varieties of Religious Experience* (Cambridge: Harvard University Press, 1985): 407.

11. Louis Menand, "William James and the Case of the Epileptic Patient," *American Studies* (New York: Farrar, Straus and Giroux, 2002), 28.

12. Ibid.

13. William James (1873), cited in ibid.

14. Gertrude Stein, *The Autobiography of Alice B. Toklas* (1933; New York: Vintage Books, 1990), 79.

15. Menand, "William James and the Case of the Epileptic Patient," 29–30.

16. William James, *Pragmatism: A New Name for Some Old Ways of Thinking* (1907; New York: Longmans, Green, and Co., 1912), 223.

17. Ibid., 53.

18. Ibid., 201.

19. Ibid., 54.

Illustration Credits

Note: All Robert Ryman paintings are keyed with numbers corresponding to his archive (and forthcoming catalogue raisonne). These appear as RR numbers at the end of each relevant credit entry.

Page 2 Group portrait in *Time* magazine, November 22, 1968. Rob Crandall, Time & Life Pictures / Getty Images.

Page 5 Robert Ryman, *Untitled* (c. 1960). Oil on stretched cotton canvas, 58 ¾ in. × 58 ¾ in. × 1 ¾ in. Paolo Mussat Sartor. RR 60.017.

Page 12 Robert Ryman, *Untitled* (c. 1965). Oil on stretched sized linen canvas, 10 ⅛ in. × 10 ⅛ in. Robert Ryman Archive. Bill Jacobson for Robert Ryman Archive. RR 65.006.

Page 15 Installation view of Robert Ryman (1972), The Solomon R. Guggenheim Museum, New York. Robert E. Mates © The Solomon R. Guggenheim Foundation, New York.

Page 16 Installation view of *Robert Ryman: Early Paintings* (1972), John Weber Gallery, New York. Walter Russell.

Page 22 Robert Ryman, *Test* (1986). Lascaux acrylic (synthetic polymer paint) and graphite on gatorboard panel, 24 in. × 24 in. Robert Ryman Archive. Bill Jacobson for Robert Ryman Archive. RR 86.537.

Page 31 Victor D'Amico, Frances Wilson, and Moreen Maser, *Art for the Family* (New York: Simon and Schuster, 1954), 19. Photograph by Soichi Sunami.

Page 35 Children's art class of the "Children's Holiday Carnival." The Museum of Modern Art, New York. December 4, 1951 through January 6, 1952. (PA307) The Museum of Modern Art, New York. Digital Image © The Museum of Modern Art / Licensed by SCALA / Art Resource, New York.

Page 36 People's Art Center, The Museum of Modern Art, New York, 4 West 54 Street (PA306). The Museum of Modern Art, New York. Digital Image © The Museum of Modern Art / Licensed by SCALA / Art Resource, New York.

Page 39 Alfred H. Barr, Jr., "Torpedo" diagrams of the ideal permanent collection of The Museum of Modern Art, as advanced in 1933 (top) and in 1941 (bottom). Prepared by Barr for the "Advisory Committee Report on Museum Collections," 1941. The Museum of Modern Art Archives, New York: Alfred H. Barr Jr. Papers, 9a.15 (MA70) The Museum of Modern Art, New York. Digital Image © The Museum of Modern Art / Licensed by SCALA / Art Resource, New York.

Page 41 First floor installation view of the exhibition, "XXVth Anniversary Exhibitions: Paintings." The Museum of Modern Art, New York. October 19, 1954 through January 23, 1955. (IN567.65) The Museum of Modern Art, New York. Digital Image © The Museum of Modern Art / Licensed by SCALA / Art Resource, New York.

Page 54 Robert Ryman, *To Gertrud Mellon* (1958). Casein, graphite, and colored pencil on paper, irregular 11 ¾ in. × 12 in. Robert Ryman Archive. Bill Jacobson for Robert Ryman Archive. RR 58.001.

Page 56 Robert Ryman, *Untitled (Orange Painting)* (1955, 1959). Oil on stretched sized cotton canvas, 28 ⅛ in. × 28 ⅛ in. Robert Ryman Archive. Bill Jacobson. RR 55.102.

Page 58 Robert Ryman, *Untitled* (1959). Oil on preprimed stretched cotton canvas, 8 ¼ in. × 8 ¼ in. Photograph by Blair Clark. RR 59.046.

Page 59 Robert Ryman, *Untitled Study* (c. 1958). Oil on unstretched sized cotton canvas, irregular 7 ⅜ in. × 7 ⅛ in. Robert Ryman Archive. Bill Jacobson for Robert Ryman Archive. RR 58.106.

Page 61 Robert Ryman, *Untitled* (c. 1957). Casein on printed wallpaper, 10 in. × 10 ⅜ in. Robert Ryman Archive. Bill Jacobson for Robert Ryman Archive. RR 57.035.

Page 64 Robert Ryman, *Untitled* (1953). Oil on canvas board set into wooden frame and backing, 19 13⁄16 in. × 24 in. Robert Ryman Archive. Bill Jacobson for Robert Ryman Archive. RR 53.001.

Page 65 Robert Ryman, *Untitled* (1954). Crayon on canvas board, 14 5⁄8 in. × 8 in. Courtesy the collector. RR 54.003.

Page 67 Robert Ryman, *Untitled* (1954). Oil on paper, 24 in. × 18 in. Robert Ryman Archive. Bill Jacobson for Robert Ryman Archive. RR 54.004.

Page 69 Robert Ryman, *Untitled Study* (c. 1954). Oil and masking tape on paper board, 3 ¾ in. × 8 ¾ in. Courtesy the collector. RR 54.009.

Page 69 Robert Ryman, *Untitled Study* (c. 1954). Oil on cardboard backing, 4 in. × 8 ¾ in. Courtesy the collector. RR 54.010.

Page 70 Robert Ryman, *Untitled* (c. 1961). Oil on unstretched partially sized linen canvas with six brass grommets, three each at upper and lower edges, no fixed orientation, irregular 29 ½ in. × 31 ½ in. Robert Ryman Archive. Bill Jacobson for Robert Ryman Archive. RR 61.030.

Page 72 Robert Ryman, *Untitled* (c. mid-1950s). Oil on stretched preprimed canvas, 18 in. × 18 in. Robert Ryman Archive. Bill Jacobson for Robert Ryman Archive. RR 55.009.

Page 73 Robert Ryman, *Yellow Drawing #10* (c. 1963). Charcoal, graphite, and pastel on yellow paper, 19 in. × 19 in. Courtesy of the artist. RR 63.059.

Page 74 Robert Ryman, *Drawing with Numbers* (c. 1963). Charcoal, graphite, and pastel on yellow paper, 19 in. × 19 in. Courtesy of the artist. RR 63.057.

Page 75 Robert Ryman, *Untitled* (1965). Enamel on stretched sized linen canvas, 10 in. × 10 in. Robert Ryman Archive. Bill Jacobson for Robert Ryman Archive. RR 65.147.

Page 76 Robert Ryman, *(Ever) Since* (1998). Oil and graphite on stretched linen canvas, 17 in. × 17 in. Ellen Page Wilson for PaceWildenstein. © Robert Ryman, courtesy PaceWildenstein, New York. RR 98.040.

Page 78 Robert Ryman, *Untitled Study* (c. 1954–1955), front. Ink and brush on both sides of paper with cut upper and left edges, torn right and lower edges, 6 in. × 5 ½ in. Robert Ryman Archive. Bill Jacobson for Robert Ryman Archive. RR 54.00205.

Page 79 Robert Ryman, *Untitled Study* (c. 1954–1955), back. Ink and brush on both sides of paper with cut upper and left edges, torn right and lower edges, 6 in. × 5 ½ in. Robert Ryman Archive. Bill Jacobson for Robert Ryman Archive. RR 54.00205.

Page 81 Robert Ryman, *Untitled* (c. 1964). New Masters vinyl polymer acrylic and charcoal on stretched linen canvas, 8 in. × 8 in. Robert Ryman Archive. Bill Jacobson for Robert Ryman Archive. RR 64.0503.

Page 82 Robert Ryman, *Untitled* (c. 1964). New Masters vinyl polymer acrylic on aluminum, 7 in. × 7 in. Robert Ryman Archive. Bill Jacobson for Robert Ryman Archive. RR 64.0512.

Page 84 Robert Ryman, *Untitled Study* (c. 1954–1955). Ink and brush on letterhead with Atlantic Mimeo Bond watermark, cut upper, left and lower edges, torn right edge, 8 ½ in. × 5 ⅞ in. Robert Ryman Archive. Bill Jacobson for Robert Ryman Archive. RR 54.00213.

Page 85 Robert Ryman, *Untitled Study* (c. 1954–1955). Ink on printed The Museum of Modern Art letterhead with Rockledge watermark, cut edges, 11 in. × 8 ½ in. Robert Ryman Archive. Bill Jacobson for Robert Ryman Archive. RR 54.00244.

Page 88 Robert Ryman, *Untitled* (1958). Oil on stretched sized cotton canvas, 53 ⅜ in. × 32 ½ in. × 2 in. Robert Ryman Archive. Bill Jacobson for Robert Ryman Archive. RR 58.045.

Page 90 Robert Ryman, *Studio View* (1959). Oil on black and white photograph, 3 ⅛ in. × 4 ¼ in. Courtesy of the artist. RR 59.097.

Page 91 Robert Ryman, *Untitled*, from "On the Bowery" print portfolio (1969–1971). Serigraph on Schoeller-Hammer paper, sheet: 25 ½ in. × 25 ½ in. Robert Ryman Archive. RR 69.G1.

Page 93 Robert Ryman, *Unresolved Drawing* (1961). Graphite and pastel on gray Rives paper, 10 in. × 10 in. Robert Ryman Archive. Bill Jacobson for Robert Ryman Archive. RR 61.060.

Page 94 Robert Ryman, *Spectrum VIII* (1984). Graphite on anodized aluminum panel, 8 ⅜ in. × 8 ⅜ in. Robert Ryman Archive. Bill Jacobson for Robert Ryman Archive. RR 84.463.

Page 95 Robert Ryman, *Untitled Study* (c. 1956). Gouache and crayon on matboard, no fixed orientation, 5 in. × 5 in. Robert Ryman Archive. Bill Jacobson for Robert Ryman Archive. RR 56.008.

Page 99 Robert Ryman, *Untitled Study* (c. 1956). Oil, casein, graphite, and colored pencil on unstretched sized cotton canvas, no fixed orientation, irregular 7 ½ in. × 7 ¾ in. Robert Ryman Archive. Bill Jacobson for Robert Ryman Archive. RR 56.005.

Page 100 Robert Ryman, *Untitled* (c. 1956). Oil on preprimed stretched canvas, no fixed orientation, 22 in. × 22 in. Robert Ryman Archive. Bill Jacobson for Robert Ryman Archive. RR 56.012.

Page 101 Robert Ryman, *The Paradoxical Absolute* (1958). Oil, casein, and graphite on printed paper, 7 ¼ in. × 7 ⅜ in. Dia Art Foundation; Promised gift. Robert Ryman Archive. Bill Jacobson for Robert Ryman Archive. RR 58.0736.

Page 102 Robert Ryman, *Untitled* (1958). Casein, gouache, and graphite on newsprint, mounted on board, irregular 11 ⅞ in. × 11 ⅞ in. Robert Ryman Archive. Bill Jacobson for Robert Ryman Archive. RR 58.003.

Page 103 Robert Ryman. *Untitled* (1959). Casein on paper, 9 in. × 9 in. Robert Ryman Archive. Bill Jacobson for Robert Ryman Archive. RR 59.0881.

Page 108 Robert Ryman, *Untitled* (2000). Oil and graphite on sized linen canvas, 11 ¼ × 11 ¼ in. Robert Ryman Archive. Bill Jacobson for Robert Ryman Archive. RR 00.006.

Page 112 Robert Ryman, *Untitled #1004* (c. 1960–1961). Oil and gesso on unstretched sized linen canvas, irregular 15 ½ in. × 14 ½ in. Robert Ryman Archive. Bill Jacobson for Robert Ryman Archive. RR 60.0711.

Page 116 Robert Ryman, *Untitled* (c. 1957). Colored pencil, gouache, casein, and oil on verso of printed wallpaper, 12 in. × 12 in. Robert Ryman Archive. Bill Jacobson for Robert Ryman Archive. RR 57.0891.

Page 117 Robert Ryman. *Untitled* (c. 1964). Pastel and charcoal on Chemex coffee filter paper, diameter 12 ⅜ in. Robert Ryman Archive. Bill Jacobson for Robert Ryman Archive. RR 64.015.

Page 122 Robert Ryman, *a painting on canvas measuring 9-¾″ × 10″ and signed in green at lower center and twice in neutral green at the bottom right corner.* (1961). Oil on unstretched sized linen canvas, irregular 9-¾ in. × 10 in. Robert Ryman Archive. Bill Jacobson for Robert Ryman Archive. RR 61.020.

Page 124 Robert Ryman, *Untitled #1005* (1962). Oil on unstretched sized linen canvas, irregular 16 ½ in. × 16 ½ in. Gordon R. Christmas for PaceWildenstein. © Robert Ryman, courtesy PaceWildenstein, New York. RR 62.067.

Page 125 Robert Ryman, *Untitled* (c. 1962–1963). Oil, gesso, and graphite on unstretched sized linen canvas, irregular 10 ¼ in. × 9 ¾ in. Robert Ryman Archive. Bill Jacobson for Robert Ryman Archive. RR 62.121.

Page 127 Robert Ryman, *Stretched Drawing* [5 × 5 grid] (1963). Charcoal on stretched sized cotton canvas, 14 ½ in. × 14 ⅜ in. Dia Art Foundation; Promised gift. Robert Ryman Archive. Bill Jacobson for Robert Ryman Archive. RR 63.122.

Page 129 Robert Ryman, *Bent Line Drawing* (c. 1970). Ball-point pen on polyester fabric over foamcore, 12 in. × 12 in. Robert Ryman Archive. Bill Jacobson for Robert Ryman Archive. RR 70.025.

Page 133 Ellsworth Kelly, *Window, Museum of Modern Art, Paris* (1949). Oil on wood and canvas, two joined panels, 50 ½ in. × 19 ½ in. Jerry L. Thompson. Private collection. © Ellsworth Kelly.

Page 138 Ellsworth Kelly, *Red Green Blue* (1964). Oil on canvas, 90 in. × 66 in. Collection Walker Art Center, Minneapolis. Gift of the T.B. Walker Foundation, 1966.

Page 139 Robert Ryman, *Untitled* (1965). Oil on stretched cotton canvas, 10 ¼ in. × 10 ¼ in. Collection of Nina and Michael Sundell. RR 65.131.

Page 149 Installation view from the exhibition "16 Americans," The Museum of Modern Art, New York, December 16, 1959 through February 17, 1960. (IN656.29) The Museum of Modern Art, New York. Digital Image © The Museum of Modern Art/ Licensed by SCALA / Art Resource, New York.

Page 151 Frank Stella, *The Marriage of Reason and Squalor, second version* (1959). Enamel on canvas, 90 ¾ in. × 132 ¾ in. Collection of the artist. Art Resource, New York. © 2008 Frank Stella / Artists Rights Society (ARS), New York. Photo credit: Art Resource, NY.

Page 159 Robert Ryman, *Delta II* (1966). Oil on stretched cotton canvas, 106 in. × 105 ¾ in. × 3 ½ in. David Heald © The Solomon R. Guggenheim Foundation, New York. Solomon R. Guggenheim Museum, New York. Purchased with the aid of funds from the National Endowment for the Arts in Washington, D.C., a Federal Agency and Mrs. Leo Simon, 1972. 72.2022. RR 66.169.

Page 161 Robert Ryman, *General 49 × 49* (1970). Enamel and Enamelac on stretched cotton canvas, 49 ⅛ in. × 49 ⅛ in. Robert Ryman Archive. Bill Jacobson for Robert Ryman Archive. RR 70.2783.

Page 162 Robert Ryman, *Untitled* (1973). Double-baked porcelain enamel on five copper panels, each: 15 ¾ × 15 ¾ in.; space between panels ca. 4 ¾ in.; overall ca. 15 ¾ × 97 ¾ in. Robert Ryman Archive. Bill Jacobson for Robert Ryman Archive. RR 73.321.

Page 162 Robert Ryman, *No Title Required* (2006). Enamel on birch plywood with cherry, maple, or oak, ten panels, each panel from 50 × 50 in. to 55 × 55 in. © Robert Ryman, courtesy PaceWildenstein, New York. Photograph by Ellen Labenski, courtesy PaceWildenstein, New York. RR 06.002.

Page 165 Robert Ryman, *Untitled, The Magazine Show, Artforum. Artforum* (December 1976). Commercial offset lithograph on paper, 10⅝ × 10½ in. RR 76.GP.

Page 168 Robert Ryman, *Standard* (detail) (1967). Swann's Down enamel on cold-rolled steel, twelve panels, each: 48 in. × 48 in. Ellen Labenski © The Solomon R. Guggenheim Foundation, New York. Solomon R. Guggenheim Museum, New York. Panza Collection, 1991. 91.3840. RR 67.182.

Page 171 Robert Ryman, *Mayco* (1966). Winsor White oil on stretched sized linen canvas, 75 ⅝ in. × 75 ⅝ in. Courtesy of Daros Collection, Switzerland. RR 66.172.

Page 173 Robert Ryman, *Winsor 34* (c. 1966). Winsor White oil on stretched sized linen canvas, 63 in. × 63 in. © Robert Ryman, courtesy of PaceWildenstein, New York. RR 66.164.

Page 176 Robert Ryman, *Dutch Boy Diamond* (1965). Enamel on stretched linen canvas, 11 ¼ in. × 11 ¼ in. Lorenzo and Marilena Bonomo Collection, Bari, Italy. RR 65.142.

Page 177 Robert Ryman, *Castell 8H #2* (1966). Graphite on Chemex coffee filter paper, diameter 12⅜ in. Robert Ryman Archive. Bill Jacobson for Robert Ryman Archive. RR 66.179.

Page 191 Robert Ryman, *Untitled, Prototype* (1969). Acrylic polymer on fiberglass panel, 20 in. × 20 in. Robert Ryman Archive. Bill Jacobson for Robert Ryman Archive. RR 69.222.

Page 194 Eva Hesse, *Contingent* (1969). Fiberglass, polyester resin, and latex over cheesecloth, each of eight units 114 in. to 168 in. × 36 in. to 48 in. National Gallery of Australia, Canberra. ©The Estate of Eva Hesse, Hauser & Wirth Zürich London.

Page 198 Robert Ryman, *Factor* (1983). Oil over Swiss Lascaux acrylic on recto, Swiss Lascaux acrylic with varnish on verso of fiberglass panel with honeycomb aluminum with epoxy edge, and metal rods with oval attachments, panel 90 in. × 45 in. × 1 in., overall 92 ¾ in. × 45 in. × 14 ¾ in. Dia Art Foundation; Promised gift. Robert E. Mates. RR 83.452.

Page 199 Robert Ryman, *Pace* (1984). Lascaux acrylic (synthetic polymer paint) on fiberglass panel with redwood edge with aluminum, stainless steel wall dowels, fasteners, and rods, overall: 59 ½ × 26 × 28 in. Gift of anonymous donor and gift of Jo Carole and Ronald S. Lauder. (452.1994) The Museum of Modern Art, New York. Digital Image © The Museum of Modern Art/Licensed by SCALA/Art Resource, New York. RR 84.453.

Page 200 Robert Ryman, *Pair Navigation* (1984). Oil on fiberglass panel with redwood edge and metal frame, with four rod fasteners, 9 in. × 47 ½ in. × 47 ½ in. Dia Art Foundation; Promised gift. Photo courtesy Galerie Lelong, New York. © Robert Ryman, courtesy PaceWildenstein, New York. RR 84.454.

Page 201 Robert Ryman, *Varese Wall* (1975). Vinyl acetate emulsion on six wood door panels, six metal rods, five blue foam blocks, 96 in. × 24 feet × 20 in. Dia Art Foundation; Promised gift. Installation at Dia: Beacon, Beacon, New York. Photo credit: Bill Jacobson. RR 75.352 .

Page 204 Robert Ryman, *District* (1985). Oil on aluminum panel with six hexagonal round-faced steel bolts, 80 ¾ in. × 30 in. × 2 ½ in. Stedelijk Museum Amsterdam. RR 85.467.

Page 208 Robert Ryman, *Untitled* (1959). Graphite, colored pencil, and casein on collaged tracing paper, 10 ¼ in. × 10 ⅜ in. Robert Ryman Archive. Bill Jacobson for Robert Ryman Archive. RR 59.0862.

Page 209 Robert Ryman, *Adelphi* (1967). Oil on unstretched linen canvas, installed with staples, waxed paper, masking tape, canvas, 102 in. × 102 in., overall with waxed paper, c. 112 in. × 112 in. Deimel+Wittmar, for Museum für Moderne Kunst, Frankfurt am Main. Museum für Moderne Kunst, Frankfurt am Main. RR 67.184.

Page 211 Robert Ryman, *Untitled, John Weber Gallery, New York, wall installation* (1973). Gloss enamel, Gripz, acrylic polymer, on wall, 294 × 114 in. Mates and Katz. RR 73.331.

Page 213 Robert Ryman, *Exeter* (1968). Oil on unstretched linen canvas, installed with staples, masking tape, canvas 98 ½ in. × 98 ½ in., with tape c. 104 ¼ in. × 104 ¼ in. Courtesy of Daros Collection, Switzerland. RR 68.194.

Page 214 Robert Ryman, *Untitled* (c. 1970). Acrylic on unstretched sized linen canvas, 7 ½ in. × 7 ¼ in. Robert Ryman Archive. Bill Jacobson for Robert Ryman Archive. RR 70.048.

Page 216 Robert Ryman, *Medway* (c. 1968). Acrylic polymer on six sheets of overlapping handmade Medway wove mounted on foamcore panels, each sheet irregular c. 30 in. × 22 ½ in., overall variable c. 79 ½ in. × 77 in. Dia Art Foundation; Promised gift. Robert Ryman Archive. Bill Jacobson. RR 68.193.

Page 217 Robert Ryman, *Impex* (1968). Oil paint on unstretched linen canvas and blue chalk line on wall, Canvas: 97 in. × 97 in.. David Heald © The Solomon R. Guggenheim Foundation, New York. Solomon R. Guggenheim Museum, New York. Panza Collection, 1991. 91.3842. RR 68.189.

Page 220 Robert Ryman, *Untitled, Surface Veil 12 1/16″ × 12 1/8″* (1970). Oil on fiberglass panel, 12 1/16 in. × 12 1/8 in. Robert Ryman Archive. Bill Jacobson for Robert Ryman Archive. RR 70.044.

Page 221 Robert Ryman, *Blue Line Drawing #5* (1969). Conté on thin matte Mylar panel, 12 in. × 12 in. Robert Ryman Archive. Bill Jacobson for Robert Ryman Archive. RR 69.043.

Page 223 Robert Ryman, *Surface Veil II* (c. 1970). Oil and blue chalk on stretched linen canvas, 144 in. × 144 in. David Heald © Solomon R. Guggenheim Museum, New York. Panza Collection, 1991. 91.3854. RR 70.275.

Page 227 Robert Ryman, *Monitor* (1978). Oil on stretched cotton canvas with metal fasteners and four bolts, canvas, 66 in. × 66 in., overall 69 in. × 66 in. Stedelijk Museum Amsterdam. RR 78.381.

Page 228 Robert Ryman, *Alliance* (1976). Acrylic polymer on blue Acrylivin panel, with four sanded plexiglass fasteners, cadmium-plated steel pentagonal bolts, panel 14 in. × 14 in., overall 15 5/8 in. × 14 in. Robert Ryman Archive. Courtesy of the artist. RR 76.362.

Page 229 Robert Ryman, *Arrow* (1976). Oil on sanded plexiglass panel, four sanded plexiglass fasteners and hexagonal cadmium plated steel bolts, panel 12 in. × 12 in., overall 13 ¾ in. × 12 in. Robert Ryman Archive. Courtesy of the artist. RR 76.530.

Page 230 Robert Ryman, *Phoenix* (detail) (1979). Varathane on eight steel panels, each with four fasteners and bolts, from 13 7/16 in. × 13 7/16 in. to 8 ½ in. × 15 in. Dia Art Foundation;

Promised gift. Robert Ryman Archive. Bill Jacobson for Robert Ryman Archive. RR 79.396.

Page 232 Robert Ryman, *Roll* (1989). Oil and graphite on gatorboard panel with aluminum frame mount, 25 ⅛ in. × 25 ⅛ in. Robert Ryman Archive. Bill Jacobson for Robert Ryman Archive. RR 89.648.

Page 234 Robert Ryman, *Untitled, P.S. 1, Long Island City, New York, wall installation* (1976). Acrylic polymer on two sheets of watercolor paper, each sheet 22 in. × 22 in. Robert Ryman Archive. Courtesy of the artist. RR 76.010.

Page 237 Robert Ryman, Installation view of the exhibition, Robert Ryman. The Museum of Modern Art, New York. September 26, 1993 through January 4, 1994. (IN1663.11) The Museum of Modern Art, New York. Digital Image © The Museum of Modern Art / Licensed by SCALA / Art Resource, New York. *VII* (1969). Enamelac on seven corrugated paper panels mounted on aluminum, each panel 60 × 60 in.; ca. 5 in. gap between panels. RR 69.229.

Page 246 Installation view of Ryman's studio. Robert Ryman Archive.

Page 248 Robert Ryman, *Untitled* (1960). Oil on stretched sized cotton canvas, 59 ¼ in. × 59 ¼ in. Robert Ryman Archive. Bill Jacobson for Robert Ryman Archive. RR 60.019.

Page 250 Robert Ryman, *Series #12 (White)* (2004). Oil, gesso on stretched cotton canvas, 42 in. × 42 in. × 1 in. Robert Ryman Archive. Bill Jacobson for Robert Ryman Archive. RR 04.012.

Page 251 Robert Ryman, *Series #24 (White)* (2004). Oil, gesso on stretched cotton canvas, 16 in. × 16 in. × 1½ in. Robert Ryman Archive. Bill Jacobson for Robert Ryman Archive. RR 04.024.

Index

NOTE: Page numbers appearing in *italics* indicate illustrations.